Thomas Coram, Gent.
1668–1751

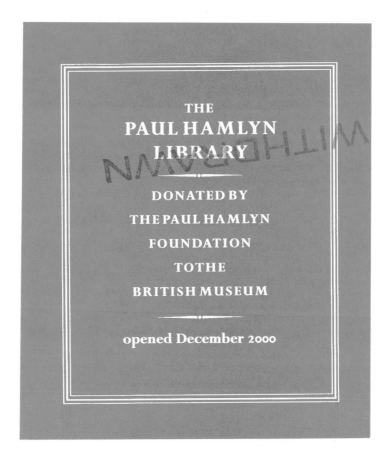

Portrait of Captain Thomas Coram by William Hogarth, 1740.

Thomas Coram, Gent.
1668–1751

Gillian Wagner

THE BOYDELL PRESS

First published 2004
The Boydell Press, Woodbridge

ISBN 1 84383 057 4

The Boydell Press is an imprint of Boydell & Brewer Ltd
PO Box 9, Woodbridge, Suffolk IP12 3DF, UK
and of Boydell & Brewer Inc.
PO Box 41026, Rochester, NY 14604–4126, USA
website: www.boydellandbrewer.com

A catalogue record for this book is available
from the British Library

Library of Congress Cataloging-in-Publication Data
Wagner, Gillian.
Thomas Coram, Gent. / Gillian Wagner.
    p. cm.
Includes bibliographical references and index.
   ISBN 1–84383–057–4 (alk. paper)
    1. Coram, Thomas, 1668?–1751.   2. Great Britain – History – 18th century
– Biography.   3. Shipbuilding – Massachusetts – History – 18th century.
4. British – Massachusetts– History – 18th century.   5. Philanthropists –
Great Britain – Biography.   6. Reformers – Great Britain – Biography.
7. Foundling Hospital (London, England)   8. Taunton (Mass.) – Biography.
9. Boston (Mass.) – Biography.   I. Title.
DA483.C69W34   2004
362.73'2'092 – dc22   2003022237

This publication is printed on acid-free paper

Printed in Great Britain by
Cromwell Press, Trowbridge, Wiltshire

Contents

Illustrations

All illustrations are by kind permission of Coram Family in the care of the Foundling Museum unless otherwise stated.

Acknowledgements

I started my research into the life of Thomas Coram in America, where as a young man he had found fulfilment and met with disaster. I would like to thank all those who helped me to get started, both in Boston and Taunton, Massachusetts. The staff at the Massachusetts Historical Society were always helpful, as were the staff at the Massachusetts Archives. I am most grateful to Fremont Prescott for his help, his unfailing interest and for being my guide in Taunton. My thanks go also to the Rev. Franklin Huntress. Dr Katheryn Viens and Jane Kennedy, Directors of the Old Colony Historical Society in Taunton, who gave me invaluable help in finding old records and in showing me some books sent to the church in Taunton by Thomas Coram. It was a special pleasure to be welcomed to Coram's House by Mr and Mrs Jim Scott, the present tenants, and to take part in a service at St Thomas's church in Taunton. My thanks also go to the staff at the Taunton Public Library, the Atheneum, Boston, and William Kuttner, King's Chapel guide and historian. I am particularly indebted to Henry Beckwith, past director of the New England Historic and Genealogical Society, for his hospitality and help. I thank his successor Henry Huff and Jerry Anderson, who gave me invaluable help sorting out the family history of the Waite family and other matters. I thank Barry Cahill of the Public Archive of Nova Scotia for his help. Dr James Taylor of the University of West Georgia has kindly shared his knowledge of Coram with me. My thanks also go to Dr Joy Parr for help with research.

Hugh Jacques, County Archivist, and his staff at the Dorset Record Office gave me valuable assistance, as did the Rev. W. Wright, vicar of St Mary's Church, Ottery St Mary, who helped me transcribe the registers of his church. Liz Anne Rawden, Honourable Curator of the Philpot Museum, Lyme Regis, and Helena York both gave me help.

I am grateful to the Chair and Governors of Coram Family for their encouragement and to the Chief Executive, Gillian Pugh, for her help. Rhian Harris, Director of the Foundling Museum, has shared her knowledge of and enthusiasm for the Foundling Museum treasures and I thank her, her assistant Jane King and Janet Broadhurst. I am grateful to the Museum Trustees for allowing me to quote from the archive and reproduce paintings, prints and drawings. I thank Jim Swinley for help with the history of the Thomas Coram Foundation for Children.

I thank Dr Alan Borg for casting light on the architectural career of Theodore Jacobsen, Dr David Hancock for sharing his knowledge of Martin Folkes, and Sir Keith Thomas for letting me have a copy of his lecture on James Oglethorpe.

The staff at the British Library, the Public Record Office and the London Metroplitan Archive were unfailingly courteous and helpful. I also thank Margaret Daley at the Central Library, Liverpool, M.K. Stammers at the National Museums and

Galleries, Merseyside, and Kay Walters, Librarian at the Athenaeum, London. James Kilvington of the National Portrait Gallery, arranged for me to see the supposed portrait of Coram. I was greatly helped by Thomas Woodcock, Norroy and Ulster King of Arms, over matters genealogical. I am particularly indebted to Pamela Tudor Craig who gave so much time to help with my research. I would also like to thank Chris Harvey, Jenny Uglow, and Dick Foster.

My thanks go to Jill Croft Murray for providing near perfect conditions for writing at her home in Tuscany; to Liz Bonython and Pamela Powell for reading the text; to my family, Roger Wagner, Mark Wagner and Lucy McCarraher, for their encouragement and help as well as giving me technical assistance. Richard and Helen Barber have been supportive all the way through, and I thank them and Ellie Ferguson and the team at Boydell for their patience in bringing order out of what at times seemed like chaos.

Introduction

The name Thomas Coram is remembered, almost entirely, because of his achievement in bringing to public notice the scandal of infants abandoned and left to die in ditches or by the roadside in eighteenth-century London. It was entirely due to his perseverance that a powerful and privileged group of men, hereditary aristocrats, landowners and wealthy merchants, members of the small circle of London's social elite, were reluctantly persuaded to join with him in petitioning the King for a charter for a hospital for foundlings. But perhaps his most astonishing achievement was in first gaining the support of twenty-one ladies of quality and distinction, his ladies of charity as he called them, to endorse his petition and promise financial support. The Duchess of Somerset was the first to sign his petition. Coram was convinced that without the support of these ladies he would never have been granted a royal charter, such was the prejudice he encountered. The charter for a Hospital for the Maintenance and Education of Exposed and Deserted Young Children, the Foundling Hospital's legal title, was granted to Coram by King George II in 1739, and Coram is rightly acclaimed for having forced society, rather against its will, to interest itself in the fate of its youngest, most defenceless, destitute and abandoned citizens.

The later renown of the Foundling Hospital is due, in large measure, to its magnificent art collection and its musical tradition rather than to an understanding of its work with foundlings. That is in no way meant to detract from the work of the hospital in rescuing thousands of children and giving them a start in life, but by the nineteenth century many other children's organisations had come into being and the hospital was no longer unique. What differentiated it in the public mind was its links with Hogarth and Handel and its artistic heritage. Hogarth's great iconic portrait of Coram remains a lasting reminder of Coram's triumph, but Coram himself had little to do with this flowering of artistic creativity and the hospital's musical tradition. Although the initial vision of the hospital was his, he was involved with its governance for only two years, before being voted off the General Committee. The aristocratic governors soon left the management of the hospital in the hands of a small group of powerful and wealthy men, nearly all known to one another, who quickly and quietly sidelined Coram, and finally, in a shameful way, engineered his dismissal from the General Committee.

So much emphasis has been placed on Coram's long struggle to obtain support for his petition that his interest in colonial development has seldom been given the attention it deserves. After a difficult childhood – he lost his mother when he was four and was sent to sea at eleven – Coram left for New England in 1694, as factor to Thomas Hunt, with a commission to build ships in Boston and Taunton. He returned to London ten years later with a Bostonian wife but deeply in debt, his shipbuilding business in Taunton having been wrecked by a small number of men, jealous of his success and suspicious of his Anglican beliefs. Despite being literally driven out of Taunton, Coram remained deeply influenced by the ways and customs of the new young thrusting country, which appealed to his independent and entrepreneurial spirit. His yearning to return to America only left him in old age.

Coram left few clues as to how he spent the first years after his return. The most likely scenario is that he worked for the merchants to whom he was indebted, trading on their behalf with America. But from 1713 to 1738 he was continuously involved, with others, with plans to help the unemployed, debtors and foreign Protestant refugees to start a new life in America, both in the unsettled lands between Massachusetts and Nova Scotia and in Nova Scotia itself, urging the supply of cheap naval stores as an inducement to the Board of Trade and Plantations to underwrite his plans. His affection and admiration for the country is acknowledged in the *Dictionary of American Biography*, where it is noted that 'Coram never returned to America but America never left his mind'.

England was at war with France and Spain during much of the early part of Coram's life, and, in a sense, the wars and their aftermath shaped Coram's career. He had sailed to Boston in 1694, in convoy under the protection of the navy, so was fully aware of the important role played by the navy in countering French and Spanish naval power. Coram returned to England convinced of the economic advantages to be had from importing cheap timber, masts, tar, hemp and other supplies from America for the benefit of the navy, rather than importing them expensively from the Baltic countries. He understood the strategic as well as the economic importance of settlements in the contested lands between Massachusetts and Nova Scotia and in Nova Scotia itself. Such settlements would not only provide a bulwark against the depredations of the French and Indians, but they would also provide opportunities for work for the many soldiers left unemployed at the end of the war in 1713, as well as for debtors and others who found it hard to make a living.

Frustrated by the Attorney General's final ruling in 1732, that the contested lands between New England and Nova Scotia did belong to Massachusetts, Coram abandoned any hope of creating a 'Royall Province' of Georgia or of settling the lands that are now northern Maine. He turned his attention to plans for the colonisation of the lands south of Carolina, becoming a trustee of what is the present Georgia. He was already accepted as an expert on colonial affairs by the Board of Trade and Plantations and frequently was consulted by them. Only when the Georgia trustees refused to allow females to inherit did Coram, a strong believer in women's rights and the importance of their role in society, give up his active involvement with Georgia, circulating a defamatory letter in an attempt to discredit the other trustees.

Fiercely loyal to king and country, with an entrenched hatred of the French and a fear of all things Roman Catholic, Coram, besides being a convinced mercantilist, was also an ardent Anglican and, influenced by the work of Thomas Bray, the founder of the Society for Promoting Christian Knowledge (SPCK), worked to encourage the spread of the Anglican Church's influence in America. He saw this as a means of countering the influence of both the Roman Catholics and the Puritans. His quarrel with the people of Taunton was provoked in part by his desire to see an Anglican school or church built among that fiercely Puritan community. His generosity in donating the land he had been given, by way of compensation for the wrecking of his shipyard, to Taunton to be used for a church or school was recognised. Even though Taunton was never able to benefit from his gift, he helped the first struggling church in other ways, arranging for books to be sent to it. When the first Episcopalian church was finally built in Taunton in 1728 it was dedicated to St Thomas. Today the third church of that name has a portrait of Coram in his red coat in one of its stained-glass windows and he is remembered with affection and gratitude by the congregation.

Coram, following his dispute with the trustees of Georgia, now turned his attention to Nova Scotia. His detailed and meticulous plans for its settlement under a civil government were all worked out in the early 1730s at the same time that he was actively engaged in seeking support for a foundling hospital. In 1737 petitions for charters for the Foundling Hospital and for a settlement in Nova Scotia were presented to the Privy Council within three weeks of each other. Robert Walpole's brother, Horatio Walpole, begged his brother, the Prime Minister, 'to lose no time in talking to Sir Charles Wager, Mr Bladon, and one Coram, the honestest and most disinterested and the most knowing person about the plantations that I have ever talked with'. Unfortunately for Coram, Robert Walpole was more interested in the European political scene than becoming involved in colonial adventures. Coram believed that, through his friendship with Horatio Walpole, he was to have had a meeting with the Prime Minister to discuss the matter. The death of Queen Caroline temporarily put a stop to business and the moment passed. This was the nearest Coram came to success in promoting a settlement in America. He hoped, as he had hoped over the years, that he would be able to return to America with the settlers. But it was not to be. Mahaffie, in his book *Land of Discord Always*, thought Coram was the most likely colonial promoter. He thought that had Coram been given sufficient official encouragement, with his strong belief in civil government, he might have been able to bring about a rapprochement between the Acadians and the new British settlers. Had such an accommodation taken place between the two peoples, the tragedy of 1755, when the entire Acadian population was expelled from the land, would have been avoided.

History is full of many a 'What if?' What if Coram had not fallen ill in 1737? What if Queen Caroline had not died and business not been held up owing to the King's grief? What if Coram's wife had not become increasingly frail? It seems almost certain that the Corams would have sailed with the settlers to Nova Scotia. Letters to friends over the years tell of his hope of returning to the country that so appealed to his independent and freedom-loving spirit. It is nonetheless some consolation to know that his plans for Nova Scotia were adopted almost in their entirety when Cornwallis, in 1749, led an expedition of thirteen ships carrying 2,576 men, women and children to that country. But, for the sake of the foundlings, it is fortunate that he remained in London, for no one else would have had the tenacity and dogged determination to raise the money needed to pay the fees demanded by the lawyers to prepare the charter, and to collect the large number of signatures that were still needed to ensure royal assent.

Coram, always conscious of his lack of education, the result of being sent to sea as a boy, was never inhibited by deficient grammar from expressing his thoughts and feelings in a robust and vigorous style. He left no diaries, apart from a notebook in which for a few months he kept his accounts, and which also fortunately contains the names of the ladies who gave him their support and the dates when they signed his petition. It is through his correspondence – starting in the 1730s with a series of letters to both

Jeremiah Belcher, Governor of Massachusetts, and the Rev. Benjamin Colman, minister of the Brattle Street church – rather than through the huge number of formal letters and petitions that he addressed to the Board of Trade and Plantations, that he can best be understood. The Colman letters are particularly important and revealing. Once Coram gets to feel at ease with Colman, he lets him have his candid opinions about people and events. Coram tells it as it is with no frills. In his last letters to Colman, he writes frankly about himself, as if wanting to ensure that at least Colman will have a true record, as understood by him, of some of the main events of his life. Coram wrote as he thought; his style is without the polish and polite mannerisms of the age. In vigorous terms he lays into those he thought had either wronged him or acted wrongly, yet at the same time, without any hint of self congratulation, his own remarkable disinterested selflessness and generosity of spirit shine through the correspondence.

During his time in New England he was involved in a long series of court cases which give invaluable background information as to how he lived in Taunton. A further Chancery court case brought against him in London for debt does much to explain his relative silence during his first years back in England. He bombardment of the Board of Trade and Plantations with memoranda and petitions shows him knowledgeable and enterprising in his views on colonial development. He was not afraid to petition the King directly on his own behalf, but without result. What emerges from these different sources is a man of startling integrity in an age of corruption, a man prepared to use his own limited resources to gain his objects, with little expectation of personal reward apart from the satisfaction of having contributed to the public good. From a modest family background, without wealth or a patron, in an age when both were considered a necessity, he triumphed through his own energy, persistence and enterprise combined with a rough charm of manner, made the more appealing on account of his patent honesty. Unfortunately, his fierce temper together with his injudicious habit of responding in an intemperate manner, both verbally and in writing, to perceived or real injustices made for difficulties throughout his life. As his first memorialist, Dr Brocklesby put it, 'free from all hypocrisy, he spoke what he thought with vehemence'.

Following Dr Brocklesby's 'Memoir of the Founder', written soon after Coram's death and included in Brownlow's *History and Objects of the Foundling Hospital*, in 1865, it was not until 1918 that a small biography of Coram appeared, entitled *Thomas Coram, Churchman, Empire Builder and Philanthropist*, by H.F.B. Compston, who wrote this before he was aware that Coram's letters had been printed and published by the MHS. This remains the only biography to have been written. American historians have paid more attention to Coram's time in America, and have been interested in his colonial projects. Hamilton Andrews Hill wrote an account of Coram's life in New England in a paper for the American Antiquarian Society in 1892, entitled 'Thomas Coram in Boston and Taunton', and an article by H.B. Fant appeared in the *Georgia Historical Quarterly*, again dealing with Coram's colonial interests: 'Picturesque Thomas Coram, Projector of Two Georgias and Father of the London Foundling Hospital'. The Colonial Society of Massachusetts was also interested in Coram's attempts to found a colony in what is now northern Maine, and published an article on 'The Proposed Colony of Georgia in New England, 1713–1733'. Coram's interest in the development of Nova Scotia has also attracted the attention of historians. In a publication entitled *The 'Foreign Protestants' and the Settlement of Nova Scotia* there is an article on 'Thomas Coram and the First Proposals for Foreign Protestants as Settlers', held in the possession of the Public Archives of Nova Scotia.

Accounts of the Foundling Hospital are naturally always preceded by a short account of the life of Thomas Coram, many of them perpetuating the myth that he returned from America a wealthy man. In their *History of the Foundling Hospital*, Nichols and Wray allow Coram just fifteen pages of text. Ruth McClure, to whom I am greatly indebted for her masterly book *Coram's Children*, does Coram the honour of looking in greater detail at his life but, as she says herself, she was not attempting a biography.

This life of Coram is an attempt to disentangle the facts from the many myths that have accumulated, particularly around his early life. My admiration for Thomas Coram has grown as I have worked on this account of his life. He fits no stereotype and was unique in being a man of integrity in an age of corruption, with a generosity of spirit and a capacity for compassion that has rightly earned him a place in the history of his time.

I

The Making of the Man, 1668–1693

Early years

> For my part I am no Judge in Learning I understand no Lattin nor English
> nither, well, for though Through Mercy I discended from vertuous good
> Parentage on both sides as any Body, they were Famelies of Strict hon'r and
> honesty and alwayes of Good Reputation amongst the better sort of people,
> Yet I had no Learning, my Mother Dying when I was Young, My Father
> Marryed again 4 or 5 years after at Hackney Near this City. I went to sea, out
> of my Native place, the Little Town of Lyme in the West of England at 11
> years and a half old until 5 years after my Father sent for me hither and put
> me apprentice to a Shipwright.[1]

Coram was at the start of a long correspondence with the Rev. Benjamin Colman,
minister of the Brattle Street church in Boston, when he wrote this summary of his
life. Anxious that there should be no misunderstanding between them, and conscious
of his lack of formal education, Coram, in those few words, gave the most informative
account of his background and early life that there is. Coram was both proud of his
family background and sensitive about his educational shortcomings brought about
by the family's impoverished circumstances and domestic difficulties.

It is difficult to identify the virtuous good family, to whom Coram refers, or to
know where they came from. In records of the seventeenth and eighteenth centuries
the name Coram appears all over the West Country, in Cornwall, Devon and
Somerset. Corams can be traced through a number of court cases, mainly concerned
with disputes over property.[2]

The Corams are variously described as clothier, yeoman or husbandman, and in
one case neither father nor son, both named John Coram, could sign their name and
left their mark on the document which concerned the non-payment of a mortgage on
Wilton Abbott in Devon.[3] Several generations of the Coram family[4] had lived at
Ottery St Mary, an important agricultural town lying some twenty miles east of Lyme,

---

[1] Letter from T. Coram to B. Colman, London, 30 April 1724, in 'Letters of Thomas Coram', p. 20. I have
used Coram's own spelling and grammar throughout the book.
[2] PRO, C9/458/120; C1/484/15; C11/107/9; C11/1711/31; C16/192/26.
[3] PRO, C11/1320/46.
[4] The name Coram is also spelt Coreham, Choram, or Corham.

until the middle of the seventeenth century. A herald's visitation in 1620 signed by
William Coram shows that the Corams were entitled to bear arms, a sign of being
accepted as a gentleman.[5] Was this what Coram was referring to when he said his
family was always of good reputation? There were so many William Corams and
Thomas Corams in the church baptismal and burial records of the town that they had
to be differentiated as William the younger, or the elder, or Thomas senior or junior.
Then suddenly they disappear. The last two entries in the record of burials are of
'Robert Coreham, an old man of ye almeshouses' who died in 1652, and Katherine, 'a
wid. An Almswoman' who died in 1654.[6] It seems likely that the family had fallen on
hard times, got into debt or become unemployed and left the town in search of work
elsewhere. There is nothing to prove that Thomas Coram's father was related to any
of these Corams, other than the prevalence of the Christian names William, John and
Thomas, names which echo those of Thomas's own family.

John Coram, Thomas Coram's father, is first recorded as being in Lyme in 1667
and he may have left home when things became difficult for the family and come to
Lyme looking for work. There is a note of both pride and regret in Thomas's description of his family circumstances, but apart from references to his father and mother
he says almost nothing about his relations. However in 1721 John Coram's sister
Mary is recorded as living at Combe Raleigh, which is only a few miles from Ottery St
Mary. In his will her brother left her thirty shillings.[7] She died in 1740.[8]

There is no record of the marriage of Thomas's parents, John and Spes Coram, in
the Lyme Regis parish register,[9] so it must be presumed that they came to live there
after they were married. They buried their first son, Thomas, on 10 November
1667.[10] It has always been accepted that the date of Thomas's birth was 1668, which
accords with all known statements, although there is no documentary evidence. It
would seem the parents called their second son Thomas to replace the child they had
lost. Three years later, in 1671, a third son was born and baptised William.[11] Eleven
days later he was buried, on 29 April 1671.[12] Nothing is known about Thomas's
mother, Spes, except that her name is unusual, being the Latin form of Hope, and that
she gave birth to three sons, only one of whom survived to adulthood. She died soon
after the death of William and was buried on 13 September 1671,[13] leaving John
Coram to bring up his motherless three-year-old son. No help seems to have come
from any other member of the Coram family, so the next six years cannot have been
easy for either father or son and they left their mark. Thomas only mentions his
father on one other occasion, so perhaps relations between the two were strained.
Early in life Thomas learned to be self reliant and independent. In later life he
displayed many of the characteristics of a loner, unable to work for long in association

5   College of Arms, MS Visitations of the County of Devon; MS Harl., f. 2626, ICI 262b. The arms were
    argent, a cross sable between four eagles displayed Gules; crest, a beaver passant Or.
6   I am grateful to the Rev. W. Wright, vicar of St Mary's Church, Ottery St Mary, for allowing me to
    consult the church baptismal, marriage and burial records.
7   PROB 11/579, sig. 66.
8   Combe Raleigh, Devon, Register of Burials, 1721–1731–1741.
9   DRO, Lyme Regis Register of Marriages, 1653–1972, PE/LR.
10 DRO, Lyme Regis Register of Burials, 1653–1958, PE/LR.
11 DRO, Lyme Regis Baptismal Register, 1543–1572, 1653–1958, PE/LR.
12 DRO, Lyme Regis Register of Burials, 1653–1958.
13 Ibid.

with others without friction, a behaviour trait which may have resulted from his solitary childhood.

Lyme[14] today – a minor but charming holiday resort with literary associations, with its Cobb the scene of Louisa Musgrave's fall in Jane Austen's *Persuasion*, and the haunting image of a woman in silhouette gazing out to sea in the film of John Fowles' *The French Lieutenant's Woman* – was a very different place in the late seventeenth century. Lyme lies cramped in a valley between crumbling cliffs and the sea. It could only extend into the hinterland, and in Thomas's time most of the land was owned by the Henleys of Colway Manor who would not part with it, so of 1,600 acres of the parish, the borough occupied only 40 acres of the old town.[15] Lyme was always subject to the destructive ravages of the sea, whipped up by the prevailing westerly winds, and its famous Cobb, which served both to protect it from the sea and offer shelter to its shipping, is first mentioned in 1294. Roger North, who was accompanying his kinsman Lord Guildford, Lord Keeper of the Great Seal of England, on a tour of the Western Circuit, has left a fascinating account of how the Cobb would have looked in Coram's time. He starts by saying that Lyme, of all the places upon the coast of England, was the least to be suspected of being a good port, but art and industry had done wonders and the Cobb supplied all the requisites of a safe harbour. He described the Cobb as 'a mole built in the sea, about two furlongs from the town and named from the cobblestones from which it is compiled. There is not anyone like it in the world: for though it is an immense mass of stone, of the shape of a demilune, with a bar in the middle of the concave, no stone that lies, was ever touched with a tool or is bedded in any sort of concrete; but all being pebbles of the sea, are piled up and hold their bearings only, and the surge plays in and out, through the interstices of the stone in a wonderful manner.' North continues his account of the way in which the citizens of Lyme repaired their famous Cobb. When a swamp appeared on the flat top on which they walked they had to take down all that part and build it up from the bottom. However, if they had to lay foundation stones, 'they search them out upon the coast and mounting them upon casks chained together, with but one man mounted upon them, he with the help of a pole, conducts it to the place where it is to lie, then striking out an iron pin, away go the casks, and the stone falls where it is to lie'.[16] Coram passed his childhood among these resourceful, sturdy, independent people and must have witnessed this strange ritual of the rebuilding of the Cobb many times.

Lyme was a mercantile town of some importance. From earliest times it had been one of the chief centres for the export of woollen goods and it was this trade in cloth that brought wealth to the merchants of Lyme. Morlaix and Rotterdam were their natural cross-channel partners, but their horizons were not bounded by the channel, and their ships carried on a lucrative trade with Mediterranean ports. By the end of the seventeenth century the trade in fine woollen cloth had begun to lose ground to tobacco, sugar, fish and beaver pelts, all imported goods carried in British ships from the American colonies, and the surplus goods were re-exported. The Navigation Acts of 1651 and 1660 compelled the merchants to conduct all their trade through Britain

[14] Lyme took the title Regis soon after being granted a Charter in 1284.
[15] Fowles, *Brief History of Lyme*, p. 10.
[16] North, *Life of Francis North*, pp. 117–18.

1. Print of Lyme Regis from the west showing the Cobb, from an engraving published in
1723 by J. Stukeley.

and in British-owned ships. With the growing importance of the cod fishing off
Newfoundland, the West Country ports began to develop as major fishing ports.
Although Plymouth held the record for the greatest number of ships sailing to
Newfoundland, the merchants of Lyme had a long-established tradition of fishing for
cod on the Grand Banks in the summer months. The merchants found a ready market
for their produce. They supplied the navy, which had built up a formidable fleet in
case of war with France, able to protect the transatlantic trade and to patrol fishing
grounds off Newfoundland and Nova Scotia. The West Country was also a recruiting
ground for indentured labour, that is of men willing to sell their labour for a number
of years in return for a passage to America. Their sea passage cost them £5 plus £4 for
food, the money to be repaid at a later date.

Although not as large as Bristol, the population of Lyme, because of the importance of its maritime trade, when compared to the national average, put it in the same
class as towns like Weymouth, Poole and Portsmouth. During the war years many
ships came to Lyme and other south coast ports rather than Bristol to avoid the priva-
teer-infested Bristol Channel. To give some indication of Lyme's relative wealth, its
Customs receipts were greater than those of Liverpool, although its fortunes started
to decline towards the end of the seventeenth century. The town itself had little of
commercial value to offer and was inaccessible to wheeled traffic until 1759. Until
then pack horses provided the only transport and everyone walked up and down the
steep hills.[17]

There is no certainty as to how John Coram earned his living in Lyme. Dr
Brocklesby, a friend of Thomas Coram, is believed to have been the author of the first

---

[17] Tattersfield, *Forgotten Trade*, ch. 16, 'Lyme Regis', pp. 227–76.

short memoir of Coram, written soon after his death.[18] In his memoir Brocklesby gives the title of Captain to John Coram, which has commonly been accepted and therefore it has been assumed that Coram's father was a captain in the merchant navy. In William Coram's original baptismal record, where his father's name is given, the title Captain is missing. It would seem that the title was a later insertion by the vicar of Lyme.[19] Had John Coram been a sea captain his son would almost certainly have said so instead of saying that his family were 'vertuous' and 'of Good Reputation amongst the better sort of people'. It is also curious that the vicar, having recorded William's birth, missed the entry eleven days later recording his death, which has led to further confusion, giving rise to the idea that Thomas had a brother living during his lifetime. John Fowles, who wrote a short history of Lyme for the Philpot Museum, believed that John Coram was on the Customs staff at Lyme, which seems much more likely.

If that was so, the young Thomas Coram no doubt spent much time down by the Cobb where his father would have worked, watching the ships loading and unloading their merchandise. Trade between England and the American colonies was becoming increasingly important. The new colonies needed everything from building materials and manufactured goods to food and clothing. The Staple Act of 1663 stipulated that the colonists must purchase all the manufactured goods they needed from England. These were exchanged for tobacco from Virginia, sugar and molasses from the West Indies, and fish, beaver pelts and timber from North America. Lyme ships had long been involved in transporting white indentured labour to the American plantations. Some merchants had been trading in gold and ivory from Africa, but as the demand for black labour grew Lyme merchants, by the end of the seventeenth century, had made the transition to the more lucrative slave trade.[20] It was not only the great ports like Bristol that were involved in the slave trade; it was much more widely spread and many of the smaller ports all along the south coast were involved.

The Custom House, where his father probably worked, must have been a splendid vantage point from which to watch the ships loading and unloading. There was a system using Cobb porters, responsible for carrying goods ashore via the Custom House at the Cobb Gate situated at the bottom of Broad Street. At high tide the goods were brought ashore by boat, but at low tide pack horses carried the goods to and fro without drivers. What must have seemed routine to the citizens of Lyme astonished Roger North, who left a description of the scene:[21]

> The vessels of Burthen are loaden and unloaden by horses, turning and returning upon the sand and cob and the town. And they have no drivers, but are charged with bales (for instance) at the warehouse and away they trot to their ships side, and stand fair, sometimes above the belly in water, for the tackle to discharge them; then they gallop back to the warehouse for more. And so they perform the tide's work and know by the flood when their

---

18 Brownlow, *History and Objects of the Foundling Hospital*, p. 97.
19 The then vicar of Lyme Regis had supplied Brocklesby with information about the family. The vicar quoted the entry relating to the baptism of William as 'William, son of John Coram, Captain, was baptised at Lyme, April 29th 1671.' In the original entry John Coram is entered simply as 'John Coram'.
20 Tattersfield, *Forgotten Trade*, p. 257.
21 North, *Life of Francis North*, p. 118.

labour is at an end. I must own I could scarce have believed this description if
I had not seen the place and the poor horses at work.

Once he had left Lyme, Thomas seems never to have returned. When told that he had
been given the honour of the freedom of the town he wrote expressing his gratitude
to the people of Lyme.[22] He was then an old man, over eighty, who had been living in
poverty, but the grant of a pension in the same year gave him material comfort.

Bred for the sea

Thomas Coram's later letters and petitions show that he made the most of his early
elementary education. Although he was not entirely at home with grammar and
syntax, his ability to express himself in language full of vivid imagery indicates that he
had made the most of his limited time at school. John Kerridge II ran the school in
Lyme and there Thomas must have mixed with the sons of the rich merchants, who
would have stayed on until they were old enough to be apprenticed at fifteen or
sixteen to merchants who would have taught them the necessary groundwork in
mercantile practice.[23] Instead, Thomas spent his next five years at sea, sent by his
father. His experiences during that time were very different from those of his erstwhile school fellows and this background would have served to reinforce his feelings
of not belonging and his status as a loner. While they were being given the necessary
grounding to enable them to follow in their fathers' footsteps, Thomas had to endure
a life full of hardship and danger.

It would not have been difficult for John Coram to find a berth for Thomas on any
of the ships that came to Lyme. The flourishing merchant community in Lyme meant
that Thomas could have gone to sea on vessels owned by prominent Lyme merchants
such as Robert Burridge or other local families like the Tucker brothers, the
Courtneys or the Grundys. Many of them were attracted by the financial opportunities that trade with the North American plantations offered. Thomas could have
visited the West Indies, Virginia, Boston and Newfoundland in his time as a boy. It
was not unusual for a lad of his age without prospects to be sent to sea. There was
little work to be had in Lyme other than that generated by its maritime trade. Boys
sometimes went to sea as young as six or eight in the seventeenth and eighteenth
centuries, and children commonly began their working lives at ten or twelve.

At some time while Thomas was at sea his father left Lyme for London, so the
break with Thomas's early life was final. Father and son kept in touch and Thomas
was aware that his father had married again. In his first letter to Benjamin Colman,[24]
Thomas writes of his father's marriage having taken place in Hackney. The only John
Coram on record as having married during the relevant years was a John Coram,
whose name appears in the London Parish Register as having married Grace Barnes,
the widow of James Pitts, on 4 July 1682 at St James, Dukes Place.[25] There is no refer-

---

[22] Letter in the possession of the Philpot Museum, Lyme Regis.
[23] Tattersfield, *Forgotten Trade*, p. 239.
[24] Coram to Colman, 30 April 1724, in 'Letters of Thomas Coram', p. 20.
[25] *London Parish Registers*, vol. 1, *1668–1683*.

ence to his new family in any of Coram's known correspondence, and in his letters he only mentions his father's name once more in connection with his apprenticeship. But Thomas did not lose contact with his father, who had set up as a timber merchant in Hackney. John Coram died on 26 March 1721[26] and in his will left his two daughters-in-law, Eunice, Thomas's wife, and Ann (Anna), wife of John Coram, £1 1s 6d each. It must be presumed that this John Coram, who predeceased his father, was Thomas Coram's half-brother, the son of his father's second marriage. He and Ann had a son, Richard, to whom John Coram left £1 1s. Thomas acted as his father's executor and inherited his clothes, household goods and the rest of his estate.

Boys who went to sea were in effect servants, not in the modern sense of domestics, but more as apprentices, learning their trade. Thomas described himself as having been 'bred for the sea', equating his sea-going experience as preparation for his later life as a shipwright and mariner. Seamen had to learn their trade from boyhood while they were still young and agile and could be sent aloft to work on the topgallants and the mizzen topsail. Whether on a naval vessel or on a merchant ship, boys were better able to adjust to a very different way of life and the demands made on them. They could come from any background, some aiming to become officers, others future seamen. Life at sea was arduous and dangerous. Since Lyme was a mercantile port, the likelihood is that Thomas was sent to sea in a merchant ship, where life was tougher than on a man-of-war. Owners paid no more hands than they needed, their holds were filled with cargo, leaving the minimum possible space under the forecastle for the crew. Discipline was generally slack and mutinies and murders were not infrequent.[27] The power of the Master was supreme, and there was little that a victim of ill-treatment could do. Thomas may well have benefited from the fact that in that small community the Master and his father would have known each other, but this did not always guarantee favourable treatment.

Boys would have been given formal instruction in seamanship by the Master; the boatswain and seamen would teach the arts of knotting and splicing, but the practical aspects of a seaman's life could only be learnt by practice. On a naval ship there might be a schoolmaster who would continue the boys' formal education and teach rudimentary Latin and grammar. Thomas clearly did not have this advantage, and without education he would be unable to achieve a commission or even a warrant, hence the edge of bitterness apparent in his letters at being denied the opportunity of professional advancement. No man from a respectable family would send his son to sea with the sole expectation of his just becoming a seaman unless from expediency. It seems likely that it was expediency that lay behind John Coram's decision to send his son to sea. It was a practical solution to the problem of what to do with Thomas until he was old enough to be apprenticed at sixteen, and it enabled his father to pursue his own interests unencumbered by a young lad.

There is no doubt that seafaring was an exceptionally dangerous profession, and life on board was often brutal and hard, but that was not the whole story; seafaring life had its lighter moments. Thomas Coram left no written record of his early life at sea. It is possible to get a flavour of what such a life was like for a young boy by refer-

---

[26] PRO Family Record Centre, PROB 11/579, sig.66.
[27] Rodger, *Wooden World*, p. 117.

ence to the account Jack Cremer left of his experiences.[28] Jack Cremer was sent to sea a few years after Thomas when he was eight years old, and remembered and recorded his impressions. Reading Cremer's story is as near as it is possible to get to understanding something of what life was like in a world with its own customs and way of life. 'The wooden world' that Thomas Coram was to inhabit as a young boy was a term in colloquial use at sea. It was used to refer to the navy, referring not just to a fleet but to a society in miniature with it own customs and way of life.[29] It was also an apt description of the limitations of life at sea, whether in a naval ship or a merchantman.

There are parallels between Coram and Cremer. Cremer was intelligent but uneducated, a difficult child, the fourth son of a widow who could not cope with him, but the important difference was that he had an uncle who had connections with the navy. He was sent aboard the *Royal Escape*, where life would have been marginally easier than on a merchant ship. He recorded his first impressions: 'I was not taken notice of for a day or two, nor could I think what world I was in, weather among Spirits or Devills. All seemed strange; different languidge and strange expressions of tonge, that I thought myself always asleep or in a dream, and never properly awake . . . and I was always dreading what was the matter.' Life on board was not all work, and ships often had to lie off the Downs for days, sometimes weeks, waiting for a favourable wind to take them down the channel. It was then that Jack Cremer remembered that the boys 'were always together and the greater part of our time was spent in play'. There would have been plenty of opportunity for skylarking about and playing in the rigging and indulging in practical jokes. Jack recounted how they strung up hammocks so that when the boys climbed in they would crash to the ground, and how once they had done this to their schoolmaster, who had been nearly killed and was off duty for more than a month. Flogging was the usual punishment for children and adults. Jack learnt to take this brutal punishment strapped to a gun 'and a Boatswain's Mate to wip me with a cat of Nine tailes, which at first was five lashes on my poor tender young brich almost like knives cutting. But by constancy I grew hardened.'[30]

Jack also remembered many acts of kindness and how the men looked after the younger boys, seeing they were kept clean, and lifting them into their hammocks when necessary. Although life could be brutal and dangerous, sailors, with rough understanding, sometimes went out of their way to protect the youngsters from witnessing some of the more distressing occasions. Driven ashore off Harwich in a storm, Jack's ship was in danger of breaking up when some of the crew over-persuaded the Captain to let them try to reach shore in the long boat. The boat capsized in the surf and the men drowned. A 'dismall Sight', as Jack recalled, but he and the other boys were sent below so as not to hear the cries of the drowning men. Moulded by the rigorous discipline of life at sea during his boyhood, Coram remained all his life a hard worker, both stubborn and noted for the persistence with which he pursued his objectives.

---

[28] Bellamy, *Ramblin' Jack: The Journal of Captain John Cremer*, pp. 43–50.
[29] Rodger, *Wooden World*, p. 14.
[30] Bellamy, *Ramblin' Jack*, p. 45.

Apprenticeship

It is thanks to that first letter to Colman that we know Coram was recalled from his seafaring life by his father. '5 years after my Father sent for me hither and put me apprentice to a Shipwright.'[31] His father could hardly have chosen a profession more likely to guarantee work for life. The Navigation Acts of 1651 and 1660 had been passed to preserve English ships and the jobs of English seamen. The Staple Act of 1663 restricted the trading possibilities of the colonies still further by stipulating that all goods produced or manufactured in Europe and destined for the plantations had first to be carried to England in 'lawful' ships and there be unloaded, before being carried thence in English-owned and -manned ships. The colonial governors were made responsible for seeing that the Acts were complied with, but colonial bureaucracy was in its infancy and trade violations often occurred.

English shipbuilders had to work hard to keep pace with the ever increasing demand for shipping. By the beginning of the reign of James II in 1685 the total tonnage of the merchant fleet had virtually trebled since 1629. English merchant ships did not sail unchallenged. This was the era of the privateers and, particularly in time of war, merchant ships were forced to sail in convoys under the protection of the navy to avoid being boarded by the French or Spanish and having their cargoes seized and crews held to ransom. The English privateers were also on the lookout for likely victims: gentleman buccaneers were licensed to prey on enemy ships, and a naval officer, Sir Charles Wager, became very wealthy as a result of the many treasure ships that were intercepted under his command.[32]

The expansion of the merchant fleet had been accompanied by a similar expansion of naval power. There had been a flurry of repairing and fitting out in preparation for the war with the Dutch in 1664. In 1671, Anthony Deane, Master Shipwright, had been seriously worried by the shortage of shipwrights in the royal dockyards. In 1684, the year that Coram started his apprenticeship as a shipwright, Charles II had made his brother, James, Duke of York, Lord High Admiral of the navy. When James became king in 1685 he had the biggest fleet in Europe, due to the work of Samuel Pepys, who had overseen the expansion of the navy.[33]

There is a striking paucity of information as to what was required of an apprentice, and indeed of how ships were built. Many older shipwrights were barely literate and few if any artisans could read or write. This would have given Coram an advantage, and he doubtless made the most of his situation. Many shipwrights were accustomed

[31]   Coram to Colman, 30 April 1724, in 'Letters of Thomas Coram', p. 20.
[32]   Sir Charles Wager, 1666–1743. In 1693 (the same year that Coram sailed for Boston) he commanded the *Samuel and Henry*, an armed ship which conveyed the merchant navy to New England. He saw action in the Mediterranean under Sir Cloudesley Shovell. In 1708 he intercepted a convoy of Spanish treasure ships off Cartagena and, although most ships escaped, enough treasure remained to make Wager a wealthy man. He remained on station in Jamaica until 1709, and the many prize ships taken increased his wealth. He was Rear Admiral of the Blue in 1707, Controller of the Navy 1714–18, and was appointed Lord Commissioner of the Admiralty 1718–33. He became First Lord of the Admiralty in 1733. He retired from the Admiralty in 1742 and died the following year. See *DNB*. He was a long-term friend and supporter of Coram's and became a governor of the Foundling Hospital in 1739.
[33]   As Clerk of the King's Ships, Pepys was an energetic official, a zealous reformer against abuses during the war with Holland, and worked hard to supply the requirements of the fleet. He became Secretary to the Navy in 1673 and Secretary to the Admiralty in 1668 and was twice Master of Trinity House. See *DNB*.

to work on 'recipes' of their own devising based on a preferred shape or an arithmetical formula. It is not surprising that a culture of professional secrecy grew up, for to divulge their secrets in a competitive market place was tantamount to reducing the unique value of their knowledge.[34] It is not known where Coram was apprenticed, but in the light of his lifelong association with the Navy Office, it is tempting to believe that it might have been with one of the naval dockyards or with one of those that worked on commission for the navy. The dockyards at Woolwich, Chatham and Deptford could build all the larger warships with only occasional help from private yards. The navy was increasing in size all the time and by 1690 eighteen out of thirty third- or fourth-rate naval ships, as well as many smaller vessels, were built for the navy in merchants' yards on the Thames.[35] The great Wells yard, founded by Abraham Wells in 1660 at Rotherhithe at the Commercial Dock Pier between Odessa Street and Rotherhithe Street, was one of those to work on commission for the navy.

Although the records of the Company of Free Shipwrights list all shipwrights and details of their apprenticeships in their Quarterage Books covering the period 1681–1711, Coram's name is absent. This may be because towards the end of the sixteenth century a community of shipwrights came into existence at Rotherhithe that did not belong to the Company of Free Shipwrights and were therefore known as 'foreigners' because they were not freemen of the city. This rival company constantly attempted to usurp and interfere with the privileges long enjoyed by the Worshipful Company of Free Shipwrights. A royal charter was granted in 1612 to the Master, Wardens and Commonality of the Art or Mystery of Redriff (as Rotherhithe was known in those days). The Shipwrights of Rotherhithe wanted to bring the rival, and older, Company of Free Shipwrights under the jurisdiction of their charter and a long and bitter dispute ensued. By the time Coram became an apprentice the Shipwrights of Rotherhithe had lost out despite Pepys's support and their charter had been surrendered and cancelled in 1684.[36] In the light of Coram's possible association with Rotherhithe it may be that he learned his trade in the Wells yard or one of the other Rotherhithe yards, and that would explain why his name is not recorded in the Quarterage Books of the Company of Free Shipwrights.

Thomas Coram was in the last year of his apprenticeship when William III landed at Torbay in 1688. Although James II had the biggest fleet in Europe at that time, the navy did nothing to oppose the landing. The ill-fated attempt at rebellion, led by the Duke of Monmouth, who landed at Lyme on the beach beside the Cobb, had been crushed swiftly by James at Sedgemoor. The King, with an army of 20,000 men at his disposal, had no reason to think his throne in danger. His pro-Catholic sentiments and policies had alarmed and alienated some Anglican Tories, who were also dismayed at the news from Ireland where the army and the civil service were, they thought, being catholicised. There were a number of conspiracies and plots among both Tories and Whigs, but nothing to alert James to any particular threat.

The 'Glorious Revolution' of 1688 was seen by many as providential, although the outcome could have been catastrophically different. Historians of the time chose to see it as part of the divine pattern and purpose. The Lords and Commons of the

---

[34] Ollivier, *Eighteenth Century Shipbuilding*, p. 10.
[35] Banbury, *Shipbuilders of the Thames and Medway*, pp. 139–41.
[36] Ridge, *Records of the Worshipful Company of Shipwrights*, Intro. A. Charles Knight, p. xiii.

Convention Parliament of 1689 described it as a 'miraculous delivery from popery and arbitrary power'. It was said that it was an easterly 'Protestant Wind' that in the early days of November blew Prince William's invasion force of ships at high speed down the channel. As later historians have pointed out, the success of the revolution owed more to the passivity of the people of England and Scotland than to any working of divine providence.

Across the channel, Louis XIV was not going to allow his protégé, ally and co-religionist to lose his throne without a fight. Louis had offered to send James naval support, but his offer had been spurned. Now, after James's precipitate flight, he gave him sanctuary and offered to lend him arms, money and men to help with a planned invasion of Ireland with the intention of using that country as a springboard for the recovery of England.

James landed at Kinsale on 12 March to reinforce the Irish Catholic rising, which had broken out in January. The rebellion, which had reached alarming proportions, together with the French king's refusal to acknowledge William and Mary's titles, easily persuaded the English House of Commons to vote to support William III in a war against France. Had William's new subjects known that the war would embroil England in continental wars for many years they might have hesitated. Most Englishmen probably believed it would be a short struggle to secure William's right to the throne. But England and her allies were taking on the greatest military power in Europe. The 1697 Treaty of Ryswick only ended the first stage of the European wars, and the peace that followed was an uneasy one. Although England had gone to war with France for political and dynastic reasons, by 1701 the defence of England's commercial interests was seen as equally important.

The first priority in 1689 was to crush the rebellion in Ireland. Preparations for the invasion of Ireland gave Coram, his apprenticeship now complete, his first paid job. Men and horses needed to be transported across the Irish Sea. The Admiralty ordered the Navy Office, who were housed in a handsome building in Crutched Friars, to provide shipping for 23,528 men and 4,384 horses. The Navy Office replied that they were unable to undertake the task. They argued that they were overburdened with their responsibilities for building, repairing and fitting out ships as well as mustering ships' companies. The Lords of the Admiralty, at the King's express command, thereupon appointed three captains as Commissioners to manage the business with a Cashier, Secretary and Clerk.[37] A final Order in Council was issued on 26 February 1690, appointing a Commission consisting of eight members to execute the service of providing ships and necessaries for transportation to Ireland. It was they who hired Coram to go to Liverpool to detect frauds in the stated burden of the ships taken on as transports and to report on their true tonnage. It was the beginning of Coram's long association with the Navy Office.

Since Liverpool was the nearest port to Ireland a lot of the shipping being made ready to take the troops across was anchored in the Pool. The Pool was singularly unfitted for the task. Until the end of the seventeenth century the Pool, the outstanding geographical feature of the town, was a tidal inlet, covering nearly 50 acres. There were no dockyards, and little in the way of shipbuilding was carried on.

37 Robinson, *British Fleet*, p. 125.

Only small ships could be built, as all 'docks' from which such ships were launched had to be filled up within three days and the first proper dock was only built in 1710.[38] The lack of facilities must have made Coram's task no easy one, but he clearly accomplished it to the satisfaction of the authorities. He later wrote to Colman that he had performed the service required of him with reputation and that he had been well esteemed in those parts ever since.[39] Those early Liverpool contacts would form part of his later extensive network and be used by him to gain support for one or other of his many projects.

The rates charged for shipping were calculated according to tonnage and varied between 11 shillings and 14 shillings per calendar month, so there was scope for profiteering if an accurate check to ascertain the true tonnage was not maintained. Coram told Colman in the same letter that he had been given the freedom of the city in 1691, clearly as a token of appreciation by the authorities for the money that had been saved. Again there is no record of Coram's having been presented with the freedom, other than his own word, but there is no reason to doubt his statement. It is known that Captain Phineas Pett was made a burgess in 1693 and that other captains of ships of war were similarly honoured. For Coram the gift of the freedom would have been a valuable privilege because only freemen were permitted to work within the borough limits. The son of a freeman, born within the borough limits, was admitted as a burgess practically as a matter of course. An apprentice to a freeman shipwright would be admitted at the end of his seven years on proof of his servitude, as was Roger James Junior at the same time as Coram. Admission to the privileges of working in the town as a 'foreign' or outside shipwright, such as Coram would be, was a very different matter. Practising the faculty of a freeman without being free would have meant fines of increasing severity until the culprit either left or humbly petitioned for admission as a burgess. The freedom of Liverpool would have given Coram the opportunity to set up as a shipwright, but to do so he would have needed capital which he did not possess. It is unlikely that he worked for another shipwright in Liverpool.[40] He probably returned to London and worked in one of the yards on the Thames for the next two years before leaving for New England, fully qualified and with some work experience. There is no further mention of his father in his letters, and it is clear that the decision to go to Boston was Coram's own.

---

[38] Stewart Brown, *Liverpool Ships*, p. 11.
[39] Coram to Colman, 26 July 1735, in 'Letters of Thomas Coram', p. 28.
[40] Stewart Brown, *Liverpool Ships*, p. 113.

2

Shipbuilding in New England

Boston

The ten years that Coram spent in New England would change his life. He was to find a wife, enjoy success, build a business, and put down roots. But sadly his experience of shipbuilding in New England was to end in bitter disappointment. His business ruined, he left for England encumbered by debt and never to return permanently. The years he lived in Massachusetts opened his eyes to the benefits of a nearly independent civil government and to the possibilities that existed for a man of intelligence and application to carve out a career. He saw for himself the great potential value of the forests and fisheries of North America to England. Fiercely loyal to the Crown, he was quick to understand the commercial and strategic importance of North America, both as providing a boundless supply of naval stores, and also as a means of containing French ambitions. Both were subjects that became of major interest to him, based on his practical knowledge as a shipwright and experience of trading conditions in New England. The major part of his life, after his departure from Boston, was to be spent attempting to persuade Ministers of the Crown of the need to settle and exploit the natural resources of the lands stretching from what is now Maine to Nova Scotia so as to preserve them from the depredations of the French. Although forced to abandon his hopes of living and working in New England, the experience had left him with a longing to return to what he saw as a land of opportunity, to a country where a man who had to make his own way in life would have the freedom to succeed.

Thomas Hunt was one of the many London merchants trading with New England who had a financial interest in a merchant ship. Merchants organised their business in one of two ways: either as sole trader or in a partnership. Ship-owning partnerships involved owning a share, a quarter, an eighth, or sometimes as little as one sixty-fourth part of a ship's property. A ship's affairs were managed by one partner, who would sometimes employ a factor or supercargo who became in effect the employer's representative in all matters pertaining to the selling and buying of cargoes at the different ports.

With the ever increasing cross-Atlantic trade, the need for more merchant ships to transport manufactured goods from England to the colonies in exchange for naval supplies, timber and masts, hemp and tar, as well as beaver pelts and fish, was acute.

It was cheaper to build ships in New England, as timber was plentiful and pitch and tar were easily obtained, and little was needed in the way of infrastructure. Not only were ships built in America cheaper, but they had an added advantage in that they counted as English bottoms, and were free from the restraints imposed on all foreign ships under the terms of the Navigation Acts.

Thomas Hunt must have been impressed by the competence and business acumen of the young Thomas Coram because he engaged him to act as his factor and instructed him to sail to Boston sometime in 1693/4 in charge of a number of other shipwrights, carpenters, sail-, block-, tackle-, and clothmakers. He was instructed to set up a shipbuilding business in New England. Apart from Coram's own account of his mission, his arrival in Boston was officially noted in the list of residents of Boston in 1693.[1] Coram himself subsequently gave several accounts of his mission. The first was in a memorial to the Governor of Massachusetts, Joseph Dudley, in 1703. Coram wrote that Thomas Hunt,

> a merchant of London, whose goodwill for this country is well known to the chiefe persons here, he sent me hither for the carrying on a design of ship-building, and was permitted and protected by the Government at home in my coming hither for the better Improvement of shipbuilding in these parts, and I have favour answerable there unto by the government here during the whole time of my building ships in Boston.[2]

In 1727, in a further memorial, Coram wrote that he carried 'shipwrights to New England, by His Majesty's permission, to promote shipbuilding there and so preserve British Oak fit for the Royal Navy'.[3] Later still, in 1745, in a letter to the Society for Propagating the Gospel, Coram wrote that he was 'sent from home with proper workmen, shipwrights and others to promote shipbuilding in New England where I remained ten years'.

Shipbuilding was already well established in New England. By 1676 New England yards were turning out thirty ships a year for the English market alone, and the Boston shipyards were supplying many of their own needs for coastal craft, schooners for the Newfoundland fisheries and many other ships capable of trading with Europe and England. Coram may have exaggerated the importance of his mission, as he sometimes did, but for him the opportunity of being his own master in a thrusting new country was an exhilarating experience, and his subsequent forced departure made all the more bitter as a consequence. Pepys gave it as his opinion that no ship-wright could make his fortune, but the ambitious Coram saw his shipbuilding and trading opportunities not only as a means toward greater financial reward, but as a step up in the world. Young skilled men in England had a poor economic future if they had neither land nor capital, but in America wages were higher, raw materials were cheap and there were opportunities for acquiring land. There was a clear pattern of social ascent through trade and any ambitious and hardworking man could aspire to become a merchant and so reach the highest echelons of colonial society, although

---

1   Reed, *Province of Massachusetts*.
2   Hill, 'Thomas Coram in Boston and Taunton', p. 134.
3   *Acts of the Privy Council, Colonial Series, VI: Unbound Papers* (PRO, Chancery Records).

the existing British social hierarchy was able, in a more flexible way, to recreate itself in North America.

Crossing the Atlantic was a hazardous experience. England in 1693 was at war with France and French privateers posed an ever greater threat as they targeted the English merchant fleet. Louis XIV had abandoned his battle-fleet strategy and concentrated on commerce by raiding and attacking individual vessels or assaulting convoys with 'wolf packs'.[4] Pepys estimated that between 1693 and 1697 over 5,000 ships were lost. In 1693 French privateers alone were accounting for the loss of between 700 and 800 ships.[5] For protection, merchant ships depended on the navy patrolling the coast and on naval escorts. Since there were never enough cruisers available, the merchant ships would have to wait on the Downs for a convoy to assemble. It seems very likely that Coram sailed to Boston in just such a convoy, since he wrote that he was 'protected by the Government at home in my coming'. By what may have been a remarkable coincidence, in 1693 Charles Wager, then a young naval officer, was in command of the *Samuel and Henry*, an armed ship conveying a merchant fleet to Boston. Was Coram on one of the merchant ships in that convoy and was it possible that the two met in Boston? Could that meeting have been the start of the friendly relationship that existed throughout their lives between these two men whose lives and social circumstances were to be so different?

Boston at the time of Coram's arrival was an island of just one square mile, linked to the mainland only by a narrow neck. The peninsula was dominated by three hills, Fort Hill, Beacon Hill and Copp's Hill, the last the only one to remain intact. Where present-day South Boston and Back Bay stand there was nothing but water and mud flats. Boston, with a population of about 6,000, was the metropolis of British America, a substantial city even by the standards of provincial England. The brightly painted small houses were cramped and smoky inside. Glass was expensive so windows tended to be small and fire was a constant hazard. Boston was a pleasant town to live in, with little crime and little poverty. Food was usually cheap, although manufactured goods, nearly all imported, were expensive. The townscape was dominated by the spires of Boston's churches, whose activities were central to the life of Boston. There were no theatres and mixed dancing was frowned upon, although the town boasted at least a dozen distilleries and there was a plentiful supply of wine, imported from the Canaries and Europe. Boston harbour was the scene of the greatest activity, with ships unloading their cargoes of manufactured goods from England, fish from Newfoundland, and sugar and molasses from the West Indies. They then took on board local produce: wheat, barrels of preserved beef, pork, herrings and cod, as well as timber and naval supplies. Around the shoreline there were at least a dozen ship-yards of varying size.

While there is a great deal of information about Coram's shipbuilding activities once he had moved to Taunton in 1697, there is no information as to how successful he was in Boston. The only knowledge we have as to his work in Boston comes from the records of the court case in 1705 concerning the building of a ship, prior to his departure for England, and of another case brought against him in London in 1704

---

4   Kennedy, *Rise and Fall of British Naval Mastery*, p. 78.
5   Davis, *The Rise of the English Shipping Industry*, pp. 293–4.

after his return to the port of London. There is no record of any ships he may have built in Boston prior to his removal to Taunton: nothing to say how many ships he built, no details as to their size or where they were built. He had to buy an existing dockyard or rent one or build one of his own. Samuel Sewall, a notable personage in Boston society – a merchant, a banker and a man of learning, whose property adjoined that of the Waite family – would have been at the dockside when Coram's convoy arrived, as it was his habit to question all arrivals for news from England. The Sewall and Waite families, although not intimate, were next door neighbours and so knew each other.[6] John Waite owned Bendal's dockyard, which he sold in 1694.[7] Sewall would have been aware that John Waite wanted to sell the dockyard. He was very likely to have heard that Coram had been commissioned to start a shipbuilding enterprise. Did he or someone else tell Coram the dockyard was for sale? The reason for thinking that Coram may have used Bendal's dockyard is that six years later Coram married John Waite's daughter, Eunice.

Coram, in all the subsequent legal processes in which he was involved, was referred to as Thomas Coram, Boston, shipwright, or Thomas Coram of Boston, sometime residing in Taunton. Although little is known about his business, the years he spent in Boston, before he moved to Taunton, were without major incident. His membership of the King's Chapel was unremarkable, as many leading merchants attended the Anglican church, which by that time had become an accepted part of Boston life. Although throughout the New England settlements only those in membership of one of the Nonconformist churches were able to hold a position of public responsibility, there was increasing acceptance of the role of the King's Chapel, and it was no longer regarded with the hostility that had been so marked during its early years. There was nothing to distinguish Coram, a devout Anglican, from the other citizens of Boston who chose to attend the chapel. In Taunton, however, Anglicanism was still regarded with the greatest suspicion. The freedom to practise their own form of Protestantism was part of the reason many had left England, and Coram's attachment to Anglican beliefs and forms of worship would immediately mark him out as different. Differences that were tolerated in Boston would be seen in a very different light in Taunton. What had been acceptable in Boston would seem provocative and suspect to the little community in which Coram came to live.

Taunton

Coram, in furtherance of his mission to promote shipbuilding in New England, had been looking for suitable locations other than Boston. After visiting the township of Taunton, which lies some forty miles south of Boston alongside the broad waters of the river of the same name, and which, according to Coram, was about twenty miles distant north and east from Rhode Island from where ships go up a navigable river to Taunton. He went on to describe it as 'a long good tract of land yet poorly inhabited

6   Thomas, ed., *Diary of Samuel Sewall*, vol. 1, p. 164.
7   New England Historical and Genealogical Register, vol. 31, p. 424.

and but a very small part of it cultivated and had not then more than about 150 English families in that large extent of country'.[8]

His decision to move there was a bold one. No one had attempted to build ships on the river before, the east bank being covered in forest and the west bank mainly used for farming. However, Coram quickly realised that all he needed for a shipbuilding enterprise was already in situ. A sawmill was already in operation to cut up the plentiful pine, chestnut and cedar trees that grew along the far bank. Iron ore had been discovered on Two Mile river. Henry and James Leonard had been persuaded to come from Wales and set up the first iron works in 1652.[9] He could bring some of his skilled workmen from Boston and hire local labour.

The region around Taunton had been inhabited by the Wampanoag Indians, a tribe of the Algonquin nation, for generations, but their numbers had been greatly reduced by the great plagues of 1612, 1616 and 1617. In 1663, Philip de Sachem, their chief, sitting under the council oak, agreed to the sale of the land on the west side of the river. James Walker, one of the earliest settlers, and John Richmond were authorised to make the purchase, which was to be divided among eighty-seven persons. Finally seventy-six signed the agreement, among them James Walker and his five children, James, Peter, Eleazor, Hester and Deborah, thereby becoming owners of shares in the land known thenceforth as South Purchase. James Walker senior was a large landowner, his son Peter Walker was an iron manufacturer as well as dealing in timber and was described as a husbandman.[10] He, together with his brother Eleazor, was to cross swords with Thomas Coram in an increasingly acrimonious series of court cases concerning the supply of timber and allegations of non-payment.

The South Purchase land was rough and stony. Before they could use the land, the new owners had the onerous task of clearing fields, and carting and cutting the trees. It took nearly a year to clear the rocks and stones from an acre of ground and could take as long as fifty years for a family to fully clear its farm. Trees were girdled rather than cut immediately and a farmer would cultivate the area around the dead tree before cutting it up for firewood. One of the prime objects of all early settlements was to make provision for a settled Gospel ministry, and Peter Walker had been active in providing for a minister, giving ten acres of land in 1688 toward the stipend of a minister. He later signed to bear equal cost and charge for the support of a meeting house.[11] This tight-knit community was very different from cosmopolitan Boston society, and Coram, a zealous Anglican, confident, ambitious, outspoken and successful, was soon perceived as a threat to their hard-won settled way of life.

Coram lived in lodgings when he first arrived in Taunton. He chose a site for his shipbuilding activities on the west side of the river, one eighth of a mile north of Muddy Cove in South Dighton. He described his yard as being the most commodious place on the river, with so good a depth of water that, if need be, a fourth-rate frigate might be launched there. The cove then went by the name of Zebulon but was later known as Dighton, and today there is a flourishing marina on the site. The quiet

8   Letter from Coram to the Honourable Society for Propagating the Gospel among the Indians of New England, 17 June 1745: The Newberry Library, Chicago, Edward E. Ayer Manuscript Collection.
9   Emery, *History of Taunton*, p. 137.
10 Lane, *History of the Town of Dighton*.
11 Emery, *History of Taunton*, p. 187.

beauty of the country and the silent grandeur of the river and woods must have made a pleasing contrast to the bustle of Boston, and augured well.

That the shipbuilding enterprise was financially successful must be assumed from the fact that in April 1699 Coram was able to buy from John Reed, a carpenter, a small lot with 190 feet of frontage on the river Taunton which he had previously leased. At the same time he also purchased, from the same John Reed, another lot of one and three-quarter acres which contained an orchard of fifty apple trees.[12] Considering the time it took to clear land, and this land was already being cultivated, this purchase must have meant a considerable financial outlay for Coram. His neighbour was Jonathan Hathaway, one of the original signatories of South Purchase, who had bought his property in 1668 and who later took over Coram's shipbuilding business after he left Taunton. There is no record of any house on the land in 1699, so Coram must have built the house between 1699 and 1700. The two-storeyed timber-framed house looks today much as it would have looked in Coram's time. Its central core consists of a circular brick chimney with ovens beside the open fireplaces, built from bricks shipped from England as ballast. The heat from the ovens and open fires in the lower rooms heated the whole building. The solid brick chimney stands four-square in the centre of the roof. A very steep staircase led to the upper rooms, and the interior walls were made of strong, wide, oak planks. There was ample storage space below, with room to house some of Coram's workmen on the ground floor. The present residents of the clapboard house are proud of the association with the one-time shipwright. It stands, on what is today called Water Street, and land that was once an apple orchard now belongs to the local school and has become the children's playground: something of which Coram would have approved.

It was not only the successful shipyard that showed Coram was putting down roots in South Purchase. The residents of Taunton were subject to attack from the Indians, and to defend themselves had set up the First Military Company of Taunton, which was under the command of Thomas Leonard.[13] Being part of the Company was a serious undertaking. The rules stated that 'whosoever shall not come to training at the day appointed being seasonable shall pay 6 pence for such default and if he come not one after the second call shall pay 12 pence for his default up to two shillings and sixpence; that whosoever shall depart away from the company before he be dismissed except he have leave granted shall pay 12 pence; that if any shall talk in time of exercising after silence is commanded by the chief officer shall be liable to pay a penny for every such default'.[14] Fines were also prescribed for those who did not have a gun, powder, bullets, halbert, belt, match or flint, bandolier or pouch, a bullet pouch, wire and rod. Jonathan Hathaway, Coram's neighbour, was one of those fined for not having a gun and powder at an earlier inspection.

In the register of members of 1700, which included the names of Dan Throope, Eleazor Walker and Abel Burt, was that of Thomas Coram. Coram alone, however, chose to register himself as Mr Thomas Coram, probably to emphasise his new-found status as a successful businessman, but this little act of vanity sent out all the wrong signals. There were some in the community who felt threatened by the pretensions of

---

12 Copy of deed printed in *Collections of the Old Colony Historical Society*, vol. 2, pp. 28–30.
13 Emery, *History of Taunton*, p. 353.
14 Ibid.

the newcomer, notably Nathaniel Byfield. Byfield commanded the First Regiment of the County of Bristol, of which the South Purchase Company formed part, so would have noticed the way in which Coram chose to style himself and could have been provoked by it. He had been one of the first to settle in Bristol County in 1674, and become an influential figure in the province. The fact that his aunt had married Bishop Juxton, who had attended Charles I on the scaffold, no doubt gave him a certain social status and, without even having met Coram, he was to take a leading role in the conspiracy to undermine his shipbuilding business and force his eventual departure.

Marriage

When Thomas Coram married Eunice Waite, the daughter of John and Eunice Waite, in 1700 he allied himself with one of the oldest Boston families.[15] Eunice's grandfather, Gamaliel Waite, had arrived in Boston on board the *Griffin*, in 1633 at the same time as Edward and Sarah Hutchinson, both having left their family homes in Lincolnshire to join family networks already established in Boston. They formed part of the migration of over 20,000 English men and women who came to New England in the decade between 1630 and 1640. However, that is where the similarities between the two families end. Their different histories illustrate how the existing British social order came to be replicated to a certain extent across the Atlantic.

The Hutchinsons had one of the most complete family commercial networks in existence at that time. The affluent Richard Hutchinson had become wealthy through the export of manufactured goods from London to New England and to the West Indies. Richard needed his younger brothers, Edward and Samuel, and his nephews, Elisha and Eliakim, to look after the New England side of the business. Thomas Savage and Peleg Sandford, both merchants, had married two of Richard Hutchinson's sisters and both played an important role in this family network. Edward was a typical younger son, seeking his fortune in America with the support of relatives in London who were anxious to profit from the importation of colonial goods.[16]

Gamaliel Waite, one of a family of fourteen, already had three brothers in Boston. Economic necessity had forced them all to emigrate to New England as their only chance of escaping the grinding poverty of rural England.[17] Without the money needed for the £5 fare, the only way Gamaliel could join his brothers was to cross the Atlantic as an indentured servant. Since both the Waites and the Hutchinsons lived in Alton, Lincolnshire, Gamaliel probably already worked for the Hutchinsons, and so to cross the Atlantic as Edward Hutchinson's indentured servant would have suited both parties. Gamaliel would have continued to work without pay until he had repaid his debt, after which he would have become a freeman. Edward Hutchinson would have had the benefit of unpaid labour until the debt was repaid. By 1636, at the time of Gamaliel's wedding to Grace, his indenture would have expired and he

[15] *Report of the Record Commissioners of the City of Boston Containing Boston Marriages from 1700 to 1751*, Boston 1898.
[16] Bailyn, *New England Merchants*, pp. 88–9.
[17] NEHGR, vol. 24, p. 103.

would have been at liberty to earn his own livelihood. All the Waite brothers were to do well in New England.

There must still have been, in the early days, close links between the two families because both were made to suffer as a result of what came to be known as the 'Antinomian Schism'. Puritans believed that all men were responsible for their behaviour and that salvation was to be had by strict adherence to the teachings of the Bible. Preservation of the health of the Puritan community required both isolation from contamination by the Old World and unquestioning acceptance of the authority of the Puritan magistracy. This in theory meant the most rigorous selection of newcomers, as it was important for those who wished to settle to be accepted into the Church. Richard Waite is recorded as having been admitted to the Church in 1633 and was included on the list of freemen in 1635, showing that he too came over as an indentured servant.[18]

The magistracy had steadfastly maintained that conformity with the letter of the law and careful performance of religious duties should be seen to be practised before a settler was admitted to the Church. Three years after Edward Hutchinson's arrival, his sister-in-law, Anne, was to challenge the authority of the Puritan magistracy by declaring that inner direct religious experience was of more importance to religious life than strict conformity with the law. Her belief that immediate revelation was of greater authority than scripture triggered what became known as the 'Antinomian Schism', a disagreement that was to shake the religious life of the colony for a year. Anne had the support of her own family and many Boston merchants backed the dissenters. Anne and her supporters were seen as so dangerous to Church orthodoxy and political stability that they were disarmed, meaning that their membership of the Church was revoked.

It was not only the important merchant families that were cast out from the Church. Thomas, Richard and Gamaliel Waite were all listed as supporters, but Gamaliel appears to have been marked out as more dangerous than his brothers, possibly because his links to the Hutchinsons were more recent.[19] Despite being only on the fringe of the support group, nevertheless Richard Waite was disarmed, and his formal exclusion was dated 30 November 1637.[20] He was reinstated, caught stealing, cast out again but after a full confession was finally reinstated in 1640. Gamaliel Waite left Boston, as did many of the exiled merchants who settled in Portsmouth. Gamaliel went to Salem and earned his living as a fisherman for a while. A record of him asking for exemption from military service during the fishing season in 1657 implies that he worked as a fisherman, and did not return to Boston until some time after that date.

Meanwhile his brothers were beginning to prosper. Samuel Waite was granted a lot by the town of Boston at Mount Willaston in 1637, the same day as his brother Richard was granted a lot there for five heads.[21] Gamaliel had to wait until 1670 before receiving a grant of one acre of land in Boston on the south side of Sentry Hill, to plant and improve. He seems to have made up for lost time for by 1673 he owned

[18] NEHGR, vol. 31, p. 421.
[19] Battis, *Saints and Sectaries*, p. 197.
[20] NEHGR, vol. 31, p. 424.
[21] *The American Genealogist*, vol. 67, pp. 195, 198.

land on Long Island in Boston as well.[22] In that year Gamaliel and Grace Waite gave as gift to their son John two parcels of land on Long Island in Boston Harbour, one of one and a half acres and one of one acre. In a separate deed on the same day Gamaliel also gave his son eight acres on Long Island.[23]

Now in possession of a large part of his inheritance, John married in the following year, but his wife Mary died without leaving issue. In 1677 John married Eunice, whose surname is given as Roberts, although there seems to be some doubt as to the reliability of the information. They had several children, among them two daughters, Eunice, who became Mrs Thomas Coram, and Grace, who would marry John Stirling. That the Waites were making their way in Boston is clear. When John Waite was asked to be a signatory to the will of Governor John Leverett (who became President of Harvard University), he described himself as a merchant of Boston. The term merchant covered a wide spectrum, from those who lived in a superior world closely linked to the centres of power in England and America, to the lowest reaches of the group, where a number of tradesmen, shopkeepers, mariners and fishermen would join together to invest their resources in a few voyages overseas and begin to think of themselves as merchants. At this level there were no institutional limits that could prohibit an ambitious shipmaster from calling himself a merchant. The Waites, as a well respected family, would have been somewhere in the middle of the spectrum. There is no record of their ever having become part of the governing elite. Many of the Hutchinsons, although first and foremost prosperous merchant ship owners, were, at different times, involved in public life. Their most famous descendant, Thomas Hutchinson, by becoming the last civilian royal Governor of Massachusetts in 1771, also became one of the most hated men in America. His loyalty to the Crown led to his exile and vilification.[24]

Thanks to Sam Sewall's property adjoining that of the Waites, and to his habit of recording small items of information, the circumstances of Gamaliel Waite's death in 1685 are known.

> Our neighbour, Gamaliel Waite eating his breakfast well, went to do something in his orchard where Serj. Pells dwells, there found himself not well, went into Pell's, his tenant's house and died extreme suddenly about noon and then was carried home in a chair and means used to fetch him again but in vain . . . he was about 87 years old, strong and hearty: had lately had several new teeth. People in the street much startled at this good man's death.[25]

Gamaliel died intestate and the administration of his estate was left to his wife, Grace. It totalled £254 including real estate of £210, the dwelling house, barn, cow house and land worth £170 and the land adjoining where John Pell lived. John Waite inherited the house, and it is to this house that Coram came to woo his future bride, Eunice, riding forty miles back and forth along the Old Bay Path, the only road between

22 NEHGR, vol. 31, p. 421.
23 Anderson, *The Great Migration*.
24 Bailyn, *Ordeal of Thomas Hutchinson*, pp. 1–9.
25 Thomas, ed., *Diary of Samuel Sewall*, vol. I.

Boston and Taunton. They were married on 27 June 1700.[26] The family were all staunch Congregationalists and the wedding took place at the Puritan First Church in Boston where Mr Wadsworth, who was later to become President of Harvard University, officiated. Although a convinced Anglican himself, Coram always respected his wife's right to worship as her family had always done.

Samuel Sewall, who lived on Cotton Hill between Summer Street and Bedford Street (the east side of what is now Washington Street), was sometimes incommoded by his neighbours. He noted that John Waite's cows had eaten all his last year's grafts, save one twig, so that this year he had to make the graft high up 'out of the cows reach with cions from Mr Moody's orange pear and grafted two apple stocks with Mr. Gardener's russettings'.[27] Also in 1700, Sewall records the details of a rather different marriage in the Waite household, with which he become involved. Sebastion, the Waite's negro servant, wished to marry Jane, the negro servant who worked for Mrs Thair. The families clearly could not agree as to how this arrangement would work and the wedding plans of Sebastion and Jane were held up for two years until terms agreeable to both parties were sorted out. The Waites called in their neighbour to help the proceedings along.

> Mr Waite desires that the banns might be published in order to facilitate the marriage. Mrs Thair insisted that Sebastion might have one day in six allowed him for the support of Jane, his intended wife, and her children if it please God to give her any. Mr Waite now wholly declined that, but offered freely to allow Bastion £5 in money per annum towards the support of his children and the said Jane (besides Sebastion's clothing and diet). I persuaded Jane and Mrs Thair to agree to it and so it was concluded and Mrs Thair gave note of publication to Mr. Waite for him to carry it to Wm Griggs, the Town Clerk and to Williams in order to have them published according to law.[28]

Finally it was Sam Sewall, who was also a judge, who married them on 13 February 1700.[29]

It is not clear from this account as to whether Sebastion and Jane were negro slaves or free black servants, but the restrictions under which they were placed suggest they were in fact slaves. By a Massachusetts law of 1641 slaves were guaranteed 'all liberties and Christian usages which the law doth morally require',[30] which meant they had the same protection against maltreatment as white servants, and the right to trial by jury. Overall the slave population of New England rarely exceeded 3 per cent of the labour force, but slaves were bought and sold in Boston. There was no stigma attached to the slave trade, although in Massachusetts slaves were granted greater equality before the law than elsewhere in British America at that time.

Samuel Sewall was exceptional in finding the slave trade obnoxious. He had no illusions about slaves and thought them untrustworthy and less profitable employees

---

[26] *Report of the Record Commissioners of the City of Boston Containing Boston Marriages from 1700 to 1751*, Boston 1898.

[27] Thomas, ed., *Diary of Samuel Sewall*, vol. I, p. 164.

[28] Ibid., pp. 435, 443.

[29] *Report of the Record Commissioners of the City of Boston Containing Boston Marriages from 1700 to 1751*, Boston 1898.

[30] Bremer, *The Puritan Experiment*, p. 204.

than indentured servants, but he did write what may have been the first anti-slavery tract, entitled 'The Selling of Joseph'. Here Sewall wrote:

> These Ethiopians, black as they are, seeing they are the sons and daughters of the first Adam; the brethren and sisters of the last Adam, and the off spring of GOD; they ought to be treated with a Respect agreeable. Originally and Naturally there is no such thing as slavery. Joseph was no more a Slave to his Brethren than they were to him and no more authority to SELL him than they had to SLAY him.[31]

Unsurprisingly, as the diary continues to relate, he was soon answered by John Safin in 'A Brief and Candid answer to The Selling of Joseph', refuting Sewall's arguments. Equally unsurprisingly, most citizens agreed with Safin.

Thomas Coram cannot have been unaware of the slave trade, allied as he was to the Waite family, and working in Boston, but despite his instinctive urge to champion the unfortunate, he was more concerned with the rights of the Indians than those of the slaves, possibly because he had more direct contact with the Indians than with slaves. Influenced by the Rev. Thomas Bray,[32] he preferred to interest himself in the Christian education of the Indians rather than the right to freedom of the slaves. However, when in 1730 he became a trustee of Georgia, he fully supported the law prohibiting negro slavery in the colony. It is certain that he was never directly involved in the slave trade in any form. He had, however, married into a solid if undistinguished Boston family, one of the few who had a slave to perform the duties of a servant.

---

31 Thomas, ed., *Diary of Samuel Sewall*, vol. II, pp. 16–20.
32 Vicar of St Botolph, Aldgate; founder of the Society for Promoting Christian Knowledge and the Society for Propagating the Gospel among the Indians of New England.

3

Trouble in Taunton

Hardworking, energetic and confident, for the first two or three years in Taunton Coram made a great success of his shipbuilding business. He rented rooms near his yard and built a covered double saw pit so that work could continue in all weathers. He had found men willing to work for him. He wrote with pride that his ship of 140 tons was the first to be built on the river and that he had built several more and larger ships thereafter.[1] He had entered into a contract with Dan Throope 'to build one of his vessels with his timber and plank in the yard'.[2] In 1699 Coram had entered into a second detailed contract with Peter Walker to cart and raft from the tree stumps into his building yard all the timber and wooden materials that would be needed for the completion of a new ship on the stocks. Peter Walker was to be paid £50 in all, £10 on 15 June, £30 on 30 June, and the remainder within three months. Peter Walker was to hew all the timber and all the planks on both sides, as well as the biggest masts and yards. A reasonable allowance was to be made to Walker for any timber or plank that might be needed over and above what had already been agreed. It would seem that a certain amount of suspicion already existed between Coram and Walker. Two men, mutually chosen by both parties, who had the option of choosing a third, were to make sure that all agreements and payments were carried out. Coram had also made an agreement with Robert Crossman, the son of one of the original purchasers of the land, to make all the bolts, spikes and nails he needed from the iron which he was able to purchase locally.[3]

From the start Coram had no very good opinion of the people among whom he had come to live. He was shocked to discover that during the particularly hard winter of 1697/8:

> few if any had any shelter for their Cattle tho their Land was encumbered with Timber Trees. Their Cows Calved out of dores and the Calves were Frozen to Death for want of a Shead or Covering for the Cows to Calve under. Those Lazy vermin would ly all night by one anothers fire sides contriving how to hurt their Industrious Neighbours rather than take a little paines to preserve their own Cattle.

---

[1] Coram to Popple, Secretary to the Board of Trade and Plantations, *CSP, CS: A and WI*, 12 March 1731.
[2] Massachusetts Archive, vol. 40, p. 653, quoted in Hill, 'Thomas Coram in Boston and Taunton', p. 143.
[3] *CSP, CS: A and WI*, 17 March 1731, p. 58.

He considered it a great pity that 'their bign Lords of their own Soyle should make them too Lazy to provide Fother and Sheter for their good Creaturs w'ch God has given them'.[4] It is unlikely that he kept these opinions to himself. Seen as an arrogant outsider, working for the good of the British, his preference for the liturgy of the Anglican Church would have made him an object of suspicion to the men of Taunton, and it was almost inevitable that there would be trouble.

Trouble was not long in coming. There seems to have been a concerted move to obstruct Coram. A series of court cases began, minor in nature at first, but becoming progressively more serious. Throope was persuaded to stop working for Coram, although Coram had made a first payment. Aided and abetted by the mistress of the house where Coram lodged, Throope entered his lodgings and burnt and destroyed the contract, and tried in this way to end his obligation to work for Coram.[5] Coram went immediately to the Justices of the Inferior Court of Common Pleas in Bristol County to demand a warrant to prosecute Throope, but members of the court, already prejudiced against Coram, refused. Not to be baulked, Coram took his case to the Superior Court in Boston and obtained a ruling in his favour. Unfortunately for Coram, it was Nathaniel Byfield, Throope's father's landlord, whom the court bound for the performance of Throope's work, thus ensuring Byfield's lasting enmity.[6] He warned Coram that his being bound to see that Throope carried out his obligations would result in Coram's ruin, and the warning proved all too accurate.

Shortly afterwards a large quantity of timber that Peter Walker had cut and hewed but not carted was burnt in the woods. That which was brought to the waterside was not put into the yard as specified, and was washed away by the tide and completely lost so that more timber had to be cut and supplied in its place.[7] Coram had been forced to bring an action against Peter Walker in the same Inferior Court of Common Pleas in January 1700 for 'not timely drawing all the timber and wooden materials . . . for the complete building, launching and finishing of the ship that he was building'. Coram therefore took it upon himself with some of his men to go into the wood to cut and carry away timber to enable him to finish the ship he had on the stocks, as he had already paid Peter Walker £40. Peter's brother Eleazor, set upon Coram and molested him for trespass, and Coram brought an action against him as well. The judges, Nathaniel Byfield, Eliakim Hutchinson and Andrew Belcher, whose son would become Governor of Massachusetts, gave judgment against Coram and awarded under arbitration £33 8s 0d to Peter Walker and £8 2s 0d and two three-quarter yards of cloth to Eleazor Walker. Coram immediately appealed, but matters took a turn for the worse.[8] Almost simultaneously, Coram's unguarded language gave Peter Walker another opportunity to attack Coram and he charged Coram with slander for lying under oath. Coram was granted costs of £1 10s 2d. This was but a mere side show.

Coram could not afford to allow the matter to rest: he now had a wife to support and a business at risk. If Coram was unable to deliver the ships he was building to the

4   Coram to Colman, *Letters of Thomas Coram*, 9 July 1737, MHS, pp. 36–7.
5   Hill, 'Thomas Coram in Boston and Taunton', p. 138.
6   Massachusetts Archive, vol. 40, p. 646.
7   Reasons for Appeal, September 1701, from the collection of Charles Greenough, MHS, p. 16.
8   Massachusetts Archive, vol. 40, pp. 653–5.

2. The house built by Thomas Coram in Water Street, Taunton, in 1699 and sold by him in 1742.

London merchants with money loaned to him, there was a danger that they would cease to support him financially. They also supplied the money to purchase goods that were to be sent back to London. Coram had to appeal the judgments against him. Eleazor Walker made matters worse by bringing an action for debt, alleging non-payment of the arbitration award, and was awarded £500. Peter Walker joined his brother, and also sued for damages and was granted leave to bring an action for debt also amounting to £500 – both sums grossly out of proportion to the amount of alleged debt. Coram immediately appealed to the next Superior Court in the county against this monstrously unfair award. He paid the clerk and brought certain persons to act as his sureties. So great was the prejudice against Coram that the court refused to take Coram's bond, saying that the court was adjourned because they were having dinner.[9]

Coram had at this time two ships on the stocks: one of 234 tons, not quite finished, with all the timber and plank in the yard needed to finish her; the other of nearly 130 tons, finished and, unusually, though still on the stocks, already rigged with all her sails and cables on board and her anchors at the bow. He had the double saw pit in his building yard, he had bought furniture for his new house, including a copper skillet, a kettle and many other things valued at a total of £20.[10] On the following day, without allowing Coram's side of the story to be heard, the judges delivered their

9 Massachusetts Archive, vol. 40, p. 649.
10 Ibid., pp. 649–50, Complaint of Thomas Coram to Court residing in Boston.

verdicts. Executions were issued against Coram and were immediately levied against the two vessels in his yard. The two ships were appraised at £432 and £650 respectively and the shipyard with all its equipment, his house and orchard were valued at £12. The true value of the ships, according to Coram was nearer £1,000 each and his buildings and land were worth at least £120. Thomas Coram complained bitterly that one of the appraisers was Dan Throope, 'a very Ill person who felloniously broake into my lodging at Taunton . . . so that I am like to have but little honesty'. He continued that Throope was aided and abetted by 'base prejudiced countrey fellows of their own party no way skilled in such things, but they valued the whole short of what would satisfy for the two five hundred pounds so as they might want some for an opportunity to carry my person to Goal, by which horrid treatment the business of my ships was wholly hindered for three months'.[11]

According to an affidavit sworn by James Pavior, one of Coram's workmen, a deputy sheriff

> came to Mr Coram's yard againe & a great crew of Taunton men with him, both horse and foot & then he read his Executing judgement again & turned me and other of Mr Coram's work folks out of Mr Coram's house & made such Havock of his things & at such an Inhuman manner.[12]

The deputy sheriff read out judgment and encouraged the mob to do their worst. It was a co-ordinated attempt by some of the leading citizens of Taunton to pervert the course of justice, and by encouraging the mob to smash Coram's shipyard and ransack his home, effectively to destroy him. Had they been able to do so, they would also have seized Coram and jailed him for non-payment of debt. Coram was, however, too quick for them and had already left Taunton for Boston, where he demanded justice of the Superior Court in Bristol County and the Great and Superior Court in Boston.

Coram had first to prove to the Superior Court in Bristol County that the Inferior Court had acted improperly in not accepting his bond. The Secretary of the court wrote to inform the three Justices, John Brown, Thomas Leonard and Nicholas Peck, who had pretended to be dining and so been able to refuse to accept Coram's bond, of Coram's claims and invited them to appear and be heard if they wished. The Justices met in Mr Brown's house to decide who was to go to Boston. Thomas Leonard drew the short straw and was chosen to make their case, which they must have known to be hopeless. Both Coram and Leonard were heard by the court.[13] The Speaker and Representatives retired and when they returned to the chamber they directed that all the judgments and proceedings in the Inferior Court be vacated and that all the goods and estates levied thereby or any of them be restored to Coram. Moreover, an additional resolve was passed giving Coram security to appeal to the next Superior Court for damages and costs resulting from the inconveniences he had suffered during the time his business had been disrupted. This special act was approved by the Lieutenant Governor, William Stoughton, on 12 March 1701.[14]

---

11 Hill, 'Thomas Coram in Boston and Taunton', p. 141.
12 Pavior Affidavit, 5 July 1701, MHS, *Miscellaneous Bound Items*, vol. 6, 1698–1702.
13 Hill, 'Thomas Coram in Boston and Taunton', pp. 139–40.
14 *Province Laws*, vol. 1, p. 454, quoted by Hill, 'Thomas Coram in Boston and Taunton', p. 141.

Coram may not have been well educated, but he was intelligent and quick witted, and obviously had taken legal advice before asking for damages. He, or his lawyer, quoted at length from the *Grand Abridgement of the Common and Statute Law of England* in support of his case. Coram was a young man in the prime of life, recently married, an entrepreneur with a business that had every chance of developing in importance. His ability to finance his shipbuilding operations was, however, dependent on his being able to satisfy the wishes of the London merchants whose agent he was. The delay occasioned by the lost timber, not to mention the damage done to the ships, had the most devastating consequences for Coram. In his appeal for damages he stated his main reason was the loss of his friend Mr Hunt. The

> damage for want of the timber being carted is the loss of my friend Mr. Hunt, a worthy Merchant in London, who was concerned with the appellant, who hath ordered the withdrawing of the effects out of the appellants hands, which was sent to Carry on the ship and for no other reason but because of the tediousness in building occasioned by the want of timber.[15]

If Coram was no longer able to provide the necessary means of transport for the goods he purchased on Hunt's account he was of no more use as a factor and agent. Coram was almost without means of his own so would find it increasingly difficult to pay for the timber he needed for his shipbuilding business. However he still owned the shipyard and his house and had no intention of giving up.

Abel Burt, one of the men who had taken part in the wrecking of Coram's house and yard, had not returned certain stores of value with the rest of his property. Coram brought two actions against Abel Burt, who was the son of one of the original signatories of the purchase of Dighton and a deputy sheriff, for the return of his possessions. The Superior Court gave judgment against Abel Burt, who appears to have been a violent and lawless man. He threatened, holding a gun, to kill the sheriff or any who would attempt to attack him. The sheriff, afraid of a violent encounter with Burt, sought an easier way out. He levied on Burt's property and gave Coram 59 acres of his farm. This grant of land appears to be the sole recompense Coram received by way of damages. Coram, fearing violence, took the sheriff with him for protection when he went to inspect his land. Notwithstanding the company of the sheriff, both men were shot at as they emerged onto the highway. Coram reported that they 'were fired upon out of some thick bushes near the roadside, we could not see the man that shot but the bullets whistled very near us and I am morally assured it was this deputed sheriff, whose name is Abel Burt'.[16]

Coram was still anxious to make use of his land and wanted it divided off from Burt's farm, but Burt's reputation for violence was such that no one was willing to mow the grass or to be seen on his land. On a later occasion in 1702 Burt violently assaulted Coram, who believed he would have been murdered had others not come to his aid. Coram immediately appealed to Captain Leonard, the same Justice who had gone to Boston and had suffered the indignity of having his previous judgment against Coram overturned. Coram took two people as witnesses and attempted to

---

[15] Reasons for Appeal, p. 16.
[16] Memorial to Governor Joseph Dudley, 26 August 1703, Deed in *Collections of The Old Colony Historical Society*, quoted in Hill, 'Thomas Coram in Boston and Taunton', pp. 141–2.

serve an affidavit. Unsurprisingly Leonard, seeing this as an opportunity to take revenge on Coram, would not grant him security of the peace against Burt and refused to accept the affidavits offered.

In June of that year Leonard summoned Coram to appear before him at his dwelling house to answer Eleazor Walker for pleas of debt for 40 shillings. Coram was accused, together with those he employed, of hauling and carrying away trees made into topmasts and yards, bowsprits and mizzen masts, all for the great ship he was building.[17] It seems very likely that he did go into the woods and cut down the timber he needed. What option did he have when those who claimed the land would not supply his needs? Certainly, he often walked in the woods and got to know the Indians who lived in the villages round about. He wrote that he 'found these poor Indians good natured, more Gratefull and much more honester than the major part of the English inhabiting there which I declare upon my own certain knowledge and experience'.[18]

Coram decided that he could no longer safely remain in Taunton. His life was in danger and he risked being thrown into jail for non-payment of the alleged debt. He was now so unpopular with the ruling faction in Taunton that, despite winning his court actions in Boston, he knew he could expect no protection from the law in Taunton. The citizens of Taunton had indeed made it impossible for him and his wife to live and work among them. It was a very bitter moment for him and he never forgave the injustices that had been inflicted on him. On the threshold of success, owning his own property and with a thriving business, all was suddenly snatched from him and he, with his wife, literally had to flee the town. As a result he was forced into debt to fulfil his contract with Hunt. A proud man, he never referred to the fact that his departure from Taunton had been forced on him, but that was the stark reality. He did not sell his house, hoping one day perhaps to return. Nathaniel Hathaway, his neighbour and a long-time resident, took over his shipyard and the shipbuilding business and went into partnership with David Bowen. Other shipyards were established. Most of the vessels were small coasting sloops ranging from 20 to 70 tons, but some were larger, intended for the European and West Indian trade.[19] By 1789 commercial activity and shipbuilding had increased to such a degree that Dighton was declared a port of entry and by the first decade of the nineteenth century more ships were built at Dighton than in any other New England community.[20] The industrial expansion of Dighton owed much to Coram's enterprising spirit. His experience in Taunton also marked the first of a recurring pattern in Coram's life. He had the initial vision, but all too often his uncompromising personality worked against his interests: arguments followed which resulted in Coram being ousted or withdrawing, despite being nearly always right.

Coram always retained a great regard for his mother-in-law, and it is doubtless to her house that the young Corams came after their departure from Taunton. John Waite had died the previous year and the management of the estate had been left in

[17] Collections of the Old Colony Historical Society, V W151E.

[18] Letter from Coram to the Honourable Society for Propagating the Gospel among the Indians in New England, 17 June 1745: Newberry Library, Chicago, Edward E. Ayer Manuscript Collection 60610–3380.

[19] Collections of the Old Colony Historical Society, V D569H; *Taunton Daily Gazette*, 20 August 1904.

[20] A. Forbes and Ralph M. Eastman, *Town and City Seals of Massachusetts*, p. 139.

Eunice's mother's hands. Coram was under contract to Hunt to build a ship and became heavily indebted while doing so. He was involved in two court cases brought against him for the return of monies lent, one in London in 1704 and one in Boston in 1705.[21] From the evidence contained in records of both cases, it is possible to follow Coram's tangled business arrangements. Hunt had supplied Coram with sums of money amounting to £1,000 to build a ship, and had sent over a supply of cordage which Coram was to pay for at market rates. The ship was to be freighted and when it arrived at the port of London, after all expenses had been paid, the ship would become Hunt's property and any surplus from the sale of the goods brought over was to go to Coram.

Notwithstanding the money advanced by Hunt, Coram, doubtless as a result of the losses he had sustained in Taunton, had to borrow heavily in Boston: the sum of £1,250 in New England value[22] is mentioned in the 1704 writ. This may well have been to purchase the goods to be freighted, but Coram also had to borrow to complete the building of his ship, and had made an agreement with Thomas Palmer and Benjamin Edmunds to borrow £200 to be repaid in 1703.

> An agreement made, or said to be made, by Thomas Coram, late of Boston shipwright, for and behalf of this Palmer and Edmunds in the beginning of the summer anno 1703 with Jacob Wyman; that the said Wyman was to provide and seasonably lay and place at or near the building yard of John Parker timber, whales, blocks, shores and stagings, spaules and standers necessary and suitable for the building and launching and finishing a new pinto of seventy seven foot to the main deck, with two decks and a small round house, which Pinto or vessel was built near the South Front in Boston and plant and turnels being accepted.[23]

Coram, burdened by debt, could not repay the money in 1703, but by 1705 the case ended in an 'amicable appeasing and Ending whereof the said parties have mutually condescended and concluded and agreed'. What Coram had agreed in order to enable this happy conclusion to be reached was to make out a bill of sale to Palmer for a quarter part of the hull and body of the ship which would become void on payment. In the meantime Hunt had died. Unfortunately for Coram, although he had managed to satisfy Palmer and Edmunds, Hunt's partners were far from pleased to discover that some parts of the ship had been sold to others, when they claimed the right to sell it to defray their losses.[24]

Coram had one other matter to settle before he left Boston, namely the disposition of his 59 acres. In a gesture both generous and astute – but he had few options – he arranged for the land he had been awarded to be entrusted to the safe hands of the vestrymen of the King's Chapel. He had no intention of allowing Abel Burt to reclaim it, and hoped that by transferring the land to the King's Chapel he was safeguarding its ownership. He employed the Attorney General, a Mr Newton, to draw up the

---

[21] *Proceedings MHS*, vol. 56, p. 11.
[22] Most colonial notes were 'bills of credit', notes meant to be redeemable in coin. Colonial paper money rarely lasted long as too much was issued and inflation made bills worthless.
[23] *Proceedings MHS*, vol. 56, p. 11.
[24] PRO, C9/466/84.

deed, 'amply strong and in due form', between himself and the vestrymen so that 'none of the crafty New Englanders might ever find flaw in it, I knowing to well what sort of folks the major part of the inhabitants then were'.[25] The indenture, dated 8 January 1704, was between Thomas Coram and Joseph Dudley, then Governor of Massachusetts, Sir Charles Hobby and other vestrymen. Among Coram's three witnesses was Gamaliel Waite, his wife's brother. Coram gave his land, which abutted on the river on the west side and on the north side was bounded by land belonging to Abel Burt with 'all meadows, feedings, pastures, trees, timber, woods under woods, easement rights, profit, emoluments, privileges and appurtances whatsoever' to the gentlemen of the vestry. It was an unusual gift, but it was given with a proviso which was to give rise to much acrimonious controversy in the future. The gentlemen of the vestry were to warrant and defend the granted premises against 'all people whomsoever', which might be difficult enough. But they were also to agree

> before the signing and sealing hereof, that if ever the Inhabitants of the town of Taunton aforesaid should be more civilised than now they are, and if they should incline to have a Church of England built amongst them or in that Town, then upon application of the Inhabitants of the Town that is to say, forty rateable men of them, upon their application of petition to the said Vestry of successors above said, for any suitable part of said land in this present deed given, to build a Church of England or School house for the use and service of the said Church, that upon such application at any time the Vestrymen for the time being shall have liberty to grant and convey for such use to such persons who shall apply and petition them.[26]

The way in which Coram's gift was subsequently treated was to anger and distress him in his old age.

Had the inhabitants of Taunton known then that Coram wished to see a Church of England church or school built in their town they would have felt that their worst suspicions were confirmed. Coram, in expressing a wish to see the Church of England established in some form in Taunton, had perhaps been influenced by the Rev. Thomas Bray. Bray had been sent to Maryland in 1700 by Bishop Compton to act as his commissary. His ship had been blown off course and landed first in Newfoundland before calling in at Boston and then finally reaching his destination. Bray, on his return to London, concerned at the lack of Christian teaching in America, set up the Society for Promoting Christian Knowledge. Bray was to become a trusted friend to Coram and it is possible that the two men met in Boston and that Coram's idea of establishing a church in Taunton came about through listening to Bray's concerns about the lack of missionaries in America.

The church that subsequently was built in Taunton, dedicated to St Thomas, was Coram's most lasting memorial in America. He had been driven from Taunton and forced to leave his home. When he left Boston with his young wife he was burdened by debt. But notwithstanding all the difficulties he had encountered in New England,

---

25 *Collections of the Old Colony Historical Society*, vol. 2, pp. 28–30, quoted in Hill, 'Thomas Coram in Boston and Taunton', p. 14.

26 The Deed is printed in full in *Collections of the Old Colony Historical Society*, vol. 2, pp. 30–3 and quoted in Foote, *Annals of the King's Chapel*.

Coram never lost the hope that one day he would return to America. He had encountered a way of life in this new young country that appealed to his independent spirit, but despite all his attempts to found settlements, and to find a way of returning himself, the Corams would never return and Eunice would never see her family again.

4

A New Beginning

A difficult time

While Coram was engaged in his losing struggle with the inhabitants of Taunton, the fragile Treaty of Ryswick, which had given Europe five years of peace, came to an end in 1702. Europe was plunged into another dynastic war, the War of the Spanish Succession, which would only end with the Peace of Utrecht in 1713. These were to be difficult years for Coram. When writing of his life in later years, Coram always spoke with pride of his achievements in Taunton, despite their disastrous ending. He never alluded in so many words to the loss of his shipbuilding business, but only to the vile manner in which he had been treated in Taunton. There is relatively little information about his activities during the next ten years, and this silence on his part is understandable. Far from returning as a rich and successful merchant, as is frequently suggested in later accounts of his life, he was not only deeply in debt, but also embroiled in a court case brought by Hunt's two partners, Nicholas Roberts and John Shippin.[1] Coram had been lent £1,000 by Hunt for the building of a ship, as mentioned in the previous chapter (p. 36), and in return had assigned the ship with all her tackle, apparel and furniture and all the money due for freight, profits and earnings to Hunt and his associates. Coram was to have any profit after the settlement of all debts.

Coram had had no option but to borrow money in Boston to enable him to bring the ship, fully freighted, to the Port of London. The writ against him alleged that the total borrowed from Boston shopkeepers amounted to £1,250 New England money. To satisfy two of his Boston creditors, Coram had agreed to the sale of a quarter part of the hull and body of the ship, an agreement which would become void upon payment of the debt. Roberts and Shippin claimed that the money raised in Boston had been raised on their account. Now that Hunt was dead, they claimed they were entitled to a share of the profits from the sale of the ship. Coram, however, had entered into a series of complicated agreements with third and fourth parties who also laid claim to rights in the ship, including Thomas Palmer. A consortium of merchants, among them Sir Edward Walls and Thomas Palmer, got together to obstruct the sale of the ship, which was meanwhile lying in the river at great expense and subject to being rifled and pillaged. Thomas Palmer was the man to whom

---

1   PRO, C9/466/84.

Coram had already assigned parts of the ship. Roberts and Shippin claimed that Coram and those associated with him had brought a suit in the Admiralty Court attaching the ship for the satisfaction of their claims. They petitioned Sir Nathan Wright to have the case tried in the Lord Mayor's Court and asked that Thomas Coram and his associates appear personally before him under certain pain to answer all their charges. It was obviously difficult for them to substantiate their claims as Hunt was dead and many of their witnesses lived in Boston. Judging by the fact that Palmer was part of the consortium and was paid what was considered to be his due in 1705, the case must have gone against Roberts and Shippin. If the consortium did indeed fight off the claims of Shippin and Roberts, then the ship would have become their property.

In one of the few references Coram made to his occupation during the war years, a brief Privy Council note states that he commanded several ships in the merchant navy during the war. This note accompanied Coram's petition to the King in 1727 asking for employment.[2] It is the only indication we have from him as to how he was occupied during that time. It seems likely that, following their court victory, the consortium of merchants who now owned the ship employed him as their factor, and that he continued to trade with America, sailing in that ship and other ships of the merchant navy. He stated that in 1712 he started to build a great ship to trade with the East, which may indicate that by that time he had worked off his indebtedness and was free to follow his own desires.

During his ten years in Massachusetts, Coram had gained a very considerable knowledge of the value of the natural resources of North America, and practical insights into New England ways. With England again at war and her trading routes vulnerable to French and Spanish privateers, the role of the navy and the importance of a steady supply of naval stores took on ever greater significance. He was well aware of the cost of importing Swedish tar at a time when Sweden held a monopoly of the trade. He knew from his own experience as a shipwright in Taunton that American shipwrights had no need to look other than to their own pine forests for an ample supply of pitch and tar, hemp, masts, yards and bowsprits. Although Coram was in financial trouble when he returned to London that in no way appears to have stopped him lobbying for an act to make importing tar and other naval stores from America more attractive. He claimed to have been instrumental in bringing about 'An Act for encouraging the Importation of Naval Stores from Her Majesty's Plantations in America',[3] often referred to as the Tar Act because it allowed, as a form of reward or premium, bonuses for importing tar, as well as naval stores, from America. It is difficult to know how much credence to give to Coram's claim. The most likely explanation is that the consortium of merchants with whom Coram was involved, recognising the benefits that would accrue to them from such an act, added their voices to his. The preamble to the Act echoes arguments that Coram was to deploy all his life:

> . . . the strength of this [the navy] depends on the supply of stores necessary for the same now brought in mainly from Foreign Parts in Foreign shipping at

2 *Acts of the Privy Council*, 8 February 1727, p. 172, note 4.
3 PRO, *Statutes of the Realm*, vol. viii, chap. ix, p. 354: An Act for encouraging the Importation of Naval Stores from HM Plantations in America.

exorbitant and arbitrary rates to the great discouragement of Trade and Navigation of this Kingdom . . . In regard to the said Colonies and Plantations by
the vast tracts of land therein lying near the sea and upon navigable rivers
may commodiously afford great quantities of Naval Stores if due encouragement is given . . . which will likewise tend not only to further employment
and increase in English shipping and seamen.

Coram was unusual in that he had experience of shipbuilding on both sides of the
Atlantic. As he was to demonstrate in later life, he had great powers of persuasion. He
also had first-hand knowledge of the country, and contacts with a number of
merchants, for whom he traded. All these points lend weight to his contention that he
was indeed the instigator of the Tar Act.

There is no doubt that Coram gave himself great credit and was proud of the part
he had played in achieving the legislation. In the Privy Council note it is stated that

considering that naval stores could be constantly and cheaply produced in
North America instead of being procured in a precarious manner and at arbitrary rates from Sweden and Russia he [Coram] returned to England in 1704
and solicited strongly at his own expense the Act, passed a few months later,
to encourage the making of tar and pitch in the Plantations which had the
effect of reducing the supplies from the Baltic and obtaining from the Plantations more tar and pitch than were required so that some was exported to
other countries.[4]

This was Coram's own account. It is of particular interest because he stated that he
solicited, at his own expense, for the Act to be passed, a phrase he was to use many
times in his various petitions. It was very unusual for a man in his circumstances, with
little or no money of his own, to work for the good of his country, at his own expense
with no expectation of reward. This was far from the only occasion when he acted in
this way.

If there was any doubt as to the truth of Coram's own assertions, the merchants
who agreed to subscribe to a pension for him in old age certainly did not believe that
he was exaggerating. First among his achievements, cited as reasons for their support,
was the fact that

he was very instrumental in planning and procuring an Act of Parliament in
1704 for the encouragement of the making of tar in the Northern Colonies of
British America by bounty to be paid on the importation thereof; but not
only does a good livelihood arise to thousands of families employed in that
branch of the colonies of North America, a million stirling has been saved to
this nation which was formerly obliged to buy all the tar from Sweden at a
most exorbitant price in Swedish bottoms and by the same gentleman's solic-
itations an Act of Parliament was obtained.[5]

Perhaps some of the merchants who signed were themselves the beneficiaries of the
Act. But, to put the matter into context, the two other achievements cited as reasons
for giving Coram a pension were, firstly, his part in negotiating the importation of

4   Ibid.
5   LMA, A/FH/A01/7/2: Subscription List, 1749.

deal and timber boards from Germany instead of expensively from the Baltic states, and, secondly, that after twenty-two years of solicitation he obtained a charter for the Foundling Hospital. Coram's personal situation in 1704 makes it legitimate to question the weight given to his role in getting the Tar Act on to the statute books. However, the evidence seems to prove him right, and his direct experience of the situation together with his forceful personality add credibility to the assertion.

While war raged in Europe, the colonies along the eastern seaboard of North America, although without interest in the causes of the European conflicts, were not immune from their effects. European monarchs used their overseas possessions as pawns in a political game, to be bartered against more immediate gains. The Massachusetts Bay Colony with its 1692 charter, giving it independent government under a royal colonial governor, could not be touched, but the lands to the east were under no such protection.

Acadia, so called by the French, comprised Nova Scotia, parts of what is now New Brunswick and the coastal strip of land to the Kennebec river, now eastern Maine, and was seen as expendable. The boundaries, however, were never precisely defined, giving rise to endless disputes as to their ownership. These were the lands that Coram would spend the major part of his life trying, with whoever shared his vision, to persuade a reluctant English government to settle on a permanent basis. From the knowledge he had gained from trading up and down the eastern seaboard, Coram understood better than most the great benefit that would come from a settled population, loyal to the British Crown. Quite apart from the rich fishing grounds offshore, Coram had an eye for the strategic position in terms of commercial geography as well as the economic advantages to be had in terms of naval supplies from the vast forests. Masts, spars, tar and pitch, hemp and timber were all to be had for the asking, cheaply and plentifully, for the benefit of the Royal Navy.

The Treaty of Ryswick in 1697, temporarily ending the war between France and England, gave back to Louis XIV the countries, islands, forts and colonies that were French before the war. Thus Acadia was restored to France, although in truth it had never been British. The change made little impact on either the Indians or the Acadians, for lines of communication from the French seat of government in Quebec were difficult and at times impossible. The French had gone to great lengths to cultivate the friendship of the Indians, with resident Jesuit priests gently introducing them to the Roman Catholic faith. As a result of this policy the French had little to fear from their subjects, but neither did they gain much in economic terms. Quebec could be reached only by porterage and canoe via the St John, Penobscot or Kennebec rivers, or, in the ice-free months, down the St Lawrence and across the stormy gulf. Trade flowed instead between the Acadians and their powerful neighbours, the New Englanders of Massachusetts. The Treaty of Ryswick meant little to the New Englanders, who laid claim to a big piece of the land and meant to dominate all of it, whatever the legal claims of the European powers. The outbreak of war in 1702 merely legitimised their actions which could be seen as part of the war against France.

The War of the Spanish Succession was started to prevent the unification of the dynasties of France and Spain. The threat posed by Louis XIV, the expansionist King of France and monarch of the most powerful country in Europe, when he nominated his second grandson, Philip of Anjou, to succeed to the throne of Spain, a country in decline but which still held an empire reaching from the Philippines in Asia to

Central and South America, Florida, Mexico, Naples, Sicily and Belgium, was not to be tolerated. When Louis XIV proclaimed James Edward, the son of the fugitive King James, the legitimate successor to the throne of Britain, the British Parliament was easily persuaded to join with Holland and Austria to go to war with France.

Little is known of Coram's activities during the remainder of the war years apart from the fact that he said that he commanded several ships of the merchant navy. He certainly knew the coast of North America well, probably buying his supplies from traders living in small settlements along the shores of what is now Maine, because in 1710 he wrote to the Lords Commissioners of Trade and Plantations warning them of the corrupt practices of the Surveyor General of the Woods, Mr Bridger.[6] He warned them that the bill for preserving pines would not be effective because Mr Bridger was corruptly taking money and allowing people to cut what they pleased. No one, he wrote, could cut pine trees without having first lined Mr Bridger's pockets, but, most damning of all, he accused Bridger of sailing on a Spanish ship knowing that the masts, yards, standers and other timber were for the King of Spain's use. His allegations went unheeded, Bridger survived and was duly reappointed. Perhaps because Coram felt rebuffed, for the first and almost only time in his life, he gave up on America and his thoughts turned to the possibilities of trading in Asia. He started to build a great ship for that purpose, but when the war ended he sold his ship.[7]

The Peace of Utrecht in 1713 marked the beginning of France's decline and the rise of Britain to world power status. The bargaining at the treaty table was tough. Spain kept her overseas possessions but lost Gibraltar; Louis XIV gave the Dutch a string of border fortresses and solemnly promised that the crowns of France and Spain would never be united; Britain got Hudson Bay, the Assiento contract,[8] Newfoundland, St Christopher and the greater part of Acadia.[9] Acadia, from Acadie, the name given by the French to Nova Scotia, was once again used as a pawn in European power politics, but was, unfortunately, only described by reference to its ancient boundaries. The Board of Trade and Plantations had warned that unless Nova Scotia 'does comprehend what the French call Acadie bounded by the river St. Croix to the West, by the sea to the South and East and by the St. Lawrence to the North' there would always be disputes with the French, and so it was.[10]

Coram always wrote with pride and satisfaction of the ten years he spent shipbuilding in Boston and Taunton. The years that followed must necessarily have seemed less rewarding in terms of personal satisfaction. But with the coming of the Peace of Utrecht new and exciting possibilities opened up. For the next twenty-five years Coram would spend much time and energy pressing for the settlement, first, of the disputed lands between New England and Nova Scotia, and then of Nova Scotia itself. For a brief period, as a trustee of the new colony of Georgia, he became

---

6   *CSP, CS: A and WI*, 9 January 1710, p. 207.

7   *Acts of the Privy Council*, 8 February 1727, p. 172, note 6.

8   An exclusive contract awarded by the Spanish crown for the supply of slaves (normally negroes from West Africa) to Spain's New World colonies.

9   The texts of the treaties between Great Britain and France, Great Britain and Spain, and Spain and Austria are in *Major Peace Treaties*, vol. 1, pp. 177–260.

10 Board of Trade and Plantations to Henry St John, 5 April 1712, *CSP, CS*, 26, pp. 256–7; Mahaffie, *A Land of Discord Always*, p. 146.

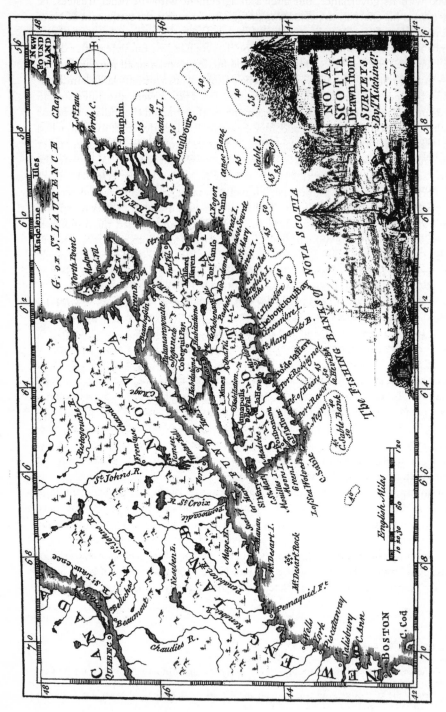

3. Map of Nova Scotia, drawn from surveys by T. Kitchin and engraved for the *London Magazine* in 1749, showing Boston and the disputed lands between the Kennebec and St Croix rivers.

involved with its governance, but after a disagreement with the other trustees, he finally turned his energies to persuading the government that the settlement of Nova Scotia would be of great benefit to British interests.

While the English armies under Marlborough were handing out defeat after defeat to the French in Europe, Massachusetts was conducting its own small wars against the French in Nova Scotia, but for very different reasons. Massachusetts laid claim to all the land between its borders and Nova Scotia. The French were also interested in these disputed lands and were a continual menace. They incited the Indians to harass and burn down homes and barns and after a particularly bloody attack in 1704, when fifty settlers were killed, the Bostonians retaliated. In 1704, under the leadership of Joseph Dudley, Governor of Massachusetts, 550 men attacked and laid waste the Acadian settlements in the fertile lands of Beau Bassin and Chignecto. The main town, Port Royal, was left untouched, probably because it was too well defended, although there were those who said Dudley had trading interests in Port Royal and that was the real reason the city was spared.[11] In 1705 Dudley tried the diplomatic approach and sent his son William with Samuel Vetch[12] to talk to the French, but to no avail. Dudley had to convince the New Englanders that he was no friend of France, and so in 1707, with more than a thousand men, he set sail from Boston for Port Royal. The labourers and fishermen of New England were no match for the disciplined, professional French defenders; the New Englanders were defeated as much by their own incompetence as by the aggressive French defence. Vetch returned to England to try to persuade the British government to allow him the necessary men to return and subdue the troublesome French. A new committee, the Board of Trade and Plantations – which had replaced King Charles's Lords Commissioners of Trade – had been given powers to oversee the colonies. Vetch handed the Board a long memorandum arguing for the conquest of New France, entitled: 'Canada surveyed or the French Dominions upon the Continent briefly considered in their situation, strength, trade and number, more particularly how vastly prejudicial they are to the British Interest and a method proposed of easily moving them'.[13] Francis Nicholson, to whom the Board turned for advice, was another larger than life character. He had a choleric temper and an abrasive personality, but nonetheless had risen in the colonial service and had been Lieutenant Governor and Governor of Maryland, and from 1698 to 1705 was Governor of Virginia. As a Tory he had lost his place when the Whig government of Walpole took power but, seeing an opportunity for himself, he gave his support to Vetch.

By 1709 Vetch had the Queen's order for an invasion and the promise of the governorship of Canada. From Maine to New Jersey, men were enlisted and barracks built. Nicholson took command of the army and Vetch would join with the regulars as soon as they arrived and sail up the St Lawrence river. Unfortunately, the regular British soldiers never arrived, having been diverted to Portugal. Nicholson returned the following July in 1710 with 400 regular soldiers. The invasion was now limited to the

11 Mahaffie, A Land of Discord Always, p. 124.
12 Samuel Vetch, 1668–1732, a Scot and a merchant adventurer, had been part of the Darien Company whose attempt to settle Panama failed. He arrived in Boston in 1705 married to Margaret Livingstone, the daughter of one of New York's richest merchants. See DNB.
13 CSP, CS: A and WI, 27 July 1708; 60, pp. 41–51.

capture of Port Royal. The cost of training the New England irregulars for the aborted 1709 invasion had been considerable, and to encourage them to take part in the 1710 invasion Nicholson had been authorised to give an assurance that

> such of them as contribute to the reduction of Port Royal and of any of the country or places adjacent belonging to the enemy, shall have preference, both to the soil and trade, when reduced, to any other of our subjects. And when they shall have concerted among themselves any reasonable proposals for securing to their respective colonies the benefits of the said soils and trade, We shall not be wanting to give Royall Sanction for the same, and you are hereby empowered to give all fitting encouragement to any such as shall offer themselves to go on this expedition, whether gentlemen or others.[14]

There was plenty of room for differing interpretations as to what was really meant, but Vetch later gave as his understanding that 'the Crown had promised land to its captors and that substantial groups of those captors might fulfil the condition if they concerted together'.[15]

The French general, Subercase, realising that his garrison was no match for Vetch's men, agreed an honourable surrender. Nicholson and Vetch wrote that all of Acadia and Nova Scotia from the river St Croix to Cape Gaspe was the Queen's. Vetch's suggestion of removing all the inhabitants was overruled: the danger of leaving the country depopulated had to be weighed against having the land cultivated, even if its people, the Acadians and Indians, were not to be trusted. Port Royal was named Annapolis Royal in honour of the Queen. Vetch was left in command of 200 Royal marines to deal with 2,000 independently minded Acadians. These were widely scattered and only interested in cultivating the rich and fertile lands, which gave them all they required for a pleasant simple life apart from the need for some manufactured goods. The native freedom-loving Mic Mac Indians had co-operated with the French, having little reason to oppose their lightly imposed government. After the Peace of Utrecht, when Nova Scotia became British, things were very different. A military government was imposed whose laws were binding, in theory, on Acadians and Mic Macs alike, guaranteeing trouble in the future.

The Royall Province of Georgia

With the coming of the peace the disbanded soldiers began to make claims for the land they had been promised. Jeremiah Dummer, the agent for Massachusetts and New Hampshire, claimed that it was he who first made use of Coram to head up the soldier's claims.

> In the project now on foot to settle the Eastern parts with disbanded soldiers, I made use of Captain Coram (formerly in New England) as an active busy fellow, to head the soldiers in presenting their petitions.

[14] 'Thomas Coram and the First Proposals for Foreign Protestants as Settlers', in The 'Foreign Protestants' and the Settlement of Nova Scotia (Public Archives of Nova Scotia), p. 30, note 2.
[15] CSP, CS: A and WI, Vetch to Lords of Trade and Plantations, 24 November 1714, pp. 42–3.

This, Dummer recognised, was a mistake on his part, for he continues

> Till at last he prevailed on me to present him in person to *My Lord Treasurer* and other great men. But in a little time I found he was making his merit with those very persons (to whom I had recommended him) by aspersing my country and all the worthy gentlemen in it. Coram endeavours to justify himself by talking of hardship in New England. I entirely flung him off and have never spoken to him since.

He went on to write that Mr Watts, a ship's captain, told him 'how insolently Coram talks to him and of Colonel Hutchinson of whom he speaks everything that is vile'.[16]

Dummer's request to Coram to head up the soldiers' petition for land gave Coram the opportunity to involve himself in a pro-active way with affairs in North America. He was not slow to exploit this new opportunity. It was just the opening he was looking for and must have helped him to decide to sell the ship he was building for trade with Asia. It explains what it was that led Coram to become involved with plans for the settlement of Maine and Nova Scotia. Apart from the trading opportunities, he may also have seen the settlement of these lands as providing an opportunity for him to return to America, the land he had left so reluctantly ten years earlier. So much of the free and independent spirit of the New Englanders appealed to him. But as a fully subscribed believer in the spirit of mercantilism, he also supported the view that a colony's duty was to supply raw materials to the mother country and to buy the manufactured goods it produced. As an active Anglican he saw it as a duty to confront and stop the spread of Roman Catholicism, and, insofar as possible, to provide a Protestant alternative to the dominant practices of the dissenters. Finally, from a strategic point of view he saw settlers loyal to the Crown as a defence against any further French and Indian encroachment.

Dummer's letter also reveals how quick Coram was to make use of any new and useful contact, a skill which he was to develop and use with great effect all his life. Operating outside the tight English social circle of court and society, Coram was learning to build up a network of contacts at all levels, people who could be useful to him in the furtherance of his projects. He was never able to operate in this way in Massachusetts, despite his wife's Boston background. He was outraged at the way he had been treated by the courts in Taunton and did not hesitate to make his feelings known in uncompromising terms. This made him enemies among the powerful New England families. They would always oppose him if they could, and they mistrusted him all the more because they knew he would always put British interests ahead of those of Massachusetts.

Coram was not the first, nor the only one, to start petitioning the Board of Trade and Plantations for grants of land, but he was one of the most persistent and vigorous. Several other groups of disbanded soldiers were making proposals apart from those headed up by Coram. He opened his campaign by writing directly to the Lord Treasurer with his request. The response was discouraging, for unbeknown to him, at the foot of the letter was scribbled the unhelpful remark 'unknown'.[17] Without patronage

---

[16] Massachusetts Archive, vol. 1, 3rd series. Edward Hutchinson Papers, Dummer to Massachusetts General Court, 13 February 1717.

[17] Coram to the Lord Treasurer, 20 June 1713: HMC MSS, *Portland MSS*, V, 297.

or influence among the great men of the day there was little hope of any request being listened to, let alone acted upon. Dummer did Coram the greatest service when he was prevailed upon to introduce Coram personally to the Lord Treasurer. Coram immediately followed up this advantage with a second letter to the Lord Treasurer. This letter is interesting as much for its contents as for what it reveals about Coram. He begins, not unnaturally, by reminding the Lord Treasurer that they have met. He goes on to introduce himself as the faithful factor of Thomas Hunt to tell of his ship-building activities in North America. Interestingly, he carefully avoided any mention of his own troubles, giving Hunt's misfortunes as the reason for his return to England. He cites General Nicholson as backing his plans for a settlement of the waste lands between New England and Nova Scotia which would complete the settling of a 'sea coast fifteen hundred miles in length and be one of the glories of His Majesties reign'.[18]

Part of the bargain struck by Nicholson was that the soldiers should have concerted among themselves their proposals. The Lord Treasurer had used the fact that they had not done so as a reason for leaving their requests hanging fire. Coram explained the reason why this had not happened. One or more members of the Board of Trade and Plantations had objected to the settlement and had proposed Nova Scotia. Some soldiers would have accepted, given a year's pay. Coram argued that it was not practicable for such indigent persons to survive and be of service to the Crown, but as the only alternative to starvation they were willing to agree to almost anything. Coram then makes clear his role in the affair:

> It was I, my Lord, that put these men upon petitioning for that settlement and have for more than five months past, been at great pains and some charges, to put them in a way that they and their posterity may be happy and the Crown and nation have an advantage from their being well settled.

This is a second example of Coram working at his own expense for the public good, in this case to alleviate the plight of the impoverished and needy. His own experience of hardship and indebtedness may have given him a greater understanding of the meaning of poverty, but this generosity of spirit where others were concerned was one of Coram's most attractive characteristics. He was also essentially a practical man. He suggested that the Lord Treasurer should sanction a general collection of voluntary contributions for the settlement, and intimated that he already knew some 'persons of character' who had assured him that there would be money enough to settle all the distressed soldiers without any charge to the Crown. It was a bold assertion. It shows Coram already using his skills as a petitioner, skills that he would continue to develop all his life, always confident of his ability to persuade others to share his hopes. Those who backed him would have been more interested in the benefit to themselves than in what the exploitation of the fisheries and the trade in hemp and other naval stores 'could bring to the Nation'. It seems fair to suggest that when Coram wrote 'that I presumed to concern myself to promote this matter and shall be glad to be an instrument of having that waste country settled with so many distressed families' he saw himself as part of that settlement. Coram had no family ties, his wife

---

[18]   Coram to the Lord Treasurer, 20 August 1713: *CSP, CS: A and WI*, 460, p. 222.

was a New Englander, he had found success in America and perhaps hoped to find it again in the unsettled lands of what would later become Maine.

The land that Coram wanted for his disbanded soldiers lay between the Kennebec and St Croix rivers, the St Lawrence and the Atlantic coast.[19] It was so extensive that the colonists proposed a loan of £15,000, to be paid back in naval stores. The Board faced a dilemma. It was reluctant to recommend any more proprietary or charter colonies. The latter had long been recognised as a dangerous tendency in government, and because of the government's financial situation any plan had to involve no expense to the Crown. Expense was only one of the problems. The unsettled lands were subject to many conflicting claims. Under its charter of 1691, Massachusetts claimed the land Coram wanted to settle. In 1629 the Plymouth Council had made grants of land to two merchants, Beauchamp and Leverett. Beauchamp died, but Leverett's patent descended to his son, Governor Leverett of Massachusetts, and in 1714 to John Leverett, President of Harvard College. Governor Leverett had found the territory too big to manage, so parcelled it into ten shares. The ten proprietors subdivided their shares among twenty associates, among them Samuel Waldo,[20] a merchant adventurer who dealt in fish and naval stores from Maine to the West Indies. Others, including several well known Bostonians, claimed they had bought grants of land from native Indians. Major Thomas Clarke had piled up an impressive collection of Indian deeds to lands in the region. His heirs were Sir Bibye Lake and Anne, wife of Increase Mather, and Edward Hutchinson, who was a member of the Massachusetts General Court and no friend of Coram's. Coram was particularly incensed by claims of grants from Indians, writing that 'simple Indians, would for a bottle of strong liquor sign any paper presented to them, which conveyances the tribe will never consent to'.[21] The opposition to Coram's plans only became more strident when two years later he put forward a better-thought-out project that was taken seriously by the Board of Trade and Plantations. But he soon became involved in disputes with those who believed they had prior claim to the land – 'these cobweb pretensions', he called them, but the cobwebs were not so easy to blow away.

Coram was now not only concerned with the New England ex-soldiers, but the many English soldiers unemployed as a result of the peace and their families. He also seems to have been one of the first to make proposals to attract displaced foreign Protestants as settlers. He was confident that once they had taken the oath of allegiance they would forthwith become loyal subjects of the King and should have the same liberties and immunities as the others.[22] He had recruited the help of the Marquis de Wignacourt and others and was ready in 1717 to put forward a well-prepared proposal:

> that the disputed lands between New England and Nova Scotia should become a Province by the name and title of the Royall Province of Georgia; to grant the same to thirty or so more good men in trust with full power for

---

19 *CSP, CS: A and WI, 1712–14*, 4 June 1713, 357, p. 187; 12 June 1713, 364, p. 186; MHS, Nova Scotia Papers, Gay Transcripts, vol. 34, pp. 255–71.

20 *Maine Historical Society*, 2nd series, vol. 9, pp. 75–113.

21 *CSP, CS: A and WI*, 20 December 1717, 268, pp. 128, 129.

22 Public Archives of Nova Scotia: *The 'Foreign Protestants' and the Settlement of Nova Scotia*: 'Thomas Coram and the First Proposals for Foreign Protestants as Settlers', f. 100b.41 1919, p. 33.

settling it. Twelve hundred families are now ready to go over as soon as the patent shall be granted.[23]

In return for a hundred acres of land, after seven years the settler would pay quit rent of 28 pounds of hemp fit for His Majesty's Navy. He explained the principal reason for this was to supply stores to the navy and suggested that the province should be under the First Commissioner of the Admiralty, who would nominate a Lieutenant Governor. Then there was to be an Upper House or General Assembly elected from among the patentees, and a Lower House chosen annually from the freeholders by the freeholders and other inhabitants. This model of civil government is one that Coram would continue to press on the Board of Trade and Plantations, and it became more detailed over the years. Coram also wanted the mines and fisheries to be wholly free. He had seen too many corrupt practices among licence holders to be satisfied with anything less.

This was no ill-thought-out scheme. Among the fifty persons listed for the first patentees were the Earl of Berkeley, First Commissioner of the Admiralty, Sir James Bateman, Lord Mayor of London, Samuel Shepherd, Micajah Perry, Jonathan Belcher and William Browne, both of Boston, George Vaughen of Pyscatagna, James Wignacourt and Coram himself. In a further memorandum to the Board, Coram had been able to add the names of two more Commissioners to the Admiralty, one of them Sir Charles Wager, who was to prove a true friend and supporter. Several of these names would recur as supporters of other proposals, including the petition for a foundling hospital. Coram had by this time become something of an expert on North America and his advice was sought on a range of subjects, from the amount of bounty to be paid for good hemp to the quality of iron ore.

Coram's ideas were backed up by a carefully drafted proposal in the form of a legal brief entitled 'An Abstract of the Scheme of Government in so far as it relates to the Grantees in Trust for Settling the Land lying between Nova Scotia and Province of Maine in New England in America'.[24] In this rare document Coram's ideals of fair play have been considerably watered down. The trustees were to be allowed to strip the land of timber and minerals before granting it to the settlers and before any quit rents became due. And after granting the land they could claim any quit rents not due to the Crown and engage in shipbuilding and erect saw mills for their own benefit. It was more realistic, perhaps, to expect future trustees to subscribe to a scheme if they saw profit in it for themselves rather than expect them to share Coram's altruistic ideals. Providing a living for the needy and at the same time supplying the navy's wants, without much benefit to themselves, did not have much appeal.

The Board of Trade and Plantations took this proposal seriously, but they were alive to the trouble it might cause in Massachusetts. On the same day as Coram presented his second proposal, Jeremiah Dummer was instructed to let the Board know as soon as possible if Massachusetts Bay had anything to offer for or against it and what powers they had.[25] The real question was whether jurisdiction lay with the Crown or with Massachusetts. In the charter of 1691 Nova Scotia had been included,

---

[23] *CSP, CS: A and WI*, 22 May 1717, 577, p. 308.
[24] MHS, Nova Scotia Papers, Gay Transcripts, p. 257.
[25] *CSP, CS: A and WI*, Popple to Dummer, 22 May 1717, p. 308.

although at that time it was in the hands of the French. It was detached in 1713 and made a separate colony without any protest from Massachusetts. Nova Scotia also included the land between the St Croix and Kennebec rivers although the boundaries were not clearly established.

It was Dummer who asked that the matter be put to the Attorney General but, he being ill, it fell to the Solicitor General to pronounce on the rights and wrongs of the matter. Dummer wrote to Edward Hutchinson to keep him informed of what was taking place.

> My last gives an account of Coram's attempt, under the umbrage of some great names, to get a grant of your lands to the Eastward of that whole country. The matter still lies with the Solicitor General (the Attorney General being ill) and as soon as any progress is made in this affair I will acquaint the General Court with it and send them copies of all proceedings. In the mean-time I enclose you Coram's answer to my several memorials which you see is very weak and very false.[26]

It took the Solicitor General some months to sort out all the various claims and his reply in December was a blow to Coram. In his long and detailed response, which relied on the information he was given, he said that the memorialists had been at great expense to improve and re-settle their possessions which had been destroyed by the Indians and that the Duke of Hamilton, Sir Bibye Lake, Ann Mather, Edward Hutchinson and Josiah Walco were all entitled to the land as stated.[27] It took Coram exactly two days to get in his rejoinder to the Board of Trade and Plantations, a remarkably quick achievement. Coram claimed that the conveyance from a certain Robert West on which the Solicitor General had been relying was got on purpose to prevent the settlement, and that Robert West had no power to make the conveyance. With regard to the purchases from single Indians, Coram waxed indignant, 'for those single Indians, when drunk, woud for a bottle of strong lequers signe any paper presented to them which conveyancies the Tribe will never consent to and that was the true cause of so many of H.M subjects being murdered'.[28] He argued that the Governors of Massachusetts Bay, in the shape of the Governor

> had no more right to concern themselves with any land in this tract than the people of Guarnnezy or Jersey have to the Highlands of Scotland. If those grants from the Indians should be confirmed it would create new warrs with the Indians and make it impracticall ever to settle this noble tract of 180 miles front to the sea for raising Naval Stores or be any wayes advantageous to the Crowne. This tract of land is not desired for ye interest of privat persons but to have it an intire Province on a better foot than most of the other Planta-tions for ye service of H.M. and the publicke benefits of the Kingdome.

---

[26] Dummer to Edward Hutchinson, 26 July 1717, *Proceedings MHS.*
[27] *CSP, CS: A and WI,* Mr Solicitor General to Mr Popple, 18 December 1717, 261, p. 125.
[28] *CSP, CS: A and WI,* Thomas Coram to the Board of Trade and Plantations, some remarks upon the Solic-itor General's report, 20 December 1717, 268, p. 128.

Coram could see his altruistic vision of a plantation – governed by its own citizens under the Crown, its lands rich in natural resources and with ample naval supplies – being handed over to be exploited by people who were out to make what they could for themselves. He may temporarily have been defeated, but he had invested too much in this project to give up easily his vision of a Royall Province of Georgia.

5

A Seed is Sown

Shipwreck

Temporarily halted in his tracks by the Solicitor General's ruling, although far from convinced of the strength of his arguments as to the ownership of the contested lands, Coram began to look around for other options. The first to present itself was an offer from Jeremiah Dummer, the agent for Massachusetts, a somewhat surprising offer as he had been unremittingly hostile to Coram. Dummer had contrived the removal of Bridger from his post as Surveyor General of the Woods and offered it to Coram. He may have calculated that by offering Coram the job, he was killing two birds with one stone. Coram would be beholden to him for the job, and at the same time the job would keep him occupied and deflect his ambition to establish a settlement on the contested lands. Bridger had written to Popple, Secretary of the Board of Trade and Plantations, that 'I am very well informed that the agent offered my post to Mr. Coram, but he asked so much money that Coram refused'.[1]

Bridger, although he had his detractors, Coram among them, and had clearly made a nice living from bribes and levies, nonetheless at this critical moment showed that his heart was in the right place. He wrote that he would continue to act as Surveyor of the Woods until his successor arrived, as it was the only hope of saving the mast trees. He said that the rumour of his removal had made 'all the timber men cut and destroy all before them. Many thousands of fine masts would be destroyed in a month.'[2] Coram would have been ideally suited to take on the job. He knew the country well and had been trading in timber and naval stores for the Navy Office for years. The salary may not have been generous but there was plenty to be made on the side, hence the stiff price that was asked for the job. Coram may not have had the money, but more likely it would have gone against his principles to pay for a job and then recoup the cost by lining his own pocket at the expense of the Crown, despite the fact it was accepted practice and that a blind eye was turned in the knowledge that the home government was powerless to prevent it. The job went to Burniston, a placeman who knew nothing of the business and never visited the country.

There is no record of when Coram met Thomas Pearse, a London merchant who

---

[1] *CSP, CS: A and WI*, 26 June 1719, p. 139.
[2] PRO, CO, vol. 1717–1720, Preface, p. xv.

gave his address, when he became a governor of the Foundling Hospital in 1739, as the Navy Office. Both Coram and Pearse would of necessity have frequented the Royal Exchange in pursuance of their business interests. Addison left a lively account of the Royal Exchange, writing that there was no place in town that he so much loved to frequent as the Royal Exchange.

> It gives me secret satisfaction and in some measure gratifies my vanity as I am an Englishman, to see so rich an Assembly of countrymen and foreigners consulting together upon the private business of mankind and making this metropolis a kind of emporium for the whole earth.[3]

Coram, temporarily unable to progress his ideas in North America, and looking for other opportunities to import timber and other naval stores for the Royal Navy, decided that a visit to Germany, now that Hanover was part of George I's domain, might be profitable. There was, however, a problem, in that a law had been passed in 1673 prohibiting the importation of deal boards and fir timber from Germany.[4] Pearse was equally anxious to open up trade with Germany and so it was agreed that Coram should sail as supercargo on Pearse's ship, the *Seaflower*,[5] with a load of wheat to sell in Hamburg. With part of the money he was to load the ship at Haarburgh, across the Elbe from Hamburg, and return with her to London.[6] Part of Coram's remit was to negotiate favourable terms with the German timber merchants, so that they would see that there would be benefit to themselves if the ban on imports were lifted, and would join with him in pressing their government to have the law changed.

The offices of factor and supercargo were very similar, and although it was as supercargo that Coram sailed on the *Seaflower*, Addison's description of the role of a factor fittingly describes the task Coram had been given:

> Factors in the trading world are what ambassadors are in the political world. They negotiate affairs, conclude treaties and maintain a good correspondence between those wealthy societies of man that are divided from one another by seas and oceans or live on different extremities of the continent.[7]

The relationship between a master and a supercargo was a delicate one. The supercargo had authority to direct the ship to the ports he thought suitable and in such cases the master was the executive agent for taking the ship where the supercargo ordered her. Instructions to the master of the *Seaflower* on an earlier voyage give a flavour of the difficulties that could arise. The master, John Berron on that voyage, was instructed

> to sail to such parts as he should be directed from time to time. It was mutually consented unto and agreed by and between the aforesaid owners and

---

3   C. Knight, ed., *London*, 1841, p. 300; *Spectator*, no. 69, 19 May 1710–11, pp. 266–70.
4   PRO, Public General Acts, 6.G I, caps. 1–30, p. 335.
5   A *Seaflower*, Slocomb, Master, carried clothing and stores to Nova Scotia in 1714: Governor's Letter Book, Annapolis, 1713–17, Public Archives of Nova Scotia (Halifax, NS 1900) 11.6.
6   A/FH/Mo1/oo5/176–202: Copy of affidavit relating to the Spoyling and Plundering of the Ship *Seaflower* on the River Elbe, 2 June 1719; quoted in Compston, *Thomas Coram*, pp. 47–62.
7   *Spectator*, no. 69, 19 May 1710–11, p. 267.

freightors, that one John Woodward should be constituted and appointed to be and should be and go in the said ship and for the said voyage, merchant and supercargo, and that the said master should observe the orders of the said John Woodward.

The master was further instructed:

> Mr John Berron you are to sail with our ship *Seaflower*, whereof you go commander, first fair wind and to observe the order of John Woodward from time to time, doubting not that you will both continue loving friends. So God send you prosperous voyage and safe return. We remain your loving friends.[8]

Coram and Henry Pearson, the master of the *Seaflower* for the voyage to Hamburg, would have received similar instructions. The final sentence of the instructions, 'you will both continue loving friends', speaks volumes. Such divided authority must all too easily have led to arguments and difficulties, and on this particular voyage such instructions were very necessary. Supercargos were costly and the master's authority was becoming more circumscribed. However, the master's navigational skills were necessary and it was up to him to prevent damage, get watering done quickly and the cargo loaded. Experienced agents like Coram would have been empowered to give orders on behalf of the owners.

Almost nothing is known of Coram's life at sea, of the dangers he must have faced during his many voyages across the Altantic. He never wrote of the hazards and misfortunes that are the lot of all mariners except in the case of this particular voyage. The stranding and plundering of the *Seaflower* is recorded in great detail in an affidavit signed by Coram on 2 June 1719 in Hamburg.[9] Coram's account gives a vivid picture of what took place. The ship had sailed from Gravesend on 4 March, 'very tight and in every way very well provided'. She arrived off the river Elbe ten days later and took on a pilot named John Strosolt from Heligoland and sailed up the river until evening when they anchored. In the early hours of the morning a strong wind got up, the cable parted and the ship started to drift. The second best anchor was dropped but did not hold and the ship was driven onto the sand. Coram blamed the pilot for ordering the cable to be cut at this juncture, and because it was high tide the ship was driven up the shore and became embedded in the sand. It was snowing and freezing, but by morning the wind had dropped and it could be seen that the ship was virtually undamaged, but she now had no anchors to pull herself off the sand.

Coram had never sailed up the Elbe so he was at the mercy of the pilot John Strosolt, who, when asked for advice, recommended their going to Cuxhaven to get another anchor and cable and assistance to get the ship off the sand. As Coram climbed down the ladder at eight in the morning to walk to Cuxhaven he saw many men coming with axes and sacks to cut up the ship and carry away what was in her. The pilot sent them packing, saying the master and crew were still on board and the ship was watertight. Coram hired two horses and for the sum of forty dollars found the captain of the pilots very willing to help and send assistance to lighten the ship and get her afloat. He sent messengers back to the captain to tell him to expect pilots

---

8 Davis, *Rise of the English Shipping Industry*, p. 171.
9 Compston, *Thomas Coram*, pp. 47–62.

to arrive in their vessel with anchors and cables to heave the *Seaflower* off the sand into deep water. Coram then negotiated with sixteen other boatmen to take their flat-bottomed boats as near as possible so as to take on board as many sacks of wheat as were necessary to lighten the ship. The pilots, in cahoots with the neighbouring villagers, never meant to reach the ship that evening. Unfortunately, the captain and crew, being wet and cold and tired of waiting for the pilots made a cardinal error. They left the ship and went to warm themselves in the neighbouring village. It is hard to blame them; the one thing sailors hate is being wet and cold, and the spray was still frozen on the rigging. How Coram reacted to the master's unwise decision is not recorded, but as soon as the men he had hired learnt that the ship was unmanned Coram noticed an immediate alteration in their behaviour. Instead of being eager to earn the promised fee for refloating the ship they made all sorts of excuses, saying the wind was too high that afternoon and it would be better to go after midnight, which Coram, being an experienced sailor, knew to be untrue.

As the affidavit states:

> The sudding alteration in the behaviour of those at Cuxhaven, Together with reflecting on the frequent Barbarities reportid of those People when any English Ship happens to be drove upon their shore, causid a Jellousy [sic] in the said Coram that they had some Ill Designe against the ship, not to assist her, according to their Agreement, but to make a Wreck of her & her Cargoe for their owne advantage, which Jellousy increasid upon his Observing the Holygland Men who came on board as a Holygland Pilot before mentioned, To be very busy amongst those at Coxhaven, as if they were agreed in some Ill Confederation.[10]

Causing ships to founder and then plundering the wrecks was a recognised hazard on both sides of the channel, and men of Cornwall were as well versed in the art as the men of Heligoland. What made this particular plundering remarkable was the level of official connivance in the affair, but it is understandable considering the long-term commercial rivalry between the two countries.

Coram set off for the village to find the master of the ship, but the master had gone to Cuxhaven by another route to hurry up the pilots. By the time the two men met it was dark, the tide had risen and there was no way of returning to the ship. No one would hire their horses to the master and two of his men, nor would they even lend a lantern and candle to help the master and mate return to the ship. While Coram went back to Cuxhaven to try to persuade the pilots to take him to the stranded *Seaflower*, the master and mate bravely set out over the treacherous ground in the dark to return to the ship. Neither succeeded and the ship remained unmanned that night. The following morning Coram, with much difficulty, hired a wagon from the villagers to take back to the ship those seamen who were not sick with fatigue and cold.

The account in the affidavit continues:

> As he came on the Strand Towards the said Ship which was setting dry upon the Sand at a good Distance from the Water, he percieved that her Ensigne was taken Away and when he came nearer he saw many boats & Waggons

[10] Ibid., p. 54.

round about her and many more Waggons driveing hastely towards her and abundance of men on board her having broken down her Great Cabin. Also cutt up her Decks in several places, some were hoisting out or Lowereing down the sacks of Wheate and other things from every quarter & part all round her into their Waggons & boats whilst others were cutting & takeing away the Rigging and sails, and abundance of Waggons goeing away loaded & comeing empty, the said Coram also saw two holes that had been cutt in her on the Starboard Side under the Wales and that the Capstand was throwed overboard & the pump Geere Taken away (which are said to be their methods to prevent Ships from being saved) and when the said Coram & the said Master and Seamen came on board to endeavour to put a Stop to their plundering, they on board laid hands on the s[d] Coram and threw him down on the Deck and Grossly abusid him and they treated the s[d] Master bad or worse than they did to the s[d] Coram.[11]

Coram and the master realised they needed help from the government, and set off to make application to the Governor of Ritzebuttel that everything that had been removed from the ship be brought to the Admiralty storehouse in Cuxhaven, and that those who plundered it have a third and Coram, as owner, have two-thirds. Coram received 233 dollars for his share, part of which he used to pay all the charges due.

However Coram was far from satisfied with the deal. He observed that the dry wheat and many other things that had been taken to the neighbouring villages had not been returned. In particular he noticed that both the pilot, John Strosolt, and the captain of the pilots, who had agreed for 40 dollars to refloat the *Seaflower*, were with their men dismantling the rigging and cutting and carrying away the shrouds. When Coram tried to restrain them they threatened to kill him. It was not the first time in his life that he had been threatened with murder, and he had to watch as all the masts, yards and the bowsprit were taken off. The holes that had been cut were sealed up, and the naked hull was towed into Cuxhaven by the pilots. To add insult to injury, the pilots told Coram that the Governor had sent two soldiers to guard the ship while it was stranded, and that he should pay for their victuals. Coram paid, but it must have gone against the grain, for he reported seeing one of them standing without arms doing nothing to prevent the plundering.

A lesser man might have given up, but Coram was never one to sit down under injustice, and he sent again to the Governor. He had noticed that less than a tenth of the cargo of wheat had been deposited at the Admiralty and he complained to the Governor and asked for protection to search for the concealed goods. The Governor sent the provost and two soldiers to accompany Coram, the master, the mate and the carpenter to search all the suspected houses, but such was the behaviour of the provost that Coram suspected that he was alerting the villagers and giving them time to conceal the stolen goods. At the first house, as a woman was about to open a large cupboard at the master's request, a soldier dragged the master away, drew his sword and threatened to use it if the master persisted in searching there. Coram and the master returned to complain to the Governor, who told them to return with the provost and soldiers, but in the light of their previous experience they decided it

---

[11] Ibid., p. 56.

would be useless as well as dangerous to return. The treatment Coram received from the authorities in Ritzebuttel echoed the treatment he had received from the authorities in Taunton where also his ships had been wrecked and his life threatened. Again, as in Taunton, Coram refused to be defeated and applied to higher authority. He went to Cuxhaven because he had heard that some of the cargo had been taken there by boat, but the magistrate, who was himself a fisherman, would not even allow Coram to question the events that had taken place at Ritzebuttel.[12] The stakes were not so high on this occasion as in Taunton, when his whole career had been destroyed, but on both occasions Coram had been threatened with violence and death when he tried to assert his rights. He had done his best to save Thomas Pearse's ship and cargo, and although he had failed in that part of his mission he did not forgo Thomas Pearse's friendship.

He continued to Hamburg to negotiate with the German authorities, and his successful lobbying resulted in an Act of Parliament which stated that, as from the first day of August 1720, the Act prohibiting the importation of fir timber, fir planks, masts and deal boards from Germany would be repealed.[13] This had the effect of reducing the price of deal boards from Denmark which fell by 20 per cent, and is cited as one of Coram's achievements in the appeal for subscriptions for his pension.[14]

Closely following Coram's activities in Germany, Jeremiah Dummer's report to the General Court of Massachusetts adds some interesting detail.

> Mr. Coram has also been inactive this winter, but is now renewing his efforts and is sure of carrying his point. He has lately been at Haarburgh, a city on the Elbe belonging to His Majesty, which having a good harbour, and being well situated over against Hamburg, he proposed the government and magistrates there the getting of an Act of Parliament for importing fir timber and deal boards and from thence to Great Britain, by which means their city was to become the magazine of all the timber in Germany and the mart for its sale and exportation. The Governor and magistrates, pleased with this scheme, gave him commendatory letters to the German minister at our Court, under whose favour and influence a bill was brought into the House of Commons for this purpose, but could not be carried for Haarburgh exclusively, though great interest was made for it. However Mr. Coram takes great merit to himself for what he has done and fancies he has thereby secured a sufficient interest at court to carry favour with his favourite design on our Eastern land on which he has fixed views and indefatigably laboured for so many years. I sent him several times to let him know that if he and his friends will be content to make Penobscot their western bounds I'll give him no opposition. But he is a man of that obstinate persevering temper, as never to desist from his enterprise, whatever obstacles lie in his way.[15]

Dummer's opaque reference to the proposal he had put to Coram concealed a scheme of his own for a proposed settlement which he and his associates meant to

---

[12]   Ibid., p. 62.
[13]   PRO, Public General Acts, 6 George I, p. 335.
[14]   LMA, A/FH/Ao1/7/2: Subscription List, 1749.
[15]   Jeremiah Dummer to the General Court of Massachusetts, 8 April 1720: MHS Collection, 3rd series, 1:42.

exploit solely for their own benefit. He had written to the General Court of Massachusetts in 1720 to report that he proposed a scheme to raise hemp flax on the lands between St Croix and Penobscot, the lands to be granted by charter to a group of notable figures.[16]

> Being strong, I had no reason to take notice of Coram and friends or to have any apprehensions of what they were doing or capable of doing against me, yet for quietness sake, I sent word, that if they would withdraw their petition and give me no more trouble, they should find an account of profit from this undertaking beyond what they could ever expect if it were to be under their own conduct.[17]

Coram made the mistake of believing Dummer, and withdrew his own petition on the understanding that there would be advantage to both, but when he found out that the country between the Kennebec and Penobscot had been left out, and discovered Dummer's real intentions, his anger knew no bounds. Dummer reported that 'he ran about in a mad rage declaring the whole design was only a trick to save that fine country for those villaneous people of New England'.[18]

Notwithstanding all the difficulties and setbacks Coram had met with in 1720, he was widening his network of acquaintances, and, through contacts with ministers and at court, becoming more widely known – an advantage that would be increasingly useful to him. While in Hamburg he may well have met Theodore Jacobsen, a successful merchant in the Steelyard, the London headquarters of the Hanseatic trade. At that time Jacobsen was involved in a lawsuit with the Hanse towns concerning a franchise.[19] Coram had not yet become aware of the plight of the foundling children, so his and Jacobsen's interests would have been concerned with matters of trade and commerce. But Coram must have won Jacobsen's support at some time during his long crusade to rouse public awareness of the shameful lack of any provision for the care of the infants born to women so lacking in the basic necessities of life, and with nowhere to turn for help, that their only option was to abandon the child. Jacobsen was not only one of the gentlemen who signed the charter in 1739, but he also became a very active member of the General Committee and later his designs for the hospital won the committee's approval and he was appointed architect of the Foundling Hospital. Unhappily, very soon afterwards Coram and Jacobsen fell out. The evidence as to the nature of the disagreement has been destroyed, but for Coram the outcome was sad. He was not re-elected to the General Committee and after May 1742 played no further part in the affairs of the hospital.

---

16 Hutchinson, *History of the Colony and Province of Massachusetts Bay*, vol. 11, pp. 244–5.
17 Jeremiah Dummer to the General Court of Massachusetts, 17 September 1720, Massachusetts State Archives, vol. 28, pp. 188–9.
18 Ibid.
19 I am indebted to Dr Alan Borg for this information.

A seed is sown

It was only a few days after Coram's furious outburst in response to Dummer's treachery that the price of shares in the South Sea Company began to fall,[20] and Dummer's 'bubble from the Eastern Lands', so called by Thomas Hutchinson in his history of the Province of Massachusetts Bay,[21] burst as well. Such had been the extraordinary success of the company that in April it had purchased the whole of the National Debt for £7,567,000, with investors from all walks of life scrambling to invest. It had given rise to a host of smaller speculative companies who put forward a series of chimerical proposals for extracting money from the public, including one for a wheel of perpetual motion. There was nothing the company, which had no assets and did no business, could do to stem the fall once it had lost the confidence of its investors, and London found itself in the grip of a full blown financial storm. Investors all around the country watched fortunes collapse and share debts mount. By the end of September, thousands were ruined and many fled the country to escape their debts. Nearly every family of any social standing had suffered. In December, Parliament was recalled to discuss the situation but there was little they could do to stem the tide of disaster, with so many families and businesses devastated. The memory of the catastrophic collapse of the South Sea Company would last for many years and make future investors much more cautious. A secret committee was set up in 1721 to probe the scandal, and proved that there had been fraud and corruption on a massive scale, reaching to the heart of government, and it was discovered that over £1 million had been spent on bribes to cover up the fraud.[22] Concealing his own involvement in the scandal, Walpole, having succeeded Sunderland as First Lord of the Treasury, pushed through his plans for financial reconstruction and succeeded in protecting many of the guilty parties from the full force of justice.

It seems likely that Coram's own business affairs were affected by the general collapse, for many of the merchants for whom he traded would have been victims of the disaster. For the next three years, Coram made no attempt to further his plans for an American settlement. But in 1724 Coram once again put himself at the head of a small group of unemployed officers who presented themselves to the Board of Trade and Plantations asking the Board to consider another plan to settle and plant the disputed lands.[23] The matter was referred to the Privy Council and Mr Coram and the others were invited to come and bring an account in writing of the numbers of persons who intended to go, how they proposed to settle the land, what encouragement they expected, and what they proposed to do in return for the Crown. Unusually for Coram, when he next appeared before the Board he was not well

---

20 The South Sea Company was formed in 1711 and granted a monopoly of British trade with South America and the Pacific Islands. Its promoters were a reckless, venal coterie who sold paper shares in a company which had no assets and did no business. Such was its success that the company was able to take over the national debt. Annuitants of the state were persuaded to exchange their annuities for South Sea stock. Investors came from every level of society from the king downwards. When the collapse came Robert Walpole kept his head down, and when he came to power he tried to deal with the wreckage. The South Sea Company continued to exist without success, and its commercial history ended in 1750. See Carswell, *The South Sea Bubble*, and Balen, *A Very English Deceit*.

21 Hutchinson, *History of the Colony and Province of Massachusetts Bay*, vol. 11, pp. 244–5.

22 Balen, *A Very English Deceit*, p. 195.

23 *Journal for the Commissioners for Trade and Plantations, 1722–28*, 12 May 1724, p. 90.

prepared, and as he had not brought his proposals in writing he was told to come back on 3 September.[24] Because of Coram's fear of seeming uneducated, he always had his proposals written out by a professional and this cost money. It could be that Coram simply could not afford the luxury of paying for this service at this time. Coram did not attend the next meeting when the proposals were read. Whether Coram was ill, or abroad, or just discouraged, or he had other matters on his mind is unknown. Predictably, as before, nothing came of these proposals.

Coram is generally thought to have given up his seafaring life after the disaster of the *Seaflower*. With time to walk the streets he was able to observe more closely what went on around him – and what he saw appalled him. Among all the filth and rubbish that cluttered the streets, among the dead cats and dogs he began to notice there were babies, dead or dying on the dung heaps. It must have been sometime in 1722 that he came to the conclusion that something must be done to try to save these foundlings, pathetic flotsam, abandoned by their destitute mothers. The result of the dire poverty to which they were born and the lack of any provision for such children other than the parish workhouse, where there was little chance of any infant surviving. If there was a particular incident that aroused his compassion for the plight of the foundlings it is not recorded. However, Coram remembered the date when he first decided to take up the cause of destitute infants. In a letter to Selina, Countess of Huntingdon,[25] dated 1739, he wrote

> After seventeen years and half's contrivance, labour and fatigue I have obtained a charter for establishing a hospital for the reception, maintenance, proper instruction and employment of exposed and deserted young children.[26]

This letter, written to gain sympathy for a request for further financial help, has encouraged the belief that Coram's main preoccupation during those seventeen and a half years was to solicit support for the Foundling Hospital. There is no doubt that he did spend a lot of his time trying to gain support for his idea, but he was also very preoccupied during those years with America, and his desire to further settlements in Maine, Georgia or Nova Scotia. Underlying his colonising efforts was the hope that he himself might be enabled to return to America. His lack of success should not obscure the time and energy he devoted to that cause.

Once Coram had decided on a course of action he would never willingly give up before achieving his object. Once his feelings of outrage at the treatment of these hapless infants had been aroused it would not have taken long for a man of his warm, compassionate nature to set about looking for a solution. The death of his only brother, William, as a baby, his own lack of children and the memory of how precious the lives of children were in New England could only have served to strengthen his determination to prevent this waste of precious human lives. What he had not expected was that it would take so long to achieve his object.

---

[24] Ibid., p. 93.
[25] Selina Shirley, 1707–91, foundress of the sect of Calvinist Methodists, generally called Lady Huntingdon's Connection.
[26] Coram to Selina, Countess of Huntingdon, 15 September 1739, HMC MSS, *Reginald Rawden Hastings*, vol. 3, pp. 22–3.

He soon learned that infanticide was common, babies were either abandoned or put out to barbarous nurses who starved them, or, when they were older, hired them out to others to beg and steal as a way of living, and, worst of all, were blinded, maimed or had their limbs distorted so as to gain more sympathy.[27] He was not the first to have attempted to stir up public interest in these unfortunate children. In an article in *The Guardian* nine years earlier, Addison had highlighted their plight:

> I shall mention a Piece of Charity which has not yet been exerted among us, and which deserves our attention the more, because it is practised by most of the Nations about us. I mean a Provision for Foundlings, or for those Children who for want of such a Provision are exposed to the Barbarity of cruel and unnatural parents. One does not know how to speak of such a subject without horror: but what multitudes of infants have been made away with by those who brought them into the world and were afterwards ashamed or unable to provide for them! There is scarce an assize where some unhappy wretch is not executed for the murder of a child; And how many more of these monsters of inhumanity may we suppose to be wholly undiscovered, or cleared for want of legal evidence. Not to mention those, who by unnatural practices, do in some measure defeat the intentions of Providence and destroy their conceptions even before they see the light. In all these the guilt is equal, though the punishment is not so. But to pass by the greatness of the crime (which is not to be expressed in words) if we only consider it as it robs the commonwealth of its full number of citizens, it certainly deserves the utmost application and wisdom of a people to prevent it. It is certain that which generally betrays these profligate women into it, and overcomes the tenderness which is natural to them on other occasions, is the fear of shame, or their inability to support those whom they give life to. This I think is a subject that deserves our most serious consideration for which reason I hope I shall not be thought impertinent for laying before my readers. I shall therefore show my readers how this evil is prevented in other countries as I have learnt from those who have been conversant in the several great cities of Europe. These are at Paris, Madrid, Lisbon, Rome and many other large towns, built like our colleges.[28]

Addison pointed the way, and when the ideas as to how the Foundling Hospital should function came to be discussed, it was to the European examples that its supporters looked for guidance.

According to Jonas Hanway,[29] even earlier in the reign of Queen Anne several merchants had proposed opening a subscription and solicitation for a charter for a hospital to receive 'such infants as the misfortunes or inhumanity of their parents, should leave destitute of support'. The merchants were dissuaded from implementing their scheme by public opinion. Hanway referred to 'ill grounded prejudices that such an undertaking might seem to encourage persons in vice, by making too easy

[27] Taken from the Memorial, signed by 'Ladies of Rank', quoted in Bernard, *Account of the Foundling Hospital*, p. 3.
[28] *The Guardian* 105, 11 July 1713.
[29] Jonas Hanway, 1712–1786, traveller, philanthropist and voluminous writer. Founder of the Marine Society, 1756, he became a governor of the Foundling Hospital in 1758. See *DNB*.

provision for their illegitimate children'.[30] Hanway hit the nail on the head in making explicit the reason why the merchants abandoned their project. The fear of encouraging promiscuous sex among the lower classes was a prejudice deeply embedded in the middle and upper class male psyche and it was reflected to an extent in their female counterparts, as Coram was to discover to his cost. Mrs Deborah's reaction to the discovery of the foundling, Tom Jones, in Mr Allworthy's bed reflected all too accurately respectable society of the time:

> . . . but for my own part, it goes against me to touch these misbegotten wretches, whom I don't look upon as my fellow creatures. Faugh, how it stinks. It doth not smell like a Christian. If I might be so bold as to give my advice, I would have it put in a basket, and sent out and laid at the church-warden's door. It is good night, only a little rainy and windy; and if it was well wrapt up, and put in a warm basket it is two to one but it lives till it is found in the morning. But if it should not, we have discharged our duty in taking proper care of it; and it is, perhaps, better for such creatures to die in a state of innocence, than to grow up and imitate their mothers; for nothing better can be expected of them.[31]

That short passage encapsulates both the prejudice and callous disregard for human life that Coram was to find so difficult to overcome once he had set himself the task of bringing to public notice the plight of so many abandoned infants. It made gaining acceptance for his proposed solution an uphill struggle. A very different set of rules applied to the aristocracy, where illegitimate births were seen as unfortunate but accepted as long as the 'unwritten rules of aristocratic gallantry'[32] were adhered to. The illegitimate daughters were usually suitably married off; the wealth, status and power of the family ensured an adequate place in society for bastard sons.

Coram would have been well aware of these double standards and this knowledge, no doubt, lay behind his impassioned outburst to Benjamin Colman[33] when writing of the difficulties he had encountered in bringing his 'darling project' to fruition. He was an experienced petitioner and his bluff, knowledgeable and disinterested approach had more often than not worked in his favour, so his initial lack of success came as an unpleasant surprise. He knew that for a project of this magnitude he would need powerful support, and when that support failed to materialise he was disgusted.

> I found it was Impossible to be done, for I could no more prevaile on any Arch Bishop or Bishop or Nobleman Britain or Foreigner, or any other Great Man, I tryed them all, to speake to the Late King or his present Majesty on this affair than I could have prevailed with any of them, if I had tryed it to

---

[30] Hanway, *Candid Historical Account*; quoted in McClure, *Coram's Children*, p. 9.

[31] Fielding, *History of Tom Jones*, p. 29.

[32] Tillyard, *Aristocrats*, chap. 4, 'Disaster and Renewal', gives an account of Lady Sarah Bunbury's illegitimate child, her disgrace and rehabilitation, pp. 269–338.

[33] Benjamin Colman, minister of the Brattle Street church, Boston, with whom Coram kept up a correspondence from 1734 to 1740.

putt down their breeches and present their Backsides to the King and Queen in a full Drawing room[34] such was the unchristian Shyness of all about the Court.[35]

By the time Coram wrote that letter he had almost achieved his object, the charter had been presented to the King, but his anger at the hypocrisy he had encountered during the early years of his struggle burns through the writing. Support for a charitable endeavour was also a means of flaunting status and power, and it would be a brave man who dared lend his name to such a dubious enterprise, given the prejudice against any proposal that could be interpreted as endorsing immorality. George I had refused at the beginning of his reign to appoint Charles Churchill Groom of the Bedchamber to the Prince of Wales solely on the ground of his illegitimacy.[36] Although he later relented, a marker had been put down, and the members of the court were not willing to step out of line and risk offending the monarch. The disastrous consequences of the bursting of the South Sea Bubble made it a singularly unpropitious time to invite men, so many of whom would have had their fingers burnt, to sign up to a charitable structure on the model of a joint stock company. Asked to give their backing to any proposal for an enterprise that needed financial support, with the memory of the South Sea Company so recently before them, it is hardly surprising that Coram found his attempts to gain the backing of the powerful men he would need to ensure success in gaining access to the King falling on deaf ears during the 1720s.

By 1727, Coram seems to have felt that the time had come for his endeavours to be recognised. Unable to make progress with his plans for an American settlement or to get the necessary support to put a petition for a foundling hospital to the King, he may have felt that it was his lack of any kind of official status that was preventing him from achieving his objectives. Since the unfortunate voyage to Hamburg his own financial situation may have become more precarious. He was nearly fifty and, although he had some solid achievements to his name, he had no official position. Until now he had paid, from his own limited financial resources, all the expenses incurred in gathering information and writing up his petitions for a settlement in North America, and in his other acts for the public good. Respected for his honesty but without a patron in an age of patronage, he decided to appeal directly to the monarch, the recently crowned George II. He had been content to serve his king and country for no financial or other reward, but in a petition presented on 5 July 1727 to the Privy Council[37] he appealed for some recompense for his services. An unusually large number of Privy Councillors, thirty-one in all, were present with the King on that occasion, half of whom would, twelve years later, become governors of the Foundling Hospital. It is ironic, in the circumstances, that on that occasion a proclamation for the encouragement of Piety and Virtue for preventing and punishing Vice,

---

34 This passage was seen as so indelicate that Compston, in *Thomas Coram*, p. 12, translated it into Latin, 'ut Coram omnibus pleno in atrio braccis Regis Reginaaeque oculus natus exhiberrent'. Nicholas and Wray, *History of the Foundling Hospital*, p. 19, omitted it altogether.
35 Coram to Colman, 22 September 1738: 'Letters of Thomas Coram', p. 43.
36 Thomas Wentworth, Earl of Strafford, to Peter Wentworth, 28 September 1714, *The Wentworth Papers, 1705–1739*, ed. James J. Cartwright, London 1883, p. 423; quoted in McClure, *Coram's Children*, p. 20.
37 PRO, PC 90 2, p. 39.

Profaneness and Immorality was presented to the King. The troubled South Sea Company also presented a petition, complaining of duties on the import and export of negroes in Jamaica. Coram's petition was the last business of the day. He must have gone to considerable trouble and expense, for it was beautifully written on parchment, and signed with a great flourish by Coram, the capital letters large and bold.

The humble petition of Thomas Coram of London was read,

> setting forth his having been bred to the sea from his youth and always much used to Shipping, Navigation and Commerce in and to His Majesty's Northern Plantation in America, wherein he hath spent many years of his time and much of his substance by steadily presenting his endeavours for the Public Benefit without having any consideration for that service, and humbly conceiving he is capable to rendering himself very Serviceable to His Majesty by his experience in Naval Affairs and in the Northern Plantations. He therefore prays that his case may be recommended to the Lords Commisioners of the Admiralty, whereby he may be employed in such service of the Royal Navy as their Lordships shall find him fitly qualified to execute, or that he may be allowed some recompense for his service aforesaid as His Majesty, in his great wisdom, shall judge he may have deserved.

The King ordered that the petition be sent to the Office of the Lord High Admiral of Great Britain to consider the same and report to 'His Majesty at this Board in what respects they may find the petitioner capable to serve His Majesty either in the Navy or in the Plantations'. The petition must have been one of the most unusual to have been presented to the King. Any kind of office was usually obtained through patronage, but Coram, although he was known at the Admiralty and he was acquainted with Sir Charles Wager, does not seem to have asked for the support of any great man, feeling no doubt that his actions should speak for themselves. For a man of his limited means to be actually spending his own money without the certainty of any other reward, other than to be working for the public benefit, must have been a rarity at that time. There is no traceable record of any response to Coram's petition. He was not given employment in the plantations – he may have made too many enemies – nor by the Navy Office, and had to look elsewhere for a means of earning his living.

6

Coram, Francis Grueber and David Dunbar

Realising that his carefully-thought-out petition to the King was going to bring neither office nor employment, Coram returned to his dream of establishing a colony in the disputed lands north of Massachusetts. As he saw it, his plan would bring profit to the Crown in the form of regular and ample naval stores without further dependency on precarious foreign supplies; strategically it would prevent the incursion of the Indians into unsettled land; and, lastly but not least, it would prevent the spread of French and Roman Catholic influence. Coram had stated time and again that the Government of Massachusetts were only too eager to claim and exploit the wealth of both land and sea to the disadvantage of the British, and that they were also unwilling to spend money on maintaining the defensive forts. Further benefits of such a settlement included the ability to offer employment to those at risk of becoming a burden and a nuisance to the state, and to offer sanctuary to Protestant refugees from Europe. Unfortunately, Coram did not carry enough weight, either politically or financially, to overcome the reluctance of the Board of Trade and Plantations to become involved in a project that might have monetary implications when emigrants were willing to settle in New England and the other plantations at no expense to the state.

In June 1728 Coram began his very long and detailed memorandum and petition to the Board[1] by reiterating all his old arguments in favour of being allowed to settle the lands between the Kennebec and St Croix rivers. Refuting the long and complicated claims put forward by Massachusetts to monopolise the land, Coram maintained that the whole territory from Cape Gaspe to the Kennebec had finally been ceded by the French at the Treaty of Utrecht. He therefore asked permission to take up the projects he had put forward under Queen Anne and George I to settle the land and to further the production of hemp and naval supplies. He accused the Government of Massachusetts of preventing

> your Memorialist and his associates from obtaining permission and encouragement from the Crown to plant an elegant Colony on the said tract under H.M. right and Government, whilst he and his associates for several years

---

[1] *CSP, CS: A and WI*, 18 June 1728, 285, pp. 138–40.

together used their utmost endeavours for obtaining the same; . . . which was
done with great fateigue and expense by your Memorialist . . .[2]

and drew attention once again to his own unrewarded endeavours. Coram said that
many of the men who had supported him in the past were ready to settle and pay quit
rent in hemp to the Crown, and, not only that, many of them had military experience
and would be able to build small forts to protect themselves and the country without
any expense to the Crown. Apart from the useful people who wished to settle, and
with the addition of some foreign Protestant refugees from the Palatine, Coram
proposed that future convicts should be transported at the Crown's expense to serve a
term on His Majesty's plantations clearing and cultivating the derelict land. He
argued that

> as there will continually be great numbers of future convicts condemned in
> Great Britain and Ireland to serve a term of years in H.M.'s plantations; and
> to be transported thither at the Crowne's expense as they are now trans-
> ported; they cannot be sent to any other part so advantageous to the Crowne
> as to employ them under strict and prudent management for the service of
> H.M. in clearing and cultivating the said wast land and derelict land for the
> complete furnishing in due time [of] constant and full supplies of hemp and
> masts for the Navy, each convict to have after the expiration of his sentence a
> small portion of land.[3]

When in Paris in 1718, Coram had noticed that more than eight hundred beggars,
ballad singers and other vagabonds had been seized in one day in the streets and sent
away to Mississippi. Encouraged by the French example, he now proposed that other

> persons of both sexes, who live in continual danger of being apprehended for
> criminal practices which by the faults of their parents or otherwise, they are
> constantly repeating Which renders them a nuisance and a pest to the
> publick, Especially about the Citty's of London and Westminster, and they
> could gladly be rescued from their neccesity of committing these crimes, and
> the evil consequences thereof, by volentary engageing themselves to serve
> H.M. a term of years in the said tract of Country now laying waste and
> Derelict.

He made a specific proposal that one of the largest storeships be detailed to transport the emigrants, and that two small sloops accompany them and remain there. The
storeship on its homeward journey would be laden with masts for the navy, thus
underlining the practical aspects of his plan. He ended by saying

> and forasmuch as such usefull undertaking will require absolutely to have
> some person of known integrity and experience in those part to begin the
> same, *offers himself in that capacity* (original emphasis).

What makes this proposal of particular interest is that he named himself as the
person who had the experience and integrity to put his plan into operation, making

---

[2]   Ibid., p. 140.
[3]   Ibid., p. 141.

explicit his desire to return to America and his hope that it would give him an opportunity for employment.

Coram knew that the government would never agree to a settlement that was going to cost money, so he was careful to show that the only cost that would fall on the state was that of transporting convicts, which was, in any case, a charge on the government. To uphold his claims that there were men of substance who would back him, two gentlemen, James Stirling and Joseph Watson, agreed to support Coram, writing the following day to the Board of Trade and Plantations:

> We are two of the many in good circumstances, who at their own expense will settle themselves, on the King's lands and islands, now laying waste and uninhabited, between the River Kennebeck and St. Croix, if H.M. shall be pleased to place our worthy friend, Capt. Thomas Coram, there in such a manner as he has proposed and we shall each of us carry one thousand pounds and more of our own with us.[4]

Coram had done all he could to advance his prospects for a return to North America. The two men willing to go with him under his leadership had substantial financial means, the land would be settled at no expense to the Crown, convicts would be occupied advantageously, undesirables removed from the streets of London and Westminster and naval stores guaranteed. But the Board of Trade and Plantations were not impressed with the practicability of forming a colony from such wretched material. They may well have doubted the financial ability of Coram's supporters to underwrite the costs of such a settlement, so once again Coram found his proposals shelved.

Unable to fulfil his dream of finding employment in America, Coram turned his attention to looking for gainful work in England. In a small pocket book, Coram made notes detailing his expenditure between 1 January and 23 May 1729, and this is how we know something of his short career as a powder maker.[5] The meticulous daily record of receipts and expenses incurred during that period gives a unique insight into Coram's business activities, about which very little is known. The general inference is that he traded in naval stores, either as agent or sometimes as supercargo for merchants, and that he had dealings with the Navy Office, but apart from his fateful journey to Haarburgh there are very few concrete details as to how he actually earned his living. Important though it is to learn from this record that Coram was, for a brief time, a producer of gunpowder in partnership with Francis Grueber, of even greater historical significance is the fact that Coram also used this notebook to list the names of twenty-one ladies of quality and distinction whom he persuaded to sign his petition for a charter for a hospital for foundlings. He carefully gives the date when each 'lady of charity', as he called them, signed. We therefore know that the Duchess of Somerset was the first to sign, on 9 March 1729 at Petworth. Unfortunately, the diary is mainly concerned with his business dealings, and although it covers the period when he went to Petworth to obtain the duchess's signature, there is no description of this momentous event or of how it came about. Coram had spent the previous

4   *CSP, CS: A and WI*, 27 June 1728, 300, p. 150.
5   The pocket-sized diary, entitled, *Merlinus Anglicus Junior, or the starry messenger* by Henry Coley, student in mathematics and celestial sciences, was printed by J. Read for the Company of Stationers in 1729. Coram made use of it for several years afterwards: LMA, A/FH/A1/7/1.

evening in Guildford dining with the Mayor, John Goodyer, from whom he hired horses to ride to and fro between London and Guildford. His journey from Guildford to London on 9 March cost 2s 3d. Since he noted that the duchess signed his petition that day, he must have gone to Petworth from London, riding back the same day.

How and when Coram met Francis Grueber, the son of a Huguenot immigrant, is not known, but Coram had many contacts with Protestant refugee families, seeing them as potential settlers in America. With his own attempt to return to America blocked, Coram had to look for another way to earn his living. Francis Grueber was involved in the production of gunpowder at mills along Faversham Creek, Oare and Chilworth, but he was in financial difficulties and faced bankruptcy in 1728.[6] Coram's name in the trading title, Messrs Grueber & Coram, and his numerous diary entries recording expenditure and receipts constitute the evidence for his financial involvment in the business. Francis Grueber died in 1730 and there is no further record of Coram's participation after that date. But by then he had met up with David Dunbar and become interested in yet another plan for a settlement in North America.

Coram's contribution to the partnership may have been in the provision and management of the ships and powder barges needed to transport the saltpetre, the major raw material used in the production of gunpowder, to Grueber's mills. It may also have been he who introduced Thomas Pearse, his old friend from the Haarburgh venture, to the business, for it seems from receipts in the pocket book that it was Pearse and Robert Norman who provided the financial backing for the enterprise. Robert Norman was a gunpowder producer at East Mosely and was described as a merchant.[7] Both he and Pearce were to become Governors of the Foundling Hospital in 1739. The Grueber/Coram partnership, with the financial help of Pearse and Norman, appears to have been able to pay off Grueber's debt to the Ordnance of £1,868 3s 9d. This had been done by raising short-term loans, but when these could not be repaid after Francis Grueber's death in 1730 the business was taken over by Thomas Pearse.

Coram played a very active part in the running of the business. Until he built his own powder barge he had to hire ships and barges to transport bags of saltpetre from the stores at Deptford, from the Ordnance Board and possibly the East India Company, to Chilworth. Coram used East India merchant ships for local transport along the Thames before transferring the cargo to powder barges in the river. Gunpowder had to be tested to make sure it was up to standard and the test procedure, carried out by Ordnance officials and known in the trade as proofing, took place at Greenwich. Coram had to arrange the transport for the barrels of gunpowder going for testing, and on 10 January 17 out of the 156 barrels for proofing were rejected. On another occasion Coram spent £1 2s 6d at the King's Head by the Tower on entertaining the officers of the Ordnance. This was probably a wise precaution because failing the test was an expensive business.

---

6 I am indebted to K.R. Fairclough for this information. His paper, 'Thomas Coram: His Brief Period as a Gunpowder Producer', is published in *Surrey Archaeological Collections*, vol. 86, 1999, pp. 53–72.

7 Pocket Book of Captain Coram (LMA, A/FH/A1/7/1), Transcript and research notes K. R. Fairclough, *Surrey Archaeological Collections*, vol. 86, 1999, pp. 1–32.

Coram had had a powder cart made to carry gunpowder by road. The cost came to over £22 3d, which included 6d to a shoemaker 'for sewing leather over the iron across the cart' to prevent sparks from the wheels setting fire to the gunpowder with catastrophic consequences. Coram and Grueber had decided by 1728 that it would be financially advantageous for the business if they owned their own powder barge. Coram had the necessary skills to oversee the building of a barge and chose the boatyard belonging to Mr Coffen, whose yard was immediately opposite the Houses of Parliament. The dukes of Richmond and Montagu kept their barges on the same strip of foreshore at Stangate and it is possible that this is where Coram first met both dukes and later persuaded them to support his petition for a foundling hospital.

During January and February there are numerous entry notes of visits to the yard, the cost of the timber, mast, spars and anchor, as well as the cost of the cooper, foreman and fitter. Waterage and payment for Coram's many journeys across the Thames at 6d a time also feature in the list. By the end of February the barge was finished and Coram was making his final purchases. For the price of 7 shillings he acquired two wooden shovels, a pail, a sheet, a mop, broom and a hand shovel for the boat. On 21 February he spent 10s 6d to celebrate the launch. In March he went with the barge on her maiden voyage by river to Guildford. Using the tide as far as possible, guided by oars and with the help of a sail when there was a favourable wind, the barge went as far as the river was tidal. After that it was towed by horses from the banks, passing between Petersham and Hampton Town and from Sheen to the mouth of the Guildford river at a cost of 6s 6d.[8]

In April the diary shows Coram paying the East India Company £468 for saltpetre and £3 13s 6d to the porters for shipping 200 bags onto his boat for distribution to Chilworth, Faversham and Bridgewater. He frequently hired a horse to ride from Guildford to London and back. At the end of every month he was reimbursed by Thomas Pearse and Robert Norman. The barge made at least four voyages to London and back. John Gillet was paid £1 11s 2d for a second voyage to Guildford and £1 11s for a third voyage. Andrews, another bargemaster, was paid £2 3s for a fourth voyage. Although Coram spent some of his time in coffee houses, the cost carefully noted, it was hard work, so it is pleasing to see that on one occasion he spent 12s 6d for treating and cards at dinner, which must have provided a welcome moment of relaxation. It is also unsurprising that Coram found this work unfulfilling, and kept in touch with developments in North America, ready to become involved if occasion arose.

Six months before Coram submitted his 1728 memorandum, the ambitious and energetic David Dunbar was commissioned to succeed the hopeless Burniston as Surveyor General of the Woods.[9] He had served in the army and been commissioned Lieutenant Colonel. As Governor of the Leeward Islands he had attracted the favourable notice of George II, to whom he probably owed his appointment.[10] He, like Coram, had ideas of settling a colony on the lands between the Kennebec and

8   Details of the barge's route from the Thames to Guildford are shown on a contemporary map of Surrey
     by John Senex, 1729, in *Surrey Archaeological Collections*, vol. 86, 1999, p. 65.
9   *CSP, CS: A and WI (1726–1727)*, p. xxiii (Journal) p. 373.
10   Colonial Society of Massachusetts, April 1739: *Proposed Colony of Georgia in New England*, p. 263.

St Croix rivers, which would have as its principal aim the provision of naval stores.[11] Instead of leaving for New England as his contract stipulated, Dunbar spent most of 1728 and 1729 in London making plans for his new colony, leaving his brother Jeremiah Dunbar as his deputy to carry out his duties as Surveyor General of the Woods. Although Coram was at this time involved with Grueber in the powder-making business, it would not have taken Coram long to learn of Dunbar's proposals through his contacts or at the New England coffee house. Soon the two men were working closely together to promote the idea of a new colony. At the same time the Board of Trade and Plantations was considering proposals from yet another potential colonist, Daniel Hinze. Hinze had been employed as an agent to transplant several Protestant refugee families from the Palatinate to settle in Ireland and America, and he now proposed collecting and bringing over another large group of families.[12] Dunbar was not slow to see the advantage of linking Hinze's proposals with his own: increased numbers would make for a more viable colony. He followed up his first suggestion by proposing to settle some six hundred Irish families, who were, he said, destitute in Massachusetts, and he also spoke of five hundred Palatine families, who he believed were eager for lands and who could be brought over by Hinze. His ideas were on an altogether larger scale than those put forward by Coram.

The Board would have preferred a settlement in Nova Scotia, as they were concerned about the predominance of the French Acadian population and wanted to see their own loyal subjects established in the province. They seem to have considered that the Palatines would, by virtue of settling in Nova Scotia, naturally become loyal subjects of the King. However the Palatines and the Irish families already in New England declared that they were unable to transport themselves and their cattle as far as Annapolis and Canco. Neither were they willing to mix with the Roman Catholic Acadians, as the French inhabitants were called. But as far as Dunbar and Coram were concerned there was a further difficulty. Nova Scotia was still ruled by a military government and both men were adamant that 'no good or profitable subjects could be induced to settle before a civil government was put in place'.[13] All his life Coram wrote and spoke against the evils of military government, and had put forward his own ideas when the merits of charter or proprietary forms of civil government had been under discussion some years previously.

After many meetings, the Board of Trade and Plantations decided to accept Dunbar's proposal based on Coram's initial idea of a Royall Province of Georgia.[14] Hinze was to be used as an agent for the recruitment of the Palatine families to make up the numbers needed for a viable colony. The Board said they had considered Dunbar's report and had discoursed with Mr Coram, 'A person well acquainted with these parts'. It is a mark of the increasing respect in which Coram's opinions were held that the Board used his name to give extra weight to Dunbar's scheme. The Board proposed that 'the tract of land extending from the River Kennebeck to the River St Croix be separated from the Government of Nova Scotia and erected into a province by the name of Georgia, and that a distinct Government be established

[11]   Board of Trade (1722–1728), p. 418.
[12]   *Proposed Colony of Georgia in New England*, p. 264.
[13]   *CSP, CS: A and WI*, 9 May 1729, 694, p. 364.
[14]   *CSP, CS: A and WI*, 12 May 1729, 705, p. 372.

there'.[15] The proposal embodied so much of Coram's thinking, echoing his previous petition for a Royall Province of Georgia, that he must have felt a great sense of satisfaction. The proposal continued:

> As the settlement of this country will in great measure be owing to the care of Colonel Dunbar, and as he has offered his services to be Governor of this colony without any salary until His Majesty shall be pleased to think him deserving of it, we take leave to recommend him as a person qualified to be governor during His Majesty's pleasure.

Dunbar was to be further empowered to grant land to such as were willing to settle there, upon condition of paying one penny sterling per acre per annum quit rent to His Majesty. The Board also wanted 100,000 acres of woodland to be reserved for the service of the navy near navigable rivers, in which no person should presume to cut any tree without the Surveyor's licence. Dunbar was delighted by the Board's response to his petition and he declared that he would erect a stockaded fort, to be called Fredericksburg, for defence against neighbouring Indians.[16] In one year he had apparently achieved what Coram had spent so much of his time since 1713 trying to bring about.

The Privy Council, alarmed at the speed of the northern developments, put the brakes on. They refused Dunbar's proposal to set up a Government of the Province of Georgia.

> They do not approve of your having the country which you are directed to settle called the 'Province of Georgia', because it is part of and under the same Government of Nova Scotia, and being called a Province, it may be thought distinct and not under any government. They therefore think it should be named George County in Nova Scotia; and they think it proper to give your new settlements English names with English terminations for which reason you will change the name Fredericksburg to Frederick Town or Fort.[17]

Worse was to come. The Board of Trade and Plantations despatched a severe reproof to Dunbar for his failure to comply literally with the various instructions he had been given, one of which was to reside in the country. Nevertheless, it recommended to the Privy Council that a new county to be called Georgia should be created with Dunbar as Governor. Although he learnt that the King had departed for Hanover without giving his assent to the proposal,[18] Dunbar, when he arrived in Boston on 23 September, never doubted for one moment that he had been given sufficient authority to go ahead with the settlement.[19] Alas for Dunbar, the same fate awaited him as Coram had suffered. All the documentary evidence that he possessed was his commission as Surveyor General of the Woods. He was very active in Maine

---

[15] Ibid.
[16] *CSP, CS: A and WI*, 1728–29, p. xxxiv.
[17] Ibid., p. xxxv.
[18] *Report on Canadian Archives* (1894); quoted in *Proposed Colony of Georgia in New England*, p. 264.
[19] *Documentary History of Maine*, vol. x, pp. 440–1.

during the next two years and Pemaquid was rebuilt[20] and six other towns laid out. But such efforts at settlement in the disputed part of New England excited the same opposition that Coram had encountered. The new Governor of Massachusetts, Jeremiah Belcher, had just arrived in Boston. Like Dunbar, he was ambitious, but the difference between the two men lay in the fact that he was a royal governor, while Dunbar could only wish to be one. From the start there was friction between the two men, who grew to loathe each other. An incident – the apparent illegal seizure of a Massachusetts vessel by Dunbar's men – played into Belcher's hands. Belcher, seeking to ingratiate himself with the people of Massachusetts, sent a committee to Frederick's Fort to investigate the matter. Dunbar was alarmed and refused to allow the committee to land.[21] In reply to Dunbar's frantic appeal to England for help Belcher was ordered not to attack the fort.[22]

But Belcher was to have the last word. Once again the whole matter was referred to the law officers, and all the old ground gone over. Their final and definitive opinion was, 'the petitioners, their tenants or agents ought not to be disturbed in their possession or interrupted in carrying on their settlements in the lands granted to them within the district in question'.[23] On 10 August 1732, the Privy Council ordered Dunbar to quit the lands.[24] Thus the attempts by both Coram and Dunbar to found a new colony of Georgia in lands claimed by New England finally came to an inglorious end. But by that time Coram had already made his move and become a supporter of the proposed new colony of Georgia in the south.

There is no evidence to show that Coram ever considered joining Dunbar in America, but the possibility must have been in his mind. But perhaps he saw no role for himself. His lack of interest may be attributable to his fear that Dunbar's colony would, after all, come under the influence of the military government of Nova Scotia, to which he would have been totally opposed. He may have feared that Dunbar would run into the same difficulties with Massachussetts that he had encountered. But the most likely reason is that his friend and mentor, the Rev. Thomas Bray, before he died in 1730, had suggested to James Oglethorpe the formation of an association to found a colony for the necessitous poor in South Carolina. By early 1730 Coram had already associated himself with this new venture. Accompanying Viscount Percival, Oglethorpe and several other men of consequence, he had been part of the delegation to the Board of Trade and Plantations to discuss a new settlement in South Carolina, the future Georgia,[25] a land well away from any possibility of interference from Massachusetts.

Despite all the rebuffs that Coram had suffered at the hands of the Board of Trade and Plantations, no doubt owing to the Walpole government's lack of interest in matters colonial, Coram continued to respond to the Board's requests for advice. He ended a letter he sent to the Board in 1731 with the words:

---

[20] Warren K. Moorhead, 'The Ancient Remains of Pemaquid, Maine', Old Time New England, vol. XIV, January 1924, pp. 133–41.

[21] Documentary History of Maine, vol. XI, pp. 70–85.

[22] Ibid., pp. 66–7.

[23] CSP, CS: A and WI, 11 August 1731, 353, pp. 218–19.

[24] CSP, CS: A and WI, 10 August 1731, recorded in Massachusetts House Journals, vol. X, pp. 387–403; vol. XI, p. 117.

[25] CSP, CS: A and WI, 23 November 1730, 546, p. 357.

If anything herein can be thought for the service of His Majesty and for the information and satisfaction of the The Hon Lords of Trade and Plantation and they shall require solemn attestation thereof, if it will to signify their Lordships pleasure hereon I shall cordially obey their commands at such time and place as they shall order.[26]

Obviously Coram enjoyed the access to influential men that attendance at the Board gave him. It also provided him with the occasional opportunity to bring his own accomplishments to their notice, but there is no doubting his genuine wish to promote the interests of his country.

While Dunbar was still pursuing his dream of becoming governor of the new colony of Georgia, the Board of Trade and Plantations was still hoping to get a colony of German families to settle in Nova Scotia. They had asked Coram for his ideas as to what instructions they should give to the colonists. Coram responded with a detailed plan modelled on a New England township. He suggested that a tract of ten miles square should be laid out and that all highways and principal streets should be at least 70 feet wide, straight and convenient. Only then should the land be divided into 100 acres for each person. Because of the danger of attack from 'frenchified' Indians, there should be an initial settlement of at least sixty families in each and every village. Finally, so as to encourage industry and commerce, sufficient land, at least 100 feet in breadth, should be free along the sea coast and the banks of navigable rivers. In a postscript Coram added that all fishing should be free.[27] A few days later he was back giving his opinion as to where the Palatines should settle. He argued that it would be better to settle on the north-east side of the Penobscot river toward Nova Scotia, leaving the south-west side to be settled later. He goes on to warn the Board of the dangers that would ensue if the land were governed from Massachusetts. His thesis was that the men of Massachusetts had so mistreated and swindled the Indians, making them sign away their rights when drunk, that there would always be enmity between the two. If that was not enough to encourage the government to settle, plant and people that tract of land, Coram held up the spectre of the French King being tempted to take possession.[28]

By December Coram was back again petitioning the Board. He must have given further thought to his hurriedly scribbled postscript concerning fishing rights in his letter of 10 November. He had discovered that some of the plantation governors, pretending that the whales and fish off their coasts were royal fish, were seizing them and taking for themselves fish, oil and fins. He prayed that fishing of all kinds should be entirely free to the inhabitants of Nova Scotia and all other plantations, as it was in Massachusetts. This time his plea did not fall on deaf ears. Almost immediately the Lords Commissioners of Trade and Plantations were ordered to prepare instructions putting a stop to all such claims. Less than two weeks after the Board had received Coram's petition his advice had been acted on.[29]

[26] CO, 5 873, ff. 234, 235v. This sentence at the end of the original letter was not included in the printed version, CSP, CS: A and WI, 12 March 1731, 88, p. 50.
[27] CSP, CS: A and WI, 10 November 1729, 936, p. 517.
[28] CSP, CS: A and WI, 18 December 1729, 1036, p. 563.
[29] CSP, CS: A and WI, 28 November 1729, 997, p. 539.

The Board of Trade and Plantations worried continuously about the way in which the colonists were flouting the Navigation Laws. It was a practical impossibility for them or their officials to put a stop to the manufacturing activities of the entrepreneurial colonists. The colonists on the other hand saw no reason why they should be bound by laws which could not be enforced. They no longer saw their country solely as a source of raw materials for the mother country. Manufacturing enterprises had been growing up all over the country. Not only did they produce goods for themselves, instead of importing them from England, but they had a flourishing export trade. Coram, good mercantilist that he was, did his best to help the Board. He reported on the illicit sawmills and the manufacture of iron tools. He confessed that when he had been shipbuilding in Taunton all the bolts, spikes and nails that he needed had been made by a certain Robert Crossman, who had now become a member of the Massachusetts government, and he was sure the practice continued. In reporting this he took the occasion to remind the Board that he had built the first ship on the river Taunton and several other larger ships, and now more than five hundred ships had been built on the river.[30]

His most effective intervention came when he took up the cudgels on behalf of the Hatters' Company. He went with the Master and other members of the company to petition Parliament against the making of hats in the plantations. They were told to return and lay before the Board a statement of the facts. Coram had been gathering evidence on the growth of American manufactures, and doubtless the illegal hat-making provided one more proof for a memorial he read to the House of Commons on the subject of an address concerning laws, manufacture and trade of the kingdom.[31]

He no doubt also drafted the memorial for the Hatters' Company praying that the inhabitants of the plantations 'may be prevented from wearing or selling any hat but what are made in Great Britain'. It is generally believed that it was owing to his influence that the Hat Act was passed in 1732. The Hatters certainly thought so and it is said that they would have acknowledged this service had he allowed it, but instead the company kept him supplied with hats for the rest of his life, whenever he needed one.[32] As Brownlow remarks, 'Its size spoke the good wishes of the makers in a very legible character.'[33] Coram is bare headed in the great portrait painted by Hogarth, but a large hat rests on the floor beside him, propped up between the leg of the table and his right leg, a symbol of his fight for what he believed to be right, even if the inhabitants of Massachusetts would not have agreed with him.

Although the Board was continuously asking Coram for his opinion, and he had built up a reputation as an expert on North American affairs, he was given little reward for all the thought and care that he put into his responses to their requests, still less given any thanks or acknowledgement. But for a man of his integrity and

---

30   *CSP, CS: A and WI*, 12 March 1731, 88, p. 58.
31   *CSP, CS: A and WI*, 15 February 1732, 87, p. 60.
32   Beaver hats were expensive. Melchior Wagner had been appointed hatter to King George I in about 1717 and a receipt dated 1742, preserved among the accounts of Frederick Prince of Wales, records that a fine beaver hat cost £1 10 shillings and the ostrich feather cost £1 8 shillings plus 2 shillings for a silver button and double chain loop and 3 shillings for a cockade and box'. See *The Wagners of Brighton*, Anthony Wagner and Antony Dale, Chichester 1983, pp. 4–6.
33   Brownlow, *History and Objects of the Foundling Hospital*, p. 114.

honesty perhaps the token gift of a hat was the most fitting reward. Although he was spending time dealing with matters concerning America, he had never stopped thinking of how he could best serve the interests of abandoned children. During the next few years of his life these two interests would be intertwined, but in the end it would be his work for children that brought him the greater renown.

7

First Success

Coram was a man who had overcome disappointment. If he believed that his ideas were right, opposition merely strengthened his resolve. His mental toughness sprang in part from the fact that he was seldom seeking his own personal advancement, but was working altruistically for what he believed to be a public good – a rare attribute in eighteenth-century Britain. No matter how long it took, he would never have given up his fight to bring material relief to the helpless infants he saw abandoned, destitute and dying, on the streets of London. It is only because of his letter to Selina, Countess of Huntingdon,[1] that we know that as early as 1722 he had started to seek support for his idea to found a hospital. There is no record of his having made any progress during the following six or seven years, while he must have been discussing his ideas for the rescue of abandoned infants and looking for ways to fund an institution to care for them. He had a large number of acquaintances and he was known to many of the great men about court through his dealings with both the Navy Board and the Lords Commissioners and the Board of Trade and Plantations. He was an experienced petitioner and fundraiser, his ability to persuade based on detailed knowledge of his subject, a certain bluff charm of manner and innate honesty winning him support for the various causes he espoused. But on the subject of a hospital for foundlings, he found, to his disgust, that he could make no headway.

Addison had signalled the existence of institutions in the larger European towns for the care of foundlings. On the continent many of the organisations set up for the care of abandoned children were religious in nature, the Roman Catholic Church being foremost among them. Since the dissolution of the monasteries, Britain had no such religious charitable tradition and by the eighteenth century the charitable and humanitarian instincts prevalent in Tudor times had all but disappeared. In 1552 the citizens of London, alarmed at the increase in the number of beggars and vagrants, and led by successive Lord Mayors, were inspired to obtain possession of the hospitals that had once been attached to the monasteries. Of the four foundations, the so-called Royal Hospitals, that passed into the control of the city, one was for children: the house of the Grey Friars became known as Christ's Hospital.[2] St Bartholomew's and St Thomas's were for the sick and aged poor, and Bridewell for the vagrant and thrift-

1   Coram to Selina, Countess of Huntingdon, 15 September 1739, HMC MSS, *Reginald Rawden Hastings*.
2   Pinchbeck and Hewitt, *Children in English Society*, vol. 1, pp. 127–8.

less poor. Christ's Hospital was designed to 'take oute of the streates all the fatherless children and other poor men's children, that were not able to keep them'.[3] A vigorous campaign to raise funds had been set in motion and the hospital was ready to receive 380 orphans by November 1552. The original idea had been to admit foundlings as well as orphans, but the numbers brought to the hospital were too great; by 1556 the number of foundlings was restricted to a hundred. Technically, the foundlings left at the gates of the hospital were then a charge on the parish, and as more foundlings found their way to the hospital the Governors gave in to pressure from the Poor Law authorities. The numbers of infants taken in gradually decreased, until by 1653 only three were admitted, although the hospital was caring for over a thousand children.

In the second half of the sixteenth century other larger towns followed London's example, and orphanages were founded in towns such as Bristol, Plymouth, Ipswich, Reading, York and Norwich. The children were to be cared for and given an educa-tion to enable them to become useful citizens. By the end of the seventeenth century the climate of opinion had changed, partly owing to the rapidly expanding and mobile population, drawn to London, the largest city in Europe, and putting the ad-ministration of relief to the poor under strain. In some areas workhouses were built to accommodate the destitute and to give work to the able bodied. In 1722 the Poor Relief Act enabled churchwardens and overseers of the poor to establish workhouses where children and adults could be housed, and this greatly increased the number of workhouses. Conditions varied widely, but eighteenth-century accounts of the children's workhouse movement bear testimony to deteriorating social attitudes to children of the poor. The humanitarian idea that they should be educated had given way to the idea that children as well as adults should be put to work as soon as they were old enough. Although Jonas Hanway was writing forty years after Coram started to campaign for a hospital, Hanway's description of the workhouse would have applied almost equally well to the years when Coram was seeking support for his project. Calling the workhouse 'the greatest sink of mortality in these kingdoms', Hanway wrote:

> Parish Officers may amuse themselves till Dooms-day, but to attempt to nourish an Infant in a Workhouse, where a Number of Adults are congre-gated, or where a Number of Nurses are assembled in one Room, and conse-quently the Air becomes putrid, be these nurses ever such proper Persons, I will pronounce, from the most intimate Knowledge of the subject, is but a small remove from Slaughter, for the child must die.[4]

The generous acceptance of the need for community support for the destitute child which had marked the creation of Christ's Hospital in 1552 contrasted with the cold hostility Coram met 170 years later when seeking support for a London foundling hospital.

Coram would have swiftly been made aware by the churchmen he approached that they regarded such a development with particular horror. This time there was no Nicholas Ridley, Bishop of London, to add his voice to that of the City when the four

---

[3]   Lemprière, ed., *John Howes, MS 1582*, p. 25.
[4]   Hanway, *Serious Consideration*, p. 10.

royal hospitals were being set up. How could the Church be seen to be condoning illicit sex by ameliorating the consequences of unwanted pregnancies and thus encouraging immorality? That the children were the innocent victims, not just of casual, or worse still pleasurable sexual encounters, but of mothers so destitute that they had no means of caring for their infants did not enter the argument. It was more convenient not to see bastard foundlings as individuals, but as part of an immoral coupling whose parents were at fault for having transgressed. Punishment for the sins of both fell entirely on the mothers and could be visited, without guilt, on the help-less children, and a blind eye turned to their fate. Coram's anger and disgust at the reaction of the Church was probably all the more acute as he himself was a staunch Anglican; the refusal of the Anglican hierarchy to even consider an organisation to ameliorate the fate of these destitute children must have offended his most basic moral principles. Coram was not, on the whole, a man to forgive or forget a wrong, and the behaviour of the Church left a lasting scar, so even when support for his charter became socially acceptable, as a token gesture he invited only the Archbishops of Canterbury and York and the Bishop of London to become founder governors.

In Ireland matters were no better, and the attitude of the Irish propertied class to social improvements was, if anything, worse than that of their English counterparts. The one churchman who did take seriously the plight of pauper children was the Dean of St Patrick's, Jonathan Swift. In his famous satirical pamphlet written in 1720 entitled *A Modest Proposal for preventing the Children of Poor People from being a Burthen to their Parents or Country and for making them beneficial to the Publick*, Swift had sought to shock the unheeding inhumanity of society into action:

> I have been assured by a very knowing American of my acquaintance in London that a young healthy child, well nursed is, at a year old, a most deli-cious, nourishing and wholesome food; whether stewed, roasted, baked or boiled; and I make no doubt that it will equally serve in a fricasie or ragoust.

Swift proposed that pauper children be fattened and reared at public expense for gentlemen of refined taste. The scheme he felt would achieve a number of very desir-able objects for it would prevent women murdering their bastards, greatly lessen the number of papists, relieve the poor and give some pleasure to the rich. He continues,

> A child will make two dishes as an entertainment for friend, and when the family dines alone, the fore or hind quarter will make a reasonable dish, seasoned with a little pepper or salt will be very good boiled on the fourth day.

The argument is written in the language of a learned paper and starts by calculating the number of children born, the impossibility of feeding and clothing them, thus making his final solution to the problem the more horrifically shocking.[5] The *Modest Proposal* was published in 1729 just prior to the government legislation enacted in March 1730 that decreed that all foundling children be admitted to the Dublin work-

---

[5] Victoria Glendinning, in *Jonathan Swift*, suggests (p. 166) that Swift is not being inventive, and that a hundred years before there were reports in Ireland of starving women lighting fires in the fields to lure children to them and then killing and eating them.

house,[6] and may well have been influential in getting the legislation passed. The institution assumed the name of the Foundling Hospital and Workhouse of the City of Dublin. On the orders of Archbishop Boulter, Protestant Primate of All Ireland, and Chairman of the Governors, a revolving basket was placed on the gate of the hospital into which unwanted children could be left anonymously, by day or night, a device already in use in Europe. Although preceding the establishment of the London Foundling Hospital by almost ten years, the Dublin Foundling Hospital, in terms of outcomes, could hardly be counted a success. In the first seven years of its existence, of the 4,025 children admitted, 3,235 died.[7] Nevertheless Swift had, in a devastatingly effective piece of work, drawn attention to a social evil, and it may be no coincidence that the publication of his proposal came in the same year that Coram was able to persuade the first of his twenty-one ladies of quality and distinction to sign his petition.

Coram eventually overcame the 'unchristian shyness' that afflicted the archbishops or bishops or noblemen or any other great men when he asked for their support by changing tactics. When he approached certain ladies of quality and distinction, he found them much more willing to listen to his arguments and to give him their support. In seeking to understand how Coram was able convince the ladies to sign his petition, it is not enough to say that there was 'no necessity to convince them by argument' or 'that the sweetness of their tempers supplied a tenderness that rendered arguments unnecessary'.[8] The action Coram took in approaching these ladies was unprecedented. He would not have met any of them in the course of business or socially: he being a mariner, and his wife a colonial, the social gulf between them could hardly have been wider. What gave him the idea that he might be able to break the impasse in this way? Ladies might be charitably inclined and given to helping the poor and needy in their locality, or to supporting the charity school movement. They would use their influence to petition for jobs and preferment for family, but to put their names to a petition for a hospital for foundlings, something no man had agreed to support, puts the matter in a different light. What made the ladies come to believe the question of bastardy, illegitimacy and the plight of foundlings should no longer be ignored? Were these matters being discussed more openly? Above all, who were the friends with whom Coram discussed his new approach? Who smoothed his way and gave him the introductions that he needed?

Coram had a long association with the Rev. Thomas Bray, who received the living of St Botolph without Aldgate in 1706.[9] Coram would have found himself much in sympathy with Bray's ideas and somewhat in awe of the older man's learning. They had a common interest in North America, Bray having gone out as commissary to Maryland in 1700. Wishing to recruit missionaries for work in the plantations before he left, he found that only poor clergy applied and they had no money for books, which prompted him to set up parochial libraries. The libraries gave rise to a larger scheme, the Society for Promoting Christian Knowledge (SPCK), which had its first

6   Robins, The Lost Children, p. 15.
7   Ibid., p. 17.
8   Nichols and Wray, The Foundling Hospital, p. 15.
9   Bray resided in Aldgate from 1708 to 1716 and again from 1720 to 1730: H. P. Thompson, Thomas Bray, pp. 73–84.

meeting in 1698. The Society's objects were to set up libraries at home and abroad, to establish charity schools and to send missions both to colonists and heathens. On Bray's return from America in 1700 he found the SPCK had grown to such an extent that he formed the Society for Propagating the Gospel (SPG) in 1701 to preach the Gospel throughout the plantations.

It is not possible to date Coram's association with Bray very precisely, but it is likely to have been at least since 1720, when Bray again took up residence in Aldgate. Coram himself wrote that

> the venerable Dr Bray, late minister of Aldgate Parish, wherein I had lived had the Goodness to bear a great respect for me at all Times from his first knowing me, and often Lamented the great pains I for many years took for having a proper Settlement made on the Lands Lying Wast and derelict between New England and Nova Scotia[10]

which suggests that the association was one of long standing and important to Coram. It may well be that Coram was finally dissuaded from associating himself with David Dunbar's attempts to colonise Nova Scotia by Bray, who thought 'it was too far Northward, the winters being very long there'.[11] Since Bray had clearly taken a great interest in Coram's colonisation plans, they would certainly have discussed his concerns over the plight of foundlings.

The two men thought alike on many subjects, Coram the practical man, Bray the intellectual. Coram was a member of the SPCK, and was particularly interested in the wish to evangelise the inhabitants of the colonies, colonists and Indians alike. His desire to establish a church in Taunton if circumstances permitted bears witness to his interest in promoting the Anglican faith in New England, and his wish to work for the conversion of the Indians, and in particular the education of girls, is well documented. Bray was an energetic minister, a prolific writer and an influential cleric. Having heard from a friend in Paris that there had been since 1640 an institution that cared for foundlings, L'Hôpital pour les Enfants Trouvés, he asked for details. He learnt that the day to day operation of the hospital was in the hands of the Order of the Daughters of Charity and the Association of the Ladies of Charity. Inspired by this example Bray wrote a pamphlet, *A Memorial Concerning the Erecting in the City of London or the Suburbs thereof, an Orphanthropy or Hospital for the Reception of Poor Cast off Children or Foundlings.* That Coram should have taken the trouble to send a copy of this pamphlet to Harvard University Library is a mark of how important it must have been to him.[12] In it Bray recommended that

> to induce Persons even of the highest Rank, to condescend to the taking these, the meanest of their Fellow Creatures under their Care and Management, I cannot offer to their Consideration any Thing more Moving than to propose to their Imitation what is done by the Dames and Sisters of Charity in Paris, in the Hospital of the very same Kind with this proposed to be erected . . . even Princesses and Dutchesses, and other Ladies of the Prime

10 Coram to Colman, 30 April 1734: 'Letters of Thomas Coram', p. 20.
11 Ibid.
12 Harvard Library attributed this pamphlet to Bray, and internal evidence suggests that it was written after 27 December 1727 and published in 1728 or 1729: McClure, *Coram's Children*, p. 279.

Nobility of Paris, to the Number of Two hundred and above, have associated themselves and entered into Confraternity to manage this Affair.

It is not known how widely Bray's pamphlet was circulated, but the SPCK and the SPG had large networks of supporters, including those involved with the charity school movement. If read by any noble ladies, Bray's words may well have given pause for thought to those who were charitably and religiously minded. The pamphlet almost certainly caused Coram to believe that he might get a more sympathetic response from ladies than from their husbands and fathers. Since there was as yet no foundling hospital for ladies to manage, as in France, for Coram the next logical step would be to ask English ladies for their support, an idea for which there was no precedent in England. In France, under the auspices of the Roman Catholic Church the participation of women from all walks of life would have been natural and accepted, as it was in Protestant Holland. Possibly only Coram, in a sense an outsider, a man unconcerned by the social niceties that ruled polite behaviour but yet who understood where power lay in the political world, could have succeeded in getting support from sixteen ladies of quality and distinction in just over a year.

Having once decided on a course of action Coram would immediately have talked of his plan with his friends. Having no entry to the charmed inner circle of society ladies he needed advice as to whom he should approach and how he might obtain the necessary introductions. There is nothing to indicate what criteria Coram used to select his ladies, but they do have certain characteristics in common. Coram seems not to have been merely looking for the ladies whose rank and social distinction would lend weight to his petition; there is evidence that his choice fell on those who also had stable marriages, or who could be seen as models of feminine propriety and virtue. This was important, as there was a strong connection drawn between feminine modesty and chastity and the dangers of associating with activities that could be seen to violate natural modesty and be a threat to chastity. If ladies known for their goodness and virtue could demonstrate that they were no less virtuous for having signed Coram's petition, the reluctance of the men to do likewise might be overcome.

There are many reasons for thinking that Henry Newman would have been one of the friends to whom Coram turned, not only for support but also for help with introductions. Newman, born in New England, spent most of his life in London. Before becoming Secretary to the SPCK, a job he held until his death in 1742, he had been for five years in the service of the Duke of Somerset. Newman in all probability attended court with the duke, and long after he had left the duke's service he retained an interest in court life and enjoyed its spectacles, regaling correspondents in New England with full accounts. He called himself 'a spectator at liberty and not a trainbearer or other fine thing confined to a place abounding with vanity and insincerity'.[13] Because of his contacts he received many requests for help from those who had no patron or who lacked influence. Besides his secretaryship of the SPCK he was agent for New Hampshire, and he and Coram would have had shared interests in the politics of New England.

Bray and Newman worked very closely together and looked for support across a wide spectrum. Robert Nelson, a devoted member of the SPCK, a philanthropist and

13   Henry Newman to Elisabeth Sheldon, 31 August 1727, Private Letters, p. 20.

an energetic promoter of the charity school movement, had written *An Address to Persons of Quality and Estate*, deploring the fact that there was neither school nor hospital for the distressed children, so violent and disruptive that they had become known as the Blackguard, and urging the establishment of a 'House of Charity to receive poor exposed Infants; whereby many Murders and Abortions could be prevented'.[14] This address was sent by the SPCK to anyone with an interest in the subject. Other members included Sir Hans Sloane, the physician, who, among his many important offices, was Physician in Charge to Christ's Hospital, to whom he donated his entire salary; he was also a generous benefactor to many other hospitals. Sloane had an enormous practice and a large circle of correspondents, who included the chief people of the time. Through his contacts with the SPCK he might have been aware of Coram's proposals. It is not known whether he helped with introductions, but he was a founder governor and played an active part in the administration of the hospital in the early days.

Inevitably in the small world of the fashionable elite, the ladies were nearly all connected by ties of blood or friendship. Their lives revolved around the London season and the country. In London they spent their segregated lives in houses in the elegant and fashionable London squares and streets of the West End, their days filled with social activities, attendance at court functions, visits to the opera, assemblies, and private masquerades. They dined and visited and they had access to the latest books and plays. Social and literary circles overlapped, poems were exchanged and gossip and scandal were discussed in the salons and drawing rooms, their thoughts far from the concerns that worried Coram. The season over, the ladies and their households retreated to the country and largely occupied themselves with their children and running their large houses and gardens. Women were not without influence, but when they manoeuvred to gain advantage on behalf of family or friends, they were aware that they were intruding on a man's world. However, there were occasions when, through their social activities and family connections, they were able to play a role that was not available in the same way to their husbands. Signing Coram's petition could have been just such an occasion. When Coram asked for their signatures none of the ladies could have been in any doubt that he was appealing for their support for a project whose objects were far removed from their usual concerns. It is entirely possible that their husbands were happy that ladies of such unassailable goodness and virtue should be the first to sign, opening the way for them, whose reputations may not have been so pure, to follow their examples with a clear conscience.

Coram's approach was blunt; he did not mince his words. The petition he asked the ladies to sign bears all the hallmarks of his approach:

> Whereas among the many excellent designs and institutions of charity, which this nation and especially the city of *London*, has hitherto encouraged and established, no expedient has yet been found out, for the preventing the frequent murders of poor miserable infants at their birth; or for suppressing the inhuman custom of exposing new born infants to perish in the streets; or putting out such unhappy foundlings to wicked and barbarous nurses, who

14 Nelson, *Address to Persons of Quality and Estate*, p. 212.

undertaking to bring them up for a small and trifling sum of money, too often suffer them to starve for the want of due sustenance or care; or, if permitted to live, either turn them into the streets to beg or steal, or hire them out to loose persons, by whom they are trained up in that infamous way of living; and sometimes are blinded, or maimed, or distorted of their limbs, in order to move pity and compassion, and thereby become fitter instruments of gain to those vile merciless wretches. For a beginning to redress so deplorable a grievance, and to prevent as well the effusion of so much innocent blood, as the fatal consequences of that idleness, beggary or stealing, in which such poor foundlings are generally bred up; and to enable them, by an early and effectual care of their education, to become useful members of the commonwealth; we whose names are underwritten, being deeply touched with compassion for the sufferings and lamentable condition of such poor abandoned helpless infants, as well as the enormous abuses and mischiefs to which they are exposed and in order to supply government plentifully with useful hands on many occasions; and for the better producing good and faithful servants from amongst the poor and miserable cast-off children or foundlings, now a pest to the public, and a chargeable nuisance within the bills of mortality; and for setting a yearly income for their maintenance and proper education, till they come to a fit age for service; are desirous to encourage and willing to contribute towards erecting an hospital for infants . . .[15]

Coram in his petition gave both the reasons for asking for the ladies' signatures and the benefits that would accrue, and added that such an action would be acceptable to God Almighty, a dig at the churchmen who had refused him support.

Several events occurred in 1729 to focus public attention on the question of bastards and their differing fates. Swift's *Modest Proposal*, so deliberately shocking, had been published. Coram's petition came at a time when the literary and social world were following with fascinated curiosity the drama of Richard Savage's arrest and imprisonment. Savage, a poet, was a friend of James Thomson and Pope, and had gained entry into the most influential literary circles. He was much better known as a poet in the eighteenth century than he is today. However, it was not only his poetry that brought him to public attention, but his claim to be the illegitimate son of the Countess of Macclesfield and Earl Rivers. He used his poems relentlessly to accuse his mother of the most inhuman behaviour towards him. His book of miscellaneous poems, published in 1726 and dedicated to Lady Mary Wortley Montagu, who with several others supported him financially, contained a relentless and brilliantly satirical attack on the Countess. In the introduction Savage launches into a tirade against his mother. It starts by saying that he was legally

> the son of an Earl, and naturally of another, I am, nominally No-Body's son at all: For the lady, having given me *too much father*, thought it but an equivalent Deduction to leave me *no mother*, by way of balance, – so I came spotted into the World, a kind of Shuttlecock between law and nature.[16]

---

15 Bernard, *Account of the Foundling Hospital*, p. 3.
16 Richard Savage, *Miscellaneous Poems and Translations*, published by Richard Savage, 'Son of the late Earl Rivers', London 1726, p. 95.

He then goes on to accuse the Countess of Macclesfield of the most extreme form of maternal barbarity that exists on historical record. He uses Locke's *Essay on Human Understanding* to make the point that humane behaviour is not always generated by innate or instinctively benevolent impulses, and that among some nations the practice of

> exposing children and leaving them in the fields to perish by want or wild beasts has been the practice, as little condemned or scrupled as the begetting of them.[17]

Savage then implies that his mother's treatment of him is little different: 'Were I inclined to grow more serious, I could easily prove that I have not been more gently dealt with by Mrs Brett.'[18] In effect this differed little from the way in which the citizens of London were treating their own unwanted children, as Coram was to point out.

Richard Savage's vendetta against his mother might not have been of so much interest to society had he not killed a man in a coffee house brawl, been tried and found guilty. At this juncture in Savage's life the difference between being seen as a pauper bastard and as the illegitimate son of aristocratic parents literally meant the difference between life and death. As a pauper criminal the gallows awaited him; as Lady Macclesfield's illegitimate son and a famous poet he could hope for a pardon.

In December 1727 the trial opened at the Old Bailey. The case was the talk of literary London and the public gallery was 'crowded in a very unusual manner'.[19] Through the endeavours of friends, in particular Aaron Hill, his publisher, Lord Tyrconnel, Savage's patron, and the Countess of Hertford,[20] who as a Lady of the Bedchamber to Queen Caroline had the ear of her royal mistress, a royal pardon was obtained. Thousands of copies of *The Newgate Pamphlet*, written while Savage was in jail, had been circulated in London. It is ironic that Savage's greatest success came as a result of his conviction for murder and his royal pardon. There was much speculation in salons and coffee houses as to the truth of his identity. After his release in 1728 he published a confessional poem entitled *The Bastard*, which was an instant success and ran to five editions. In it he again returned to his attack on Lady Macclesfield:

> O Mother, yet *no* Mother – 'tis to you
> My thanks for such distinguish'd claims are due
> You enslav'd to nature's narrow laws,
> Warm championess for *freedom*'s sacred cause,
> From all the dry devoirs of blood and line,
> From ties maternal, moral and divine,

[17] Ibid., p. 97.

[18] Lady Macclesfield had been married at fifteen in 1683. When she divorced in 1698 her two children, Anne, born 1695, and Richard, born 1696, by Earl Rivers were declared illegitimate. She married Henry Brett in 1700. Anne died as an infant and the existence of Richard after 1698 has never been proved conclusively. The balance of opinion, as recorded in Cokayne, *Complete Peerage*, vol. 8, p. 331, is that Savage was an imposter, on the evidence of four articles by W. Moy Thomas, *Notes and Queries*, 2nd series, vol. 6, pp. 361–5, 385–9, 425–8, 445–9.

[19] Richard Holmes, *Dr Johnson and Mr Savage*, p. 104.

[20] Lady Hertford was one of the ladies who signed Coram's petition, and Lord Tyrconnel became a governor of the Foundling Hospital.

Discharg'd my grasping soul; you push'd me from shore
And launched me into life without an oar.[21]

Savage continued, through his poetry, to blackmail his mother. Many in the literary world were intrigued by the fashionable image he presented, the Newgate poet, the literary outcast, and the orphan. Lord Tyrconnel, after Savage's release from jail, invited him to live in Arlington Street and recommended him for the official post of Poet Laureate. He failed to secure the post, and then, in an astonishingly daring move, appointed himself the Queen's Volunteer Laureate, and for seven years presented the Queen with his verses celebrating her virtues. What is even more unexpected is that Caroline responded with an annual grant of £50,[22] keeping alive in court circles Savage's poet/orphan image.

While the drama of Savage's arrest and release was being played out and the question of his parentage was a hot topic of discussion, late in 1729 polite society was shocked by another scandal, again demonstrating the narrow line between comfortable respectability and destitution. Katherine, the wife of the Earl of Abergavenny, described by the Duke of Dorset as 'young, thoughtless, gay and unfortunately fair',[23] was caught 'en flagrant délit' with Abergavenny's intimate friend, Richard Lydell. There was a rumour that the liaison was encouraged by Abergavenny in the hope of extracting money from his friend, as indeed he did to the tune of £10,000 after a court case. He set his butler and steward to spy on the lovers and, having got the proof he needed, he packed off his heavily pregnant wife to London, 'with orders to the servants, if her father would not receive her, to sett her down in the street'.[24] She gave birth to the child, but within two weeks both mother and infant were dead. The contrasting fates of the mother's two sons, one a royal godchild, the other a bastard who could have died in the street like other foundlings, underlines the gulf that existed between the respectable and accepted members of society and the awful consequences that could befall those on the other side of the divide. Lady Abergavenny's death was greeted by half a dozen poems and Hervey lauded her as a kind of martyr to love but, as Goldsmith bluntly put it later, dying was the only action that could have restored her to public sympathy.[25]

It was against this background of heightened awareness of the fate awaiting bastards who landed on the wrong side of the divide, that Coram set out in 1729 to woo his first four duchesses to his cause. He chose well. He may well have owed his introduction to the Duchess of Somerset to Newman, who had served the Duke and who had gone to some trouble to remain in touch with the court. Somerset, known as 'the Proud Duke' and who was described by Macaulay as 'a man in whom pride of birth and rank amounted almost to a disease',[26] was also said to be a lover of music and poetry, but whose imperious manner made him difficult to approach. His first

21 Savage, *Miscellaneous Poems*, p. 89.
22 Holmes, *Dr Johnson and Mr Savage*, p. 143.
23 Cokayne, *Complete Peerage*, vol. 1, p. 40, note f.
24 The story is given in Cokayne, *Complete Peerage*, vol. 1, p. 40, note f, and in Grundy, *Lady Mary Wortley Montagu*, p. 296.
25 Grundy, *Lady Mary Wortley Montagu*, p. 296; Oliver Goldsmith, 'When lovely woman stoops to folly', *The Vicar of Wakefield*, 1766, chap. 24.
26 Macaulay, *History of England*, vol. 2, p. 271.

wife, Elizabeth, already twice widowed before she married Somerset, had become heiress to the huge Percy estates and brought Petworth to her husband as part of her inheritance.[27] It was to Petworth that Coram rode to meet the second Duchess of Somerset, Charlotte Finch. It seems very possible that Charlotte signed Coram's petition with her husband's approval, something she as a woman could do, but that might have been construed as weakness in him. Her signature and the promise of financial support must have pleased Coram greatly. It was a spectacular start to his campaign.

The next two duchesses Coram persuaded to sign both had personal experience of illegitimacy in the family. The first Duke of Bolton had had four illegitimate children by his servant Martha Janes, and the great estates were divided among his bastard children. The second duke married Henrietta Needham, who was herself the illegitimate daughter of the Duke of Monmouth, one of the many illegitimate children of Charles II. The second Duke of Bolton was said to be a most lewd and vicious man,[28] and Henrietta cannot have mourned his death. She signed Coram's petition as the Dowager Duchess of Bolton, almost certainly at the behest of her daughter-in-law, the unfortunate Ann Vaughan who had signed three days earlier. As the daughter of Lord Carbury, one of the richest and most licentious men, 'she was educated in solitude with some choice books by a saint like governess, crammed with virtue and good qualities'.[29] At her father's death and as a rich heiress, she was much run after but gave her hand and fortune to the third Duke of Bolton, who lost no time 'in making an early confession of his aversion' and promptly and publicly left her. Her friend and distant relative, Lady Mary Wortley Montagu, was outraged at the way she was despised and rejected by her husband.[30] By 1728 the duke's passionate infatuation with the actress Lucinda Fenton, who was playing Polly Peacham in the *Beggar's Opera* to huge critical acclaim, was so well known that when Hogarth finished the final version of his painting of the *Beggar's Opera* a year later he had only to adorn the stiff figure of a gentleman sitting in a box beside the stage with the star of the Order of the Garter for everyone to recognise the Duke of Bolton.[31] The duke was soon to make Lucinda Fenton his mistress, and three illegitimate children would be born to them before he married her in 1754 after the death of his wife. It was just before Hogarth painted the picture that Coram approached the sad and pious duchess, whom Lady Mary described as 'despised by her husband and laughed at by the public'. Might Hogarth have given Coram the idea of approaching the duchess? More probably the duchess's piety had brought her into the orbit of the Church, perhaps as a supporter of the charity school movement, and Newman had suggested her name to Coram. The two duchesses of Bolton, the widow, who died the following year, and the rejected wife were not typical of the ladies who signed.

Lady Mary Wortley Montagu, when she was young, had a secret code when discussing marriage with her friends. Paradise stood for love, limbo meant marriage

27 Cokayne, *Complete Peerage*, vol. 12, p. 79.
28 Cokayne, *Complete Peerage*, vol. 2, p. 212.
29 Cokayne, *Complete Peerage*, vol. 2, p. 213, note d.
30 Grundy, *Lady Mary Wortley Montagu*, p. 66.
31 Uglow, *Hogarth*, pp. 138–9.

with indifference, and hell meant marriage with reluctance and detestation.[32] She had good reason to think in those terms, for the children of aristocratic parents were often used as pawns and were powerless to override family financial, political or social interests. Yet they had to make those marriages work, for marriage was seen as a key to stable social order. Sarah Cadogan was thirteen when she was married in 1713 to the heir to the Duke of Richmond, another of the many illegitimate children of Charles II. The match was part of a bargain to cancel a gaming debt of £5,000 incurred by her father, the Earl of Cadogan. The young bridegroom was said to be horrified at his first sight of his bride but he was immediately sent off on the Grand Tour while Sarah returned to the schoolroom. The marriage turned out to be a notable success, the couple devoted to each other. Horace Walpole reported that the duke 'sat by her side all night kissing her hand and gazing at his beautiful daughters'. Coram could not have chosen a better role model for his purpose, for not only was the duchess noted for her happy marriage, she was a Lady of the Bedchamber and would have had the ear of the Queen. Her husband performed a like function for the King. Given the closeness of the couple, it seems unlikely that the duchess would have signed Coram's petition without consulting her husband, but who provided Coram with the necessary introduction remains a mystery.

At the end of 1729 Coram had acquired the signatures of four duchesses. During the next five months he collected the signatures of twelve more ladies of quality and distinction, all related in one way or another to each other. He started off with two more duchesses, one the young Duchess of Manchester, the other the Duchess of Bedford. Of Isabella Montagu it was reported that 'Belle is at this instant in the paradaisical state of receiving visits every day from a passionate lover who is her first love; whom she thinks the finest gentleman in Europe and is besides the duke of Manchester'.[33] She was just twenty-two when she signed Coram's petition. She had married a rich aristocrat for love and perfectly exemplified the qualities Coram was looking for in his ladies of quality and distinction: a young woman, wealthy and happy, who yet had time to show concern for the fate of the abandoned children. Unfortunately the marriage later failed. Her cousin, the Duchess of Bedford, signed the following day. Her husband had been reported to be the wealthiest peer in England and the duchess was co-heir to John, Duke of Marlborough. Her son, the fourth Duke of Bedford, was to become the first President of the Foundling Hospital. Coram was building a network of support from ladies whose husbands were both wealthy and influential.

Coram may well have gained access to Elizabeth, Baroness Onslow, through knowing Sir Arthur Onslow, Speaker of the House of Commons. She is reported as 'a woman of the truest goodness of mind and heart that I ever knew'.[34] April 1730 was to be a productive month for Coram. Elisabeth Onslow signed on the sixth and by the end of the month Coram had six more signatures. Anne Pierrepoint, Baroness Torrington, a widow, was certainly introduced by Henry Newman. The two of them were close friends and had worked together to help the five children of the feckless Marquis du Quesne, Newman having met du Quesne through their common

[32] Grundy, *Lady Mary Wortley Montagu*, p. 25.
[33] Cokayne, *Complete Peerage*, vol. 8, p. 374, note a.
[34] Cokayne, *Complete Peerage*, vol. 10, p. 69, note e.

acquaintance with the Duke of Portland.[35] Since Baroness Berkeley signed on the same day, it seems likely that she was a friend of Baroness Torrington's and that they were together at the time. In her teens Frances Berkeley was married off, without compunction, by her father, to a husband who was fifty at the time. Her father wrote in 1720, 'I am going to dispose of one of my daughters to Lord Byron, a disproportionable match as to their ages'.[36] A week later Coram gained one of his most interesting supporters, Selina, Countess of Huntingdon. She was the supporter he asked for help, seventeen years later, when unable to find the necessary funds to pay the fees for the charter. She was known as 'the lady bountiful of her own immediate neighbourhood'.[37] As a result of seeing some books sent by the SPCK to her local church, she had written to Newman to enrol as a member of the society.[38] She was, however, to become better known as the foundress of the sect of Calvinist Methodists, generally called Lady Huntingdon's Connection, which had, at the time of her death, established sixty-four meeting houses. Her activities met with a certain amount of criticism among her contemporaries and a duchess wrote: 'It is monstrous to be told that you have a heart as sinful as the common wretches that crawl the earth. This is highly offensive and insulting and I cannot but wonder that your ladyship should relish any sentiments so much at variance with high rank and good breeding.'[39] Her frequent visits to her aunt, Lady Frances Shirley, brought her into contact with some of the chief literary celebrities of the day, among whom was the Countess of Hertford, a Lady of the Bedchamber to Queen Caroline. The countess was a gentle lady, who found happiness in gardens, books and in the friendship of poets. She was known as the patron of the poet James Thomson, who dedicated his poem *Spring* to her. She is also credited with helping to save the life of the poet Richard Savage, condemned to death for killing a man in a coffee house brawl, by intervening with the Queen to obtain his pardon.[40] She was the third Lady of the Bedchamber to the Queen that Coram had recruited to his cause, the first having been the Duchess of Richmond and the second the Countess of Burlington,[41] who signed on 19 May, on the same day as the Countess of Cardigan. The Earl of Winchelsea, whose wife had already signed Coram's petition, had no good opinion of his niece and wrote that Lord Burlington, 'besides his own debts and difficulties, . . . has the encumbrance of a wife, my niece, the wickedest, mischievous jade on earth. I can easily pardon her coquetting and her intriguing . . . but lying and making mischief, abusing everybody, imposing on her husband and exposing him only to show her own power does deserve some correction.'[42] If this judgement of the lady's character was true, she was an unusual choice for Coram, who tended to favour as his supporters ladies like the Countess of Cardigan, who was said to be 'extremely good humoured and has everything that can

35 Cowie, *Henry Newman*, pp. 165–79.
36 Cokayne, *Complete Peerage*, vol. 2, p. 456.
37 Cokayne, *Complete Peerage*, vol. 6, p. 661, note e.
38 Cowie, *Henry Newman*, p. 58.
39 Ibid.
40 See Hughes, ed., *The Gentle Hertford*.
41 Lord Burlington was an amateur architect, patron of Gay and Pope. He spent over £200,000 on his villa at Chiswick and his art collection. He was a Fellow of the Society of Antiquaries and Fellow of the Royal Society: Cokayne, *Complete Peerage*, vol. 11, p. 433, note a.
42 The Earl of Winchelsea, 12 April 1736: Cokayne, *Complete Peerage*, vol. 2, p. 436.

recommend a lady of quality'.[43] But he perhaps recognised the value of having ladies close to Queen Caroline, who might be persuaded to use her influence with the King to look favourably on his petition. The job of a Lady of the Bedchamber, ordering meals and dealing with servants, was extremely tedious, but it was the highest available position for a woman at court. As compensation for the boredom of their days, the ladies of the bedchamber tended to become the companions and friends of their mistress, a reward for the nature of their job. It was the importance of this close link with the Crown that Coram was astute enough to recognise and that in the end would pay off.

During the spring months of April and May Coram gained two more supporters, the Duchess of Leeds and the Countess of Lichfield. Both in their different ways deviated from the earlier models he had chosen for his ladies. The Duke of Leeds succeeded his father in January 1730. Quick off the mark, three months later Coram had added the new duchess to his list. He was, perhaps, becoming a little less particular about the character of the ladies he chose. The duchess was the duke's third wife and under-age at the time of her marriage. She had been a friend of the notoriously immoral Lady Vane and was mentioned in Smollett's *Peregrine Pickle*. When her husband died the following year, she rapidly remarried, nevertheless clinging to the title Dowager Duchess of Leeds, and enjoyed her jointure of £3,000 until her death sixty-three years later.[44] There was some mystery about the marriage of the Countess of Lichfield which was kept secret, perhaps because her husband was a Roman Catholic. Frances was said to be the eldest daughter of Edward Hales, who was killed in the Battle of the Boyne.[45] Her children were brought up as Catholics and if she, too, was a Roman Catholic it would have marked an even more radical departure from Coram's original ideal.

There was a gap of three years between the signatures of the first sixteen ladies of rank, obtained between 1729 and 1730, and the signatures of the last five, which were not added to the list until 1733 and 1734. Coram presented his own memorial, with the addition of the signatures of the twenty-one ladies, in a separate petition, to the King in the first instance, in 1735. Coram's thoughts were clearly on other matters between 1730 and 1733, and it is not difficult to see what it was that claimed his time and energy. Further opportunities had opened up in the New World. The projected colonisation of Georgia first attracted Coram's attention, to be followed by his plans for a settlement in Nova Scotia. The renewed possibility of becoming involved with both these projects, and perhaps of going back to settle in America, was alluring and for a while seems to have taken precedence over his interest in the creation of a hospital for foundlings.

[43] Letter, Lady Dupplin, June 1711: Cokayne, *Complete Peerage*, vol. 3, p. 14.
[44] Cokayne, *Complete Peerage*, vol. 7, p. 513, note d.
[45] *Blue Nuns of Paris*, Catholic Record Society, 1910, p. 363.

8

The Lure of America

Georgia

After his intensive lobbying to persuade the first sixteen 'ladies of charity', as he called them, to sign his petition Coram made no attempt to add to their number for the next three years. This may have been because it is known, through letters written by Jeremiah Belcher, the Governor of Massachusetts, to Coram,[1] that the Corams had been ill. Belcher wrote in December 1731, 'I am glad my good Mrs Coram found so great a benefit by your carrying her into the country and yourself so well recovered from so sharp a fit of sickness.'[2] The following year the Corams had again been ill, because Belcher wrote, 'I heartily rejoice upon your recovery to so good health after so tedious a fit of sickness and that good Mrs. Coram was pretty well.'[3] This letter seems to indicate that Coram had been laid up for some time, and so may not have had the time or energy to continue to obtain signatures from any further ladies. His pause in this activity would also be explained by his interest in a new project, the establishment of a colony in lands south of South Carolina which would take the name of Georgia.

The idea of establishing a new colony, to be called Georgia, the name Coram had chosen for his proposed northern colony, had come about partly as a result of the death of Thomas Bray. Bray had been ill during the winter of 1729 and died in February 1730, by which time he had already set up a large number of clerical libraries, both at home and abroad. He believed that libraries provided the most effective means of spreading the Christian gospel. He was also the beneficiary of the D'Allone Trust, a trust set up to promote the instruction of West Indian negroes in the Christian faith. No thought was given at that time as to the legality of their status as slaves, nor to the conditions under which they laboured. That they should become Christians was the greatest gift that could be offered to them. Bray, fearful that he might not survive a dangerous illness, had in 1723 gathered round him a group of like-minded men to carry on his work. They were known as Dr Bray's Associates. The

---

1   Belcher kept copies of all the letters he wrote and it is from the copies of his replies to Coram's letters, which no longer exist, that the subject matter of Coram's letters can be deduced.
2   Belcher to Coram, 9 December 1731: *Belcher Papers*, p. 86.
3   Belcher to Coram, 25 October 1732: *Belcher Papers*, p. 211.

fate of poor families had also been among his concerns, and, perhaps influenced by Coram, Bray had also given serious consideration to colonial settlement as a solution to the problem of the unemployed poor.

Recognising that his illness in 1729 was terminal, Bray had added the founding of a colonial settlement to the objectives of his Associates. At the same time he realised that if his Associates were to take this added responsibility their numbers needed to be increased, and shortly before he died he nominated James Oglethorpe and the Earl of Egmont,[4] among others, to carry out his wishes. Oglethorpe and Egmont had both been on the Parliamentary Committee appointed on 25 February 1729 to investigate conditions in prisons, a subject in which Bray had held a life-long interest. Oglethorpe had suggested the names of several other men who had been members of the prison committee that had been set up at his instigation to look into the appalling abuses that flourished in London's prisons, abuses that Walpole would have preferred to ignore. Bray had nominated his friend, Thomas Coram, to be one of his Associates, knowing that if a colonial settlement were to be attempted Coram was the only man among them with the relevant knowledge and experience. Becoming one of Dr Bray's Associates gave great satisfaction to Coram, and he referred to it more than once in his letters. However, Coram was not so happy about the credentials of some of the other new Associates. He thought that Bray had been misled by Oglethorpe, who 'had recommended to him and given him the names of some gentlemen to be associates which I believe he [Bray] would never have consented to if he had known them'.[5] This did not augur well for Coram's future relationship with his fellow Associates. Nevertheless he lost no time in switching his attention from Dunbar's attempts at colonisation in north Maine to supporting the establishment of a new colony to the south of Carolina. He was part of the deputation that went to the Board of Trade and Plantations in 1730 to petition for consideration to be given to such a scheme.

James Oglethorpe, a Member of Parliament, had become interested in prison conditions because of the death of his friend, the architect Robert Castell, imprisoned for a minor debt and unable to pay the fees demanded by his jailers, had died of smallpox. Oglethorpe pressed for an investigation into prison conditions and became Chairman of a House of Commons Parliamentary Inquiry into 'the State of the Gaols in this Kingdom', which resulted in a series of recommendations to abolish fees, gifts, presents or any gratuities whatsoever from jailers to judges, clerks and servants. He also secured the prosecution of Thomas Bainbridge and John Huggins, the most noto-riously corrupt jailers of the Fleet prison. Oglethorpe was not the first to become interested in the penal system; the SPCK had considered the state of the prisons as early as 1702 when Bray had visited the Fleet and Marshalsea prisons.[6] Bray had wanted to reclaim prisoners into honest employment, particularly those jailed for debt, and had sympathised with Coram's desire to have a settlement to which they could be sent. Coram told Colman that

---

4   At this time Egmont was known as Lord Percival. He became Earl of Egmont on 30 August 1733. For ease
     of reference he will be referred to as Egmont throughout.
5   Coram to Colman, 30 April 1734, 'Letters of Thomas Coram', p. 21.
6   R.S.E. Hinde, The British Penal System, p. 223.

Dr. Bray, the late minister of Aldgate Parish wherein I lived, had the Goodness to bear a great respect for me at all Times from his first knowing me, and
often Lamented the great pains I took for many years for having a proper
Settlement made on the Lands Lying Wast and Derelict between New
England and Nova Scotia.[7]

With Bray's death all three objectives – colonisation, conversion of native Americans
and reform of prisons – were merged, but the colonial ambitions of the Associates
took precedence.

Oglethorpe has been given the main credit for the establishment of Georgia, but
much of the original thinking had already been done by Coram. It was he, two years
before in 1728, who had suggested that convicts be sent out to populate the settlement; it was he who had put before the Board of Trade and Plantations the example
of the French in sending away their beggars to Mississippi; and he who had suggested
that foreign Protestant refugees would make a useful addition to the number of
settlers. But Oglethorpe was a Member of Parliament, he had powerful friends, he
had chaired the recent influential prison committee, and, most importantly, when the
charter for Georgia was finally granted in 1732 it was he who sailed with the first
band of emigrants as their leader. It is not unnatural that it is his name that is chiefly
associated with the establishment of the colony of Georgia, but both Bray and Coram
deserve more credit than they have been given for their part in setting the scene.
There was another factor that weighed in favour of Oglethorpe's plan. Robert
Johnson, the Governor of South Carolina, had long advocated the English occupation
of the region between the river Savannah in the north and the Althama in the south
to protect the colony from attacks by the Spaniards and the depredations of the
Indians. In view of this danger, Walpole was inclined to listen more sympathetically
to Bray's Associates' request for a charter for the colony than he had been to Coram's
plans for northern Maine. He assured them that he was not to blame for the long
delay in obtaining the King's signature and said the King had held back because he
objected to granting the Associates, who would become Trustees of Georgia, the right
to name militia officers, as he was wary of losing his prerogative.[8] Coram saw military
governments as the worst form of government, and had Egmont not been able to
overcome the King's preference for a military government Coram, among others,
would not have served as Trustees. After many delays and difficulties, the King finally
signed the charter on 21 April 1732.[9]

There can be no doubt that Coram saw Georgia as providing him with another
opportunity to return to America to live under civil government and to make a new
life for himself. Even before the Trustees had acquired a charter for Georgia, Coram
was writing to Belcher of his hopes. From the evidence of Belcher's letters to Coram, it
is plain that Coram was still looking for another occasion to return to America and
saw the creation of the new colony as providing the means of doing so. Belcher's
response to Coram's suggestion was clearly unenthusiastic. He wrote, 'I find the
Carolina affair is at present at a stand. I hope for your own and Mrs. Coram's sake

---

7 Coram to Colman, 30 April 1734, 'Letters of Thomas Coram', p. 20.
8 Ettinger, *James Edward Oglethorpe*, p. 118; *Egmont Diaries*, vol. 1, pp. 120–64.
9 *Journal of the Commissioners for Trade and Plantations*, vol. 6, 1729–34, pp. 314, 316.

you will think no more of the S. Carolina enterprise.'[10] The following year Belcher wrote again counselling Coram against going to Georgia:

> I observe you have some thoughts of going over with the settlers designed for the new colony of Georgia in S. Carolina; if you should I depend you will take care to be on a very good footing. I wish they pitch with a tolerable advantage for their health. The Southernmost colonies have been the graves of the people of England. If you go thither you give me hopes of visiting your friends here who will be glad to see you, none more so than myself.[11]

Belcher's concern may have been real, but there was also a distinct undertone of anxiety underlying his words at the thought of the controversial Coram arriving in Boston as his guest. Belcher's letter of 1733 makes clear that Coram was still hoping to cross the Atlantic, despite Mrs Coram's ill health, and also that Belcher was equally keen to discourage him.

> I am really, Sir, under discouragement in my own mind as to the new settlement, from the apprehensions I have of the violent heats and the terrible thunder and lightning. If it succeeds it may be a fine colony in time; yet I should be glad to hear you continue at home as a Director, and you are always too wise to try the climate, especially as you are running on to man's climacteric.[12]

Coram was 65. However it was not his age, nor Mrs Coram's health that persuaded him that it would be unwise in the circumstances to pull up stumps and relocate in America, but rather that by 1733 Coram was in dispute with his fellow Trustees about the rights of women to inherit land. It is also difficult to know in what capacity the Corams could have gone to Georgia. It was made clear from the start that the settlers were to be debtors released from prison, the unemployed, or Protestant refugees from Europe. Egmont wrote that the charter was for the necessitous poor, not to make rich men richer. The Trustees refused the request of a substantial builder for lands; neither did they want to put too much land in too few hands, a practice that had been the bane of other colonies.[13] Servants of the colony were to work without salary, an exception being made in the case of Oglethorpe, whose affairs, according to Egmont, 'were not in good order', and by 1734 he was willing to accept a salary.[14]

As soon as the petition had been drawn up, the Trustees realised that without money they could do nothing. Coram's ability to raise money was obviously already known, for the Trustees chose Coram to start collecting subscriptions, as Egmont notes

> A paper was drawn up for Captain Coram to carry to Tunbridge in order to collect subscriptions to our scheme, conditional that a grant be made us of lands desired, was showed to me and my leave desired that I might be

10 Belcher to Coram, 9 December 1731, *Belcher Papers*, p. 86.
11 Belcher to Coram, 23 April 1732, *Belcher Papers*, p. 111.
12 Belcher to Coram, 13 January 1733, *Belcher Papers*, p. 250.
13 *Egmont Diaries*, vol. 11, 30 April 1732, p. 370.
14 *Egmont Diaries*, vol. 11, 12 March 1734, p. 16.

mentioned in it, because they thought it might facilitate subscriptions and I readily gave it.[15]

Tunbridge Wells was a fashionable watering place and would have provided fertile ground for Coram's mission. Elizabeth Montague says of Tunbridge Wells to a friend:

in many respects this place is inferior to Bath, in some it is better. We are not confined here in streets; the houses are scattered irregularly and Tunbridge Wells looks from the window I now sit by a little like the village you see from our terrace at Sandleford, only that the inhabitants instead of Jack and Joan are my Lord and my Lady.[16]

Coram, an experienced fundraiser, already had the skills needed to approach the aristocracy, having done so for many years on behalf of the Foundling Hospital. He would have known all too well how valuable it would be to have Egmont's name on the subscription letter. There is no way of knowing how successful Coram was in raising funds for Georgia, but his visit to Tunbridge Wells would also have given him the opportunity to increase his network of contacts.

Egmont consulted Coram as to the amount that would be needed and reported back, 'I told them Capt. Coram, who knew the West Indies well, has declared to me that we could not set out under £12,000.'[17] The Trustees all made large contributions to the scheme,[18] a lottery was proposed, and sufficient money came in for an office to be established in Old Palace Yard. Benjamin Martyn was appointed Secretary and Harman Verelst appointed accountant, who would in time become the first Secretary of the Foundling Hospital. The Trustees met every Wednesday and worked hard. They resolved on a civil government, and that the town to be erected should be called Savannah and that it should consist of 5,000 acres. On 4 November 1732, after the signing of commissions for a surgeon, an apothecary and a chaplain, they all dined together at the Horn Tavern. Coram and the Rev. Samuel Smith,[19] although Trustees, were not appointed as Common Councillors, and it was the Councillors who had financial authority. Oglethorpe, much to the relief of Egmont, had volunteered to go out as leader and to remain in the colony for three years. Fundraising was going well. Coram worked tirelessly as Oglethorpe spearheaded an unprecedented publicity campaign to raise funds and to promote the attractions of the proposed colony. In May 1732 the government gave a grant of £10,000, and by September £2,000 had been subscribed,[20] making up the £12,000 recommended by Coram. On 16 November, Coram was at Gravesend to see the *Anne* sail for Georgia with the first party of settlers: thirty-five families, making 120 people in all.[21] Coram, his hopes of going to Georgia still alive, must have watched their departure with a degree of mixed feelings.

---

[15] Coram was sometimes referred to as Captain Coram, a title he never used himself.
[16] Climenson, *Elizabeth Montague*, vol. 1, p. 10.
[17] *Egmont Diaries*, vol. 1, 23 April 1732, p. 261.
[18] Crane, *The Philanthropists*, pp. 10–17.
[19] Smith had been Bray's curate and succeeded him as rector of St Botolph's. The Smiths were close friends of the Corams and were later to offer the Corams rooms in their house.
[20] Crane, *The Philanthropists*, p. 125.
[21] Ibid., p. 10; Coram to Newman, 20 November 1732, 'Letter of Thomas Coram to H. Newman'.

Some people were now beginning to question the wisdom of sending overseas capable artisan families when England could use their skills. There were others who could supply the needs of the colony, notably the oppressed Protestant refugees from Salzburg, who had been driven out by the Archbishop, Leopold Anton, a man determined to stamp out all heresy in his diocese. The SPCK was much concerned at the treatment of Protestants in Europe, and became involved in negotiations with the Salzburgers' leaders, Samuel Urlsberger and their pastor Martin Bolzius. Henry Newman, in his role as Secretary to the SPCK, played a crucial role in obtaining the necessary financial support, and, as Newman's Salzburger letterbooks show, in organising their departure for Georgia.[22] They left Rotterdam and arrived in Dover on 19 November 1733. Newman had instructed Coram to go to Dover to see that everything was being done for their comfort, and also to fill up the ship with as many English passengers as possible. Coram reported to Newman that the ship had to anchor on the Downs because of a contrary wind. Coram spent Christmas in Dover and organised a house for the ministers, women and children to stay in while waiting, and a special Christmas dinner. He told Newman

> I carry the Children a few apples, and sometimes give them a few plumbs, a pound of Malaga Raisins which costs 3d. fills them with above 5 pounds worth of Love for me. They shew it in a Dawn of Joy in their faces as soon as they see me coming.[23]

Childless himself, this show of affection by the children for the small treat he was able to offer them must have given him great pleasure. It is not known whether Eunice Coram was with her husband to share his delight.

By the following year Coram was beginning to have misgivings about his fellow Trustees. The Trustees and the Associates held their weekly meetings together at the Georgia Office. A split was becoming apparent between those who, led by the Secretary, Benjamin Martyn, were becoming increasingly secularised in their outlook and the remaining Trustees. Coram wrote to Colman

> There are not many of those Associates [Trustees] who give themselves any trouble about the two other Matters, but I believe, I may venture to say the better part of them do.[24]

By 1736 the split between the two sides was out in the open. The words 'religious uses' had been left out of the minutes and the committee was so deeply divided by this issue that the matter was put to the vote, Egmont's supporters narrowly winning. However, another dispute had arisen earlier between Coram and his fellow Trustees that was to lead to him changing course once again, and focusing his energies on the settlement of Nova Scotia.

It had been decided early on that Roman Catholics could not be considered as settlers, as it was believed they would only act as spies for the Spanish and French.

---

[22] See Jones, *Henry Newman's Salzburger Letterbooks*, p. 407.
[23] Coram to Newman, 11 December 1733: Jones, *Henry Newman's Salzburger Letterbooks*, p. 94.
[24] Coram to Colman, 30 April 1734: 'Letters of Thomas Coram', p. 21. Dr Bray's Associates became Trustees of Georgia.

After much discussion, Jews were also among those deemed unsuitable, although Oglethorpe had admitted a small number on his own authority. The trustees needed to enlarge the supply of Protestant emigrants. They were in discussion with other Protestant groups besides the Salzburgers, from Germany and Switzerland. It was, however, the refusal of the refugee Vaudois to accept the law of male entail that caused the Trustees to turn down their application to settle in Georgia,[25] and was the cause of Coram's dispute with the Trustees. According to Egmont, it was a Mr Pinkerton who had first brought the difficulties this rule might bring about to the trustees' attention:

> Mr Pinkerton had demurred upon going to Georgia because his lands, if he should died would not go to his heirs female. We told him we had set this rule in our grants.[26]

The Vaudois insisted on the descending in fee simple on the female heir and would not yield. Coram was vociferous in their support. His sense of fair play was outraged. He had always seen the role of women as important, and in particular had championed the education of girls as necessary because they were the mothers of the next generation. He asked that a day be appointed to debate the question. When the matter was put to the vote Coram received no support, but the question would not go away. Coram was unable to keep his opinions to himself. Egmont reported that at the meeting in May there was

> much discourse that the Vaudois desire that their females should inherit and letters from Lord Tyrconnel and Mr Digby were read. The former strenuous for allowing it, the latter much against. Mr. Towers was severe on Captain Coram for occasioning the dissatisfaction that appears against the exclusion of female heirs succeeding to the grants. He told him he was only a trustee and ought not to have vilified to the public a resolution taken by the Board of Common Council. That we should hear his opinion with pleasure, but he ought to think himself bound by the opinion of the board.[27]

Coram wrote angrily to Colman of his experience:

> You judge rightly of Georgia, The bettermost of the People are coming and going from that Wretched Colony, made so by a Wrong beginning contrary to everything I could say or do, Mr Oglethorpe found means to get almost all to be of his party . . . so that at last I had no Second out of the 37 trustees for opposing them being 8 or 9 Lords, 24 or 25 Members of Parliament most of them Zealous Oglethorpeans then . . . it is a pleasure to me they find what I said in a Written Declaration I had read at the Board on 27th March 1734 and demanded to have it lodged with the records to prove true That the Inhabitants would desert from that Province like leaves from a Tree in Autumn. I think I sent a copy to His Excellency.[28]

---

25 Ettinger, *James Edward Oglethorpe*, p. 168.
26 *Egmont Diaries*, vol. 11, 17 January 1733, p. 309.
27 *Egmont Diaries*, vol.11, 22 May 1735, p. 104.
28 Coram to Colman, 21 September 1738: 'Letters of Thomas Coram', pp. 47–8.

Egmont was clearly troubled by Coram's assault, and had been trying to engineer a compromise. He wrote:

> We have already declared in our rules that special regard shall be paid to daughters which is sufficient to satisfy the world on that head . . . Should we be more explicit the general welfare of the Colony might suffer by it by dispeopling, for persons not inhabiting the colony would marry such daughters. We know our own minds, that if such daughters marry persons approved by us, who will settle on the father's grant we shall make it new to her husband and her heirs male or we will settle the estate to one who will reside and give the daughter the profit.[29]

But Coram was not to be mollified. Saying that he had nothing personal against Egmont, he wrote to Colman:

> His Lordship is Really a Worthy, Good, Charitable man and a Wise man which shocks me the more that he has been prevailed on by mr Oglethorpe and others to Com into that Detestable Tenure Scheme (in) by which they Grant lands and Govern in Georgia whereby the Females are all Excluded from Inheriting their Father's Lands and an arbitrary military Government is set up there. There is some Extreordiany Designe in all this which I think I see Clearly into, but I would no more give my Consent to it than I would to the murder of all the Children of this Kingdome.[30]

Coram's subsequent actions show his least attractive side. Frustrated by the Trustees he tried, by writing and speaking against them, to undermine their authority and to derail the project. Egmont reveals the depths to which Coram was prepared to go to revenge himself:

> Mr Sterling, who with a party of Scots are settled in Savannah County, having received a letter full of invectives against the Trustees accusing us of pursuing our private interest at the expense of those we send, and that our constitution is military, arbitrary and tyrannical, and that in a little time we shall destroy the colony, he honestly gave it to our bailiffs to peruse, who sent us a copy of it, but the name of the writer being scratched out we can only guess the man; and him we believe to be Captain Coram, our fellow trustee, who on account of our not suffering females to inherit, left our board and prates against us. We believe it to be him the rather because mention is made in that letter of a new settlement in another place the King and Council have been applied to grant, and all the steps that application related, as far as it had proceeded, none but Captain Coram could tell, he being the person who proposes to make a new settlement far from us and absolutely distinct from us, but our integrity will, I trust, weather all storms.[31]

The Governors of the Foundling Hospital probably felt the same when Coram voiced his disagreement with the way in which the hospital was being managed some years later.

---

[29] *Egmont Diaries*, vol. 11, 25 May 1735, p. 184.
[30] Coram to Colman, 23 September 1735, 'Letters of Thomas Coram', p. 29.
[31] *Egmont Diaries*, vol. 11, 7 October 1735, pp. 199–200.

That Coram was covertly making plans for Nova Scotia, and did hope that if they came to fruition they would adversely affect the development of Georgia is plain from the letter he sent to Colman from Liverpool. He wanted his plans for Nova Scotia kept secret, even though he was in correspondence with Egmont:

> If you should write to his Lordship he would answear you with pleasure and is a Well bred man he honird me with a letter last post hither. however if you write to him I conceive you will not mention anything of Georgia to his Lordship. If I succeed, as more and more Expect from the Contents of some letters from London to me thereon in my Endeavours now under Consideration for the Settlement of Nova Scotia and Cat Island (in which I have the friendship of great men) *it will tak off from Georgia.*[32] (my italics)

Coram had worked hard for the success of Georgia. Apart from his fundraising he had attended fifty-nine meetings and he must have felt disappointed that he had been unable to become part of the settlement in some capacity. His dissatisfaction with the way in which the colony had developed is not enough to excuse his actions in 1735. After having vilified the Trustees he did not resign, he simply no longer attended meetings. But when in May 1739 there was a new discussion concerning the tenure of lands and further instructions were given, Egmont noted, 'Captain Coram, who was violent for female succession was much pleased with the intended act.'[33] At that same meeting the Trustees upheld their decision against allowing negroes as slaves in the colony. The reconciliation seems to have been complete by July because, although Egmont wanted the new law to go before the King in Council, the others said the trustees themselves had the power to enforce it. Egmont ends by writing 'I gave my consent and did it the more readily as Captain Coram was present and approved it, who had much prejudiced us in the town's opinion because we did not do it before.'[34] Egmont's comment shows how Coram's opinions were listened to and how influential he had become. Coram attended the Georgia Anniversay Day meeting at St Bride's vestry in 1740 and again in 1741, but after that he took no further part in the affairs of Georgia. The colony reverted to the Crown in 1752.

There are references to Coram in a political novel, written in 1759 after his death, entitled *The Castle Builders*. It purports to be the memoirs of William Stephens, who had been a settler in Georgia. Clearly disaffected, he accuses the Trustees of making laws inconsistent with the freedom of the British people, but his petition is voted to contain false, scandalous and malicious charges tending to asperse the characters of the Trustees. The petition is said to be signed by 130 people, and when it was rejected 'Mr Coram, who first projected the colony resigned in form'.[35] The novel ends with a panegyric to the writer of the memoir, which might also be seen as applying to Coram:

> To animate some in this age of corruption with an example of self denial; to inspire the minds of others with the sentiments of him who sacrificed himself

32 Coram to Colman, 23 September 1735, 'Letters of Thomas Coram', p. 29.
33 *Egmont Diaries*, vol. 111, 2 May 1739, p. 56.
34 *Egmont Diaries*, vol. 111, 3 July 1739, p. 123.
35 Stephens, *Castle Builders*, p. 106.

in his country's cause . . . of him who neither riches or worldly grandeur
would tempt to betray a public Trust or to deceive his neighbour . . .

and ends by saying the story was written

even in this age of profligacy to be a panegyric which exceeds the glittering
power, false honour, frothy titles and sordid wealth of his tempters.[36]

By the time this was written Coram had been dead for eight years, but had become
known to a much wider public, and was honoured for his work for foundlings.

Nova Scotia

Since acquiring Nova Scotia under the Treaty of Utrecht, and the installation of a
military government in Annapolis, very little had happened to change the way of life
of the French Acadians and the Indians who populated the province. The government
was a weak garrison government. Col. Richard Phillips, a career soldier, who had
been given the job of Governor in 1717 as reward for his loyalty to the Crown, visited
the province only twice during his long tenure of office. The administration of the
province was in the hands of junior officers who were not given the resources to
govern. No one paid taxes and the so-called 'neutral' French Acadians refused to take
the oath of loyalty to the Crown unless they were exempted from bearing arms, a
decision which ultimately led to the tragedy of their expulsion in 1755. The government felt unable to take action, fearing that if they did the Acadians might depart,
leaving abandoned fields and houses behind for the Indians to enjoy, so a series of
unsatisfactory compromises ensued. In effect, Nova Scotia was a bare military outpost
with a prosperous fishery in Canso. The French Acadians had no wish to change their
way of life. They had few needs, and with minimum effort cultivated the rich lands
round the Minas basin and Beaubassin.[37]

This was fertile ground for the restless and dissatisfied Coram to exploit. He was
well aware of the importance of the fishing grounds off the Grand Banks, and the
untouched timber forests which could be so valuable to the Royal Navy. He saw the
French as a threat. Already they had a far greater number of boats fishing for cod.
They also had access to the best salt, so necessary for curing and drying the fish for
export. It was soon after his rift with the Georgia trustees in 1734 that he began to
formulate his plans for a new settlement. Before making any move, Coram started to
discuss with his friends, and in particular with Sir Charles Wager, how best to present
his proposals. He was now a recognised expert on American colonial affairs. Martin
Bladon and other Commissioners at the Board of Trade and Plantations were
receiving letters from the nervous and morose Lieutenant Governor, William
Armstrong, alerting them to a deteriorating situation. He reported after a visit to
Canso and the Bay of Fundy that the French were 'multiplying fast' and that they
were more 'given to rebellion'. They condemned the garrison at Annapolis, said that

---

[36] Ibid., p. 210.
[37] Naomi Griffiths, *The Golden Age: Acadian Life 1713–1748*, Toronto 1984, pp. 21–34. See also Mahaffie,
Land of Discord Always.

the Crown had no right to the land, and incited the Indians to rebel, while the Indians despised the English for not giving them presents as the French did. Finally he advised that the important fishing settlement at Canso was not well defended.[38]

With increasing unease at the developing situation in Nova Scotia, 1735 seemed a propitious moment to Coram to put forward his ideas for a settlement. Before he took his memorial to the King, Coram had very carefully prepared the ground. He had been to Bristol and Liverpool to talk to the merchants and he already had the names of several 'honorable and worthy' persons willing to act as trustees if a charter was granted for Nova Scotia, most notably Horatio Walpole, brother of the Prime Minister. He had also secured the agreement of 102 unemployed men, mostly carpenters and bricklayers, willing to go to Nova Scotia and currently living in and around London and Westminster.

On 1 May 1735 Coram presented to the Board his memorial for a grant of Royal Letters Patent.[39] At his own expense he had employed someone to transcribe both his memorial and the petition of the men. Coram had clearly given thought, not only to the political advantages of a settlement, but also to the wider problems of the fishing industry. He therefore not only proposed the settlement of Nova Scotia, but also of Cat Island and Exuma, islands lying north-east of Cuba, in the Bahamas. The salt ponds of Exuma would provide the fishing industry with their own supply of salt and give the new settlers employment. Cat Island, lying to the west, was needed to protect the salt rakers of Exuma from the depredations of the Spanish who operated out of Baracoa. It was a clever idea, but unlikely to be accepted in the light of the strength of the Spanish fleet operating from the Bahamas. The possible dangers posed by the French, the importance of cod fisheries, and the increase in trade and navigation are all given as reasons for settling Nova Scotia under a civil government.

The names of 102 potential settlers, all of whom must have been approached personally by Coram, were inscribed in three neat columns. Coram described them as labouring handycraftsmen whose respective trades and callings were overstocked by great numbers of artisans and workmen who came from all parts of the kingdom to the metropolis. He had them say that being unable to obtain work and in order to escape 'the dangerous temptations and dreadful consequences which always attend extreme poverty the petitioners are desirous of being settled in some of the King's plantations in America'. Coram's hand is very evident in the drafting of the men's petition because, apart from requesting a free passage, he requests that their 'heirs and executors *whether males or females* [my italics] in free and common soccage for ever, one hundred acres of land'.[40] Calling the King their 'Common Father' he also has them ask that they may be given a year's supplies until they are able to raise food for themselves.

The Board was clearly interested in Coram's proposal and requested further details. He replied to this request on 11 July with a very comprehensive eight-page memorandum, written entirely in his own hand.[41] He said he believed that both Nova Scotia and Cat Island could be settled in a 'secure and elegant manner' at no

[38] CO, 217,7, ff. 12 and 164.
[39] *CSP, CS: A and WI*, 1 May 1733, 546, pp. 113–14; CO 217,7, ff. 111–16.
[40] Ibid., p. 115
[41] *CSP, CS: A and WI*, 11 July 1735, pp. 12–17; CO 217,7, ff. 117–20.

expense to the public purse except for transportation costs of about £8,000. He felt it was necessary to break down the figure and go into detail. The Board was unused to having to pay settlers; in the case of Georgia, the trustees had had to go to Parliament for the necessary money. For the price of £5,538 1s 3d, a very precise figure but certainly over-optimistic, 336 grown people and 34 children could be transported with provisions for a year plus a great warm coat for each man and other garments for the women. A long list of the necessary goods that would have to be brought over for the settlers followed, bringing the total cost to £7,985 1s 3d. The list is interesting in its own right, showing both Coram's experience and attention to detail. For the security and defence of the plantation the settlers would need:

> Great guns, small arms, ammunition, tents etc.; axes, saws, hoes, spades, shovels, scythes, ox yokes and bows, log chains, with other husbandry tools and necessaries; handmills for corn and malt, bricks, tiles and fire-stone for ovens, some necessary tools for carpenters, masons, bricklayers, brick makers, wheelwrights, coopers, shoe makers, tailors, tanners, paviors and some other useful tools; a smith's forge and sea coal, some bar iron flat and square and some steel, locks, hinges and nails of proper sorts, and other necessary iron work; also iron pots and kettles, some copper, brass, pewter and tin work; some earthen ware, grind stones, lanterns and glasses, a little glass and lead for small windows, and some other lead for necessary uses, handjack screws, cologn and other millstones, scales and weights, measures wet and dry, some ropes, lines and tarpaulins and fishing tackle for fishing boats, medicines, drugs and salves, surgeon's instruments, some good books and a little decent church furniture; and children's books, a small church clock and bell, two sun dials for the proper latitudes, some particular sorts of blankets and other proper presents for the Indians. The settlers will also need pine boards for building huts, as well as food for the 25 cows and three bulls, the 20 pairs of working oxen, 50 swine, 60 goats, 50 dozen geese, ducks and other poultry.

The most important aspect of his vision for a settled Nova Scotia was the establishment of a civil government. Still deeply influenced by his experience of having lived under an independent government in Massachusetts, however much he disagreed with some of its policies, he sets out in detail his views on the form and powers of a civil government. The settlers should be freeholders and able annually to elect a proper number from among themselves to be their representatives in the lower house of their assembly. The lower house will elect the Upper House of the Assembly and put forward their names for acceptance by the President, who would be the only officer nominated by the Crown. There follows a whole lot of curbs on the President's powers. He will have command of the militia, and will, with the advice and consent of the Assembly, appoint judges, sheriffs and other officers. The Assembly will impose taxes and name all civil officers.

Coram argued that if there were to be a rupture with the French, unless the province were settled, the French, who had already excluded Britain from the indigo trade and were on the way to doing the same with regard to the sugar trade, would beat Britain out of cod fishing. If that were to happen, it would be the greatest blow ever given to British navigation and be attended with the most fatal consequences. Coram ends with his now familiar hope that 'if H.M. shall be pleased to think the memorialist a proper person to execute any commands for accomplishing these important settlements as above proposed, he will be ready to render his best services therein'.

The Board responded to Coram's memorial very seriously by sending him proposals for the beginnings of civil government in Nova Scotia. Coram, who was at this time living at 36 Prescott Street, had the proposals neatly transcribed.[42] Then, on a larger piece of paper ruled down the middle, he restates the Board's proposals on one side of the paper and deals with his objections on the opposite side, all done in his own handwriting. He thinks wealthy foreign Protestants should be allowed to share in choosing the Council, otherwise they will be seduced by 'crafty New Englanders', into leaving the province. He is absolutely against the King having any say in the appointment of judges and or any other officers. In fact he is against having an Auditor General, a Surveyor or a Secretary of the province, saying the colony would be 'cramped and over pestered with needless officers long before the colony could raise any revenue, even before they could raise food for themselves, much less money for officers'. He points out that the grants of land could be recorded by a trustee or one of the trustees' nominees. Here is the authentic voice of experience and robust common sense arguing against the imposition of a bureaucratic idea that would be impossible to enforce. He won his point. His final recommendation was that the fifteen years suggested for the colony was too short a time, and as in Georgia, the trustees should have twenty-one years to settle the land. In contrast with conditions in Georgia, he points out the natural discouragements of the Northern Frontier,

> where the extreme severity of the long cold winters and foggy summers together with many dangerous difficulties will require to be sweetened with some indulgence to those who chose to settle there. Otherwise no industrious person will settle there where there are as many working days in twenty one years as there are in twelve in England.

What is most telling is that when the Board of Trade and Plantations came to recommend Coram's petition to the Privy Council in 1737 they had accepted all his amendments.

By May 1736 Coram had his list of trustees ready to present to the Board. The list included the Duke of Montagu, Viscount Torrington, the Earl of Granard, Sir Charles Wager and the Hon. Horace (Horatio) Walpole. Horatio Walpole had written to his brother Robert, the Prime Minister, to urge him to take note of Coram's ideas:

> Lose no time in talking to Sir Charles Wager, Mr. Bladon & one Coram, the honestest, the most disinterested, and the most knowing person about the plantations I have ever talked with.[43]

Coram was hoping to include the Earl of Derby, Sir William Young and Edward Southwell and two or three others who would not give him leave to mention their names until the matter was certain to go forward, as well as a number of Members of

---

[42] Coram to the Board of Trade, 14 April 1736; CO, 217,7, ff. 162–4.
[43] Coxe, *Life of Sir Robert Walpole*, vol. III, p. 243.

Parliament and principal merchants, whom he had sounded out in Bristol and Liverpool.[44]

Having done all he could to push forward his ideas for the settlement of Nova Scotia, Coram felt reasonably confidant of success when the Board of Trade and Plantations recommended his proposal to the Privy Council. He had visited the Board on several occasions along with some of the petitioners. Such was the respect in which Coram was now held that they specifically noted that they had Coram's agreement to their proposals.

> As the settlement of Cat Island is not immediately necessary to forward that of Nova Scotia, we proposed to Mr. Coram that the settlement of Nova Scotia might be the first consideration; and he has agreed to the following proposals for that purpose.[45]

The proposals took account of all Coram's amendments. The recommendation to the Privy Council ended with the words:

> The settlement of Nova Scotia with English inhabitants is of very great consequence to H.M.'s interest in America and to the interest of this kingdom from its situation with regard to the French and from the fishery now carried on at Canso and the several branches of naval stores that province is capable of producing when once it shall be settled, as we have several times represented to H.M. and to you.[46] And therefore we think it very much for H.M.'s service to give all possible encouragement to any undertaking for this purpose, especially when attended with so great an appearance and probability of success as that of Mr. Coram's.

It was signed by four of the Commissioners: Earl Fitzwalter, Thomas Pelham, Martin Bladon and R. Plumer.

Coram told Colman that there had been a meeting of some of the Lords of the Privy Council on 5 July, and that he was 'to attend a great man (almost certainly Robert Walpole) about it on the 11th instant to whom it is referred for him to give his reasons for it'.[47] This was the high point of Coram's career as a promoter of colonial settlements in America, and a letter to Colman[48] showed that he had been hoping to come to Nova Scotia as late as 1737. He was sanguine enough to know that, even with all the support he had, it could still fail, particularly if the King insisted on keeping a military government in place. But he had real hopes of it succeeding.

Coram was very ill for several months in 1737. By the time he had recovered in November, Queen Caroline had died and, because of the King's grief at her death, all business was held up. Coram wrote in 1738 that

---

[44] CO, 217,7, 8 May 1736, f. 172.

[45] *CSP, CS: A and WI*, 22 April 1737, 246, p. 243; CO, 218,2, ff. 337–41.

[46] There had been several other proposals to settle Nova Scotia. One promoter, Samuel Waldo, promised to bring thousands of Protestants from Germany, but the scheme was too grandiose and came to nothing.

[47] Coram to Colman, 9 July 1737: 'Letters of Thomas Coram', p. 37.

[48] Ibid.

the affair of Nova Scotia Sleeps ever since the fore part of February last when the Ministry seemed Intent on Sending out of hand One hundred of Industreous proper families to be settled under a Civil Government with 4 Independent Companies of English under its Direction, each Company to have Contained 100 private soldiers, one Captain, one Lieut, one Ensigne, 3 Sergeants, 3 Corporals, 2 Drums a Chaplin and a Surgeon.[49]

He feared, and probably rightly, that it was 'the Dread of a War put these matters out of their heads so that Nova Scotia seems like to remaine as it is a charge of £16,000 per annum to the Government'. He believed, however, that the progress he had made would excite others to accomplish what he had not been able to do for Nova Scotia. Coram obviously felt very deeply about the fate of Nova Scotia, for later in the same letter he wrote

> I wish somebody or other whether an honest man or a Byfield friend or Enemy would get Nova Scotia Settled under an honest Safe Free Civil Government for I believe I shall no further give myself any trouble about it. I believe I have not one enemy living in England. I wish there was more Regard than there is for the British Plantations those valuable Blessings to the Kingdome if suffered to be so.[50]

That Coram could even consider a man like Byfield – whom he regarded as his enemy, who had done him so much harm during his time in Taunton, and whose career he had tried to derail – taking on the settlement of Nova Scotia is a measure both of his concern for his proposed colony and of his generosity of spirit.

Coram's wish was granted, but not until nine years later. There was a shift of power in London. The Duke of Newcastle, who had never been interested in the American colonies, was replaced as Secretary of State by the Duke of Bedford, who named the Earl of Halifax as President of the Board of Trade and Plantations. Halifax was an even more ardent imperialist than the duke, and the two men saw Nova Scotia as a counterpoise to French Canada. A new capital, to be called Halifax, was rapidly established in Chebucto Bay on the western coast of Nova Scotia, to replace Annapolis. The Board moved with speed to promote colonisation. One look at the advertisements that appeared in the London Gazette shows that the Board simply adopted Coram's ideas.[51] Officers and men discharged from the army and navy were invited to settle, their fares and a year's keep guaranteed. A civil government would be established and arms, tools and building materials would be handed out. Land was to be free. The one inducement that Coram had not been able to offer was freedom from taxation for ten years, otherwise it was Coram's original plan re-used. It was Coram's misfortune that the shift in colonial policy came too late for him personally to benefit. Imagine his pleasure, had he had the political backing and the finance available to Halifax. Emigrants flocked to join what has been called 'the greatest pork barrel yet opened in North America'.[52] He was old and poor, a widower living in Leicester Fields, when Cornwallis, who had replaced the doddering old Colonel

[49] Coram to Colman, 22 September 1738: 'Letters of Thomas Coram', p. 45.
[50] Ibid., p. 47.
[51] London Gazette, 7 March 1749.
[52] Clark, Acadia: The Geography of Early Nova Scotia to 1760, p. 351.

Philipps as Governor, set off in his flagship followed by thirteen more ships carrying 2,576 people. If he was not at Gravesend to see the flotilla depart it still would have rejoiced his generous heart to know that his long-hoped-for plans had come to fruition, even though he could no longer be a part of the new generation of settlers.

Coram's contribution to the history of Nova Scotia has largely been unrecognised. There is said to have been a print showing a rowing boat approaching the shore with a figure waving who is believed to have been Coram. In a letter to the *Acadian Recorder*, a certain L.M. Fourtier suggests that Halifax owed Coram much and should keep his memory alive:

> The opportunity of the 175th anniversary ought, if possible to rehabilitate and properly honour the memory of Thomas Coram. His services to Nova Scotia in its early formative period were memorable and I trust the committee in charge of the arrangements for next year will recognise them in some way.[53]

In his book on Acadia,[54] Charles Mahaffie writes that Coram was the most likely promoter. He even thought that if Coram had been given encouragement, friendships might have grown up between his settlers and the Acadians, which could have led to an accommodation between them and the Britons who governed them. This might have prevented the estrangement and the debacle of the 1755 expulsion. Coram himself would have been satisfied to know that the importance of Nova Scotia had been recognised and the land settled, but he would also have been gratified to know that his contribution had been recognised.

---

[53] Letter from L.M. Fourtier, *Acadian Recorder*, 24 November 1923.
[54] Mahaffie, *Land of Discord Always*, pp. 158–9.

9

American Correspondence

Background

It is unfortunate that so few of Coram's letters to New England have survived, apart from his correspondence with his friends Benjamin Colman and Jeremiah Belcher. After the failure of his shipbuilding enterprise he continued his trading links with America, and a settlement in northern Maine remained a prime objective until 1730. He would have been in contact with other New Englanders besides Dummer, the agent for Massachusetts, during his long struggle to gain support to exploit those unsettled lands. His wife's family kept him in touch with events in Boston and he wrote regularly to his mother-in-law and to his wife's sister, Mrs Sterling. She in turn sent him the *Boston Weekly News Letter*. No family letters have survived. His sister-in-law died in 1736 and he only ceased writing to old Mrs Waite, 'an ancient good woman', when told in 1740 that she had become senile. Coram was in touch with other members of the Waite family and he still owned his house in Taunton.

It was not until the 1730s that Coram began to correspond with two notable Bostonians: Jeremiah Belcher, Governor of Massachusetts, and the Rev. Benjamin Colman, minister of the noted Brattle Street church. Coram's own letters to Belcher no longer exist, but Belcher kept copies of all his public and private letters – including his letters from Coram – which have been printed.[1] From Belcher's replies to Coram's letters an interesting picture emerges of the relationship that existed between the two men, and the surprisingly wide range of subjects discussed by them. The correspondence spans the decade from 1731 to 1741. The Colman correspondence provides the most important documentary evidence of Coram's early life, his achievements and his views on many subjects. The letters, written in Coram's unvarnished style, reveal his qualities of mind, and the style, though prolix, with long and detailed accounts of events of minor importance, gives a valuable insight into Coram's personality. The final letters, when he is assured of Colman's interest, become longer. It is as if Coram came to use these last letters to unburden himself; they can almost be seen as an apologia for his life.

Both sets of letters, taken together, give an insight into Coram's private life, his health, his views on people and events, both great and small. Both Thomas and

---

1 *Belcher Papers.*

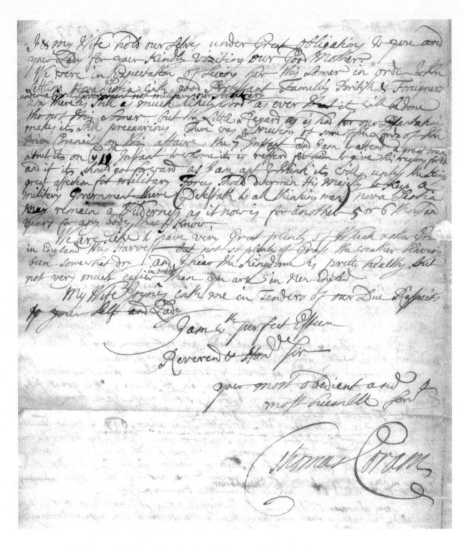

4. Coram's letter to the Rev. Benjamin Colman, 9 July 1737.

Coram's letter to the Rev. Benjamin Colman, 9 July 1737, *opposite*

Transcription:

I and my Wife hold ourselves under Great obligation to you and your Lady for Kindly visiting our Good Mother. We were in Expectation of seeing her this Somer in order to the Settling of Nova Scotia with good Protestant Famelies British and Foreigners under a Civil Government not military nor Arbitrary, and there is still as much likelyhood as ever that it will be done tho not this Somer but the Little Regard as is had for our Plantations makes it Still precaarious. There was a meeting of some of the Lords of the Privy Council on this affaire the 7 Instant and I am to attend a great man about it on the 11 Instant to whom it is referred for him to give his reasons for it and if it should go forward as I am apt to think it will, unless the Kings great affection for Military Forces should determin His Majesty to keep a military Government there (detestable to all thinking men) Nova Scotia may remain a Wilderness as it now is for another 5 or 6 thousand years for any body that I know.

We are like to have very Great plenty of Wheate and other Grains in England this Harvest but not so plenty of Grass the weather having been somewhat dry and I hear the Kingdome is pretty healthy, but not very much easier in mind than you are in New England.

My Wife Joynes with me in Tenders of our Due Respects to your Self and Lady
    I am with perfect Esteem
    Reverend and Hon'rd Sir
    your most obedient and
    most humble servant,
    Thomas Coram

Eunice Coram suffered bouts of ill health during the 1730s, and by inference Eunice Coram became increasingly frail during that period. Coram, at a critical time in 1737, when his Nova Scotia project was in the balance and when his memorial for the Foundling Hospital had been presented to the King, suffered a long and debilitating illness from which he nearly died. When he recovered he proudly boasted that he was still able to walk ten miles a day. Perhaps the most surprising and significant point to come to light was confirmation of Coram's continued wish to settle in America. He was frequently cautioned against going to Georgia by Belcher, and when he believed that his project for a settlement in Nova Scotia would go ahead, he made clear to Colman that he expected to come to Boston en route to Nova Scotia. He had a vision of living in America under the British Crown under a civil government, whose members would be elected locally, free from the inhibiting barriers of the class system that existed Britain. It was only when his plans for Nova Scotia collapsed that Coram, then over seventy, finally accepted the fact that time had run out, that his dream would never be realised.

The Belcher/Colman letters provide enough evidence, taken with what was already known, to show that Coram's tireless search for an American settlement outside the confines of Massachusetts was also motivated in part by his personal wish to leave England. His petitions to the Board of Trade and Plantations span a period of twenty-five years, from 1713 to 1737. His reasons for the proposals encompassed a variety of objects, but one constant was the provision of cheap supplies of timber for the navy. This went hand in hand with his desire to provide work for the unemployed soldiers, the resettlement of debtors and foreign Protestant refugees, all of which he saw as a means of safeguarding the borders of England's American colonial possessions from the depredations of the French and Spanish. But always there is the underlying wish that he, Coram, would have a role. Given the fact that the letter to Colman, written on 7 July 1737, giving notice of the Corams' expectation of coming to Boston, was written only three weeks before Coram presented his memorial for a charter for the Foundling Hospital to the King, it is reasonable to ask what would have happened to the charter had the Corams left for America with the intention of settling in Nova Scotia. Would any of Coram's supporters have had the commitment to see the charter through all the necessary expensive legal processes? In the event Coram had to find over £200 to pay the legal fees, money he found difficult to raise. Without his persistence, would any of those who had signed have had the will or the necessary perseverance to see the hospital established? The answer must be in the negative.

Coram's letters to Colman reveal just how tirelessly he worked from 1735 to 1737, both to collect signatures for his petition for the Foundling Hospital, and to finalise his plans for Nova Scotia. He wrote he would only go if Nova Scotia was governed by

> a perfectly free Civil Government, where every body may be fully free in Every Respect as in England but much freer in some Respects, and to have the Detestable military Government now Exercised there to be utterly abolished.[2]

It was this uncertainty that caused him to hesitate. 'I cannot yet say whether I shall come to America or not.'[3] But later in the year Coram believed he had carried his point.

> I and my Wife hold ourselves under Great obligations to you and your Lady for your kindly visiting our Good Mother. We are in expectation of seeing her this Somer in order to the Settling Nova Scotia with good Protestant Famelies British and Foreigners.[4]

Coram added 'there is still as much likelihood as ever that it will be done tho not this Somer', but being a realist he added 'the Little Regard as is had for our Plantations makes it Still precarious'.[5] Unfortunately for him, his comment proved all too prescient. His plans for Nova Scotia were shelved, but this left him free to concentrate all his energies on his darling project, a hospital for foundlings.

The Belcher letters

Jeremiah Belcher became Governor of Massachusetts in 1730 because, conveniently, he happened to be in London at the right time. The previous Governor, Burnet, had just died and Belcher was able neatly to step into his shoes. Belcher was a merchant, a man of means with a large estate in Meridon. He was known for his ungovernable

---

2   Coram to Colman, 2 March 1737: 'Letters of Thomas Coram', p. 34.
3   Ibid.
4   Coram to Colman, 9 July 1737: 'Letters of Thomas Coram', p. 37.
5   Ibid.

tongue and for a recklessness that made his standing with the Crown uncertain.[6] In his correspondence Belcher often refers to 'restless enemies, alert and pertinacious in prosecuting their ends'. The editor of the letters comments:

> they could scarcely have surpassed the Governor himself, watchful of his own interests and always watchful to circumvent the plans of others. He aroused personal and political opposition in Massachusetts and even men he had advanced became his adversaries, with conspicuous exceptions, they all came under his displeasure. While zealously contending for what he was wont to call the honour of the crown, he quietly weakened the hold of Great Britain and Her New England subjects.

It is to be wondered how much Coram, so zealous himself to promote the interests of his country, was aware of Belcher's double standards.

The correspondence between the two men was steady and cordial. The Governor, choosing his words with care, addressed Coram in a slightly patronising manner as 'my hearty friend', 'my worthy Sir', or 'my very worthy good friend', forms of address that struck a balance between the servile flattering tone he adopted when addressing those above him, and the arbitrary manner he adopted when addressing those below. Edward Hutchinson called him 'the perfect example of a New England courtier in an age of corruption'. Coram and Belcher both expressed their thoughts in forthright terms and both were able practitioners in the art of networking, a particularly American habit. The decisive difference between them was that, though Coram was not without ambition, he worked to promote the good of his country, while Belcher's ambition was limited to his own advancement and that of his family.

The underlying reason for the correspondence was that both men needed to be kept informed about developments in each other's countries. Belcher wanted Coram to keep his name to the fore in court and political circles. In an early letter Belcher makes it quite clear why Coram's letters are so important to him.

> Your letters are of very great service to me on many heads. I must enjoin you as often as you see these folks [doubtless Coram's contacts at the Board of Trade and Plantations] to be very particular to me. Pray give them my duty and respect to the Speaker when you see him. I wish it was in my power to return his friendship . . .[7]

Coram appears to have been happy to promote the interests of the Governor in so far as he was able to. In the following year Belcher is asking more of Coram.

> I charge you to give me a long letter on the affairs of Europe and Great Britain, with some London prints, the King's speech etc., in this don't fail me for we are very hungry in the winter for news from England.[8]

Coram did not fail although Belcher's requests must have made heavy demands on his time. Coram was clearly the more eager of the two correspondents, for Belcher

[6] *Belcher Papers*, Preface, pp. xvii–xxii.
[7] Belcher to Coram, 9 Dec. 1731: *Belcher Papers*, p. 86.
[8] Belcher to Coram, 24 April 1732: *Belcher Papers*, p. 1 1 1.

frequently answers three or four of Coram's letters with only one of his own. Coram took great care over this correspondence and he sent not only British news, but news from Europe. He took the trouble to introduce Belcher's son, Jonathan, to the Speaker, and when he dined with Sir Charles Wager, to talk of the Governor.

> I am much gratified with the very intelligible account you give me of the state of Europe and I really think Great Britain seems to bear too tamely the intrigues and affronts of the Princes about her, but more especially the unpardoned insults and depredations of the Spaniards.[9]

In the same letter he goes on to complain of the taxes imposed on Massachusetts Bay, particularly those concerned with the pine trees, the Hat Act and the Sugar Act. Coram must have concealed from Belcher the fact that it was he who had been the moving spirit behind the Hat Act.

Coram knew well that Massachusetts was totally opposed to the idea of a settlement in northern Maine, yet Belcher wrote disingenuously, thinking to please Coram,

> And why the Plantations (so capable of supplying the mother country with naval stores) are so little encouraged is a mystery out of my conception . . . I think it would be happy for this Province if the Crown would take to themselves the large tracts of land to the Eastward that may lay waste for years to come for anything that this Province can do.

Coram's lengthy and detailed letters were clearly very acceptable, for Belcher wrote:

> You will see that I am very fond of your correspondence by the length of this and I pray you will not fail writing me when you have anything worth handing to this remote province.[10]

Belcher had a second more personal reason for writing to Coram. His second son, Jonathan, was in London at the Temple, and his father was very anxious for him to marry advantageously while he was in England and cast Coram in the unlikely role of matchmaker. In a letter to his son he insists that 'Coram is a good friend of mine and your very good friend'. Jonathan is obviously not so sure that he wants Coram as his good friend, even though, as his father points out, it is through Coram's influence that he has been brought to Mr Speaker's notice. Belcher asks his son to deliver a letter to Captain Coram, 'with your own hand and treat him with good manners and respect. He is my hearty friend'. One can imagine the scene: the smart young man about town, busy establishing himself with his peers, would find making himself agreeable to an unfashionable elderly gentleman a bore. A further letter reveals that his father is clearly displeased with his son's cavalier attitude, and he writes sternly, 'Capt. Coram is mine and your very good friend and you will do well to own it on all occasions.' Six years later Jonathan had become Coram's good friend. His father wrote, 'I remember you formerly had but a slight opinion of Capt. Coram whom you

---

9 Belcher to Coram, 31 May 1733: *Belcher Papers*, p. 297.
10 Belcher to Coram, 6 October 1733: *Belcher Papers*, p. 311.

now think mightily well of. I am considerably wiser than you are and no wonder. So much for that.'[11]

Jonathan drafted the speech Coram made when he presented the charter for the Hospital for the Maintenance and Education of Exposed and Deserted Young Children to the Duke of Bedford and to a large gathering of distinguished supporters at Somerset House on 20 November 1739. His father wrote approvingly, 'I am well pleased with the handsome speech you made for him.' Jonathan also became one of the Governors.

Belcher had very clear ideas as to the attributes he wanted to see in a future daughter-in-law. She 'should be of strict virtue, good nature, agreeable (no matter whether beautiful) passable good sense (no matter whether quick or sharp) and a plentiful fortune'. He also wanted to know how much such a marriage would cost and asked the expense of clothing, furniture, hire of house, servants, eating and drinking, firing of candles. Thomas Coram for his part suggested the daughter of Sam Reed, whom Belcher remembered as a pretty child, and the daughter of Samuel Holden. The girls of the Lethulier family came under consideration and an orphan cared for by one Mr Bucks. Belcher indicated that the fortune to be expected must be in the region of £10,000 and that the whole affair must be managed wisely and silently. Jonathan was enjoined to consult with Mrs Coram as well. 'Can't our choice friend Coram and his good spouse assist?' There is a hint in one letter that Coram had been offered a consideration for his help with one of the prospective daughters-in-law who lived in Roehampton, but this was accompanied by the stern warning that if the answer was not promising to entirely desist.[12] Henry Newman even suggested that one of the du Quesne girls, the daughters of the feckless Marquis, might be suitable, but the young Belcher was too canny to get involved with a penniless girl. His father had warned him,

> should you presume ever to make court to any person without my knowledge and consent I shall freely own that I own myself more deceived in you than any person I have had to do with, and that you are void of the strict duty that you owe me.[13]

Nothing came of these attempts at match-making. Jonathan married the daughter of Jeremiah Allen after his return to America, and in later life became Chief Justice of Nova Scotia.

What did Coram get for all the effort he put into his letters to Belcher? Belcher provided him with information about New England politics and personalities. Coram believed he was an ally who could be relied on to support his plans for a settlement in Nova Scotia and he used him as a post office, asking him to forward his letters to others. It was indeed through Belcher's good offices that Coram's first letter reached Benjamin Colman. Coram also asked him to convey letters to the Speaker of the House of Representatives and Secretary Wolland, with the request that they should be read to the House of Representatives. Belcher did as Coram asked, and then,

[11] Belcher to Coram, 16 October 1739: *Belcher Papers*, p. 210.
[12] Ibid., p. 212.
[13] Belcher to Belcher, 25 May 1734: *Belcher Papers*, p. 49.

without comment, enclosed an account of the response given by the House of Representatives.

> In as much as the letter contains sundry injurious and scandalous reflections of the Hon. Paul Dudley Esq., a member of this house, and the suggestions therein are without support, therefore voted it is unworthy of the notice of this house, save of their displeasure and that therefore the said letter be delivered by the Speaker to the said Paul Dudley so that he may better have his remedy against the author of the same.[14]

The letter, written to avenge some perceived wrong, provides yet one more example of Coram's lack of judgement in publicly blackening the names of those he considered had injured him in some way. It is not known whether Paul Dudley replied, but the response of the House of Representatives served to remind Coram that he still had powerful enemies in Boston.

An arch intriguer himself, in the 1740s Belcher found himself being plotted against. The correspondence with Coram ends with a series of frantic letters from Belcher imploring Coram's help. He wrote saying that for the past eleven years he had faithfully served the Crown and strictly observed all the King's orders and was now cruelly and barbarously treated, superseded in his commission with little or no pension. He begged Coram to intercede with Sir Charles Wager and any others at court and to write to advise him as to whether he should come to London to solicit for justice. Even had Coram wanted to help his friend, Belcher had too many powerful enemies. He was ousted from the governorship in 1741 and the letters between the two men cease.

The Colman letters

Benjamin Colman was born in Boston and studied under Increase Mather at Harvard, at a time of intense religious and intellectual transformation in New England. The Puritan ideal needed to broaden its appeal so as to embrace wider geographical communities. Colman, who had gone to England, was asked to return to take charge of the Fourth Congregational Church, known as the Brattle Street church. He took Presbyterian ordination and taught the rationality of revealed religion. He secured many patrons for Harvard and his church became fashionable and well attended. He was said to be 'all things to all men' and 'a master of compromise'. In a harsh summing up of his qualities it was said that his 'character would have been greater could it be said of him that he excelled as much in strength of reason and firmness of mind as in many other good qualities'.[15]

Coram's letters to Colman were of a very different nature to those written to Belcher. Coram was clearly anxious to start up the correspondence and, taking advantage of the fact that he was one of Dr Bray's Associates, sent an unsolicited gift of twenty-four Latin copies of *Ecclesiastes, sive de Ratione concionandi*, with the consent of

14 Belcher to Coram, 25 October 1740: *Belcher Papers*, p. 332.
15 *Dictionary of American Biography*.

the Associates, to be used by the professors and tutors of divinity at Harvard. The correspondence opens with Colman acknowledging and expressing gratitude for the gift. There is something on the one hand rather touching about Coram, no Latin scholar himself, anxious that those about to preach the Gospel should be properly instructed. On the other hand, the gift of books provided him with the opportunity for starting up a correspondence with another prominent Bostonian.

Coram had learned from the *Boston Daily News Letter*, sent to him by his sister-in-law, that Colman had ordained three missionaries to preach to the Indians. Coram had a long-standing interest in the education of the Indians and was far more interested in their welfare than in the conversion of the negroes to the Protestant faith. Pleased with the success of his first gift, Coram wanted to build on his relationship with Colman; and arranged to send the missionaries some books to encourage them. The French had sent Jesuit priests to live with the Indians, so had not only gained converts to their faith (albeit often in form rather than spirit), but they had also gained friends and allies willing to join forces with the French against the English. As Coram noted in his robust manner,

> the Romanist spares no pains to Instruct those Indians in their Way to Consider English men as the Posterity of the Jews that murthered our Saviour and the Virgin Mary and I know not What.[16]

He believed the conversion of the Indians was not only a necessary good, but of strategic importance, a way of countering the influence of the French in northern Maine and Nova Scotia.

Before Coram was allowed to appropriate any more books for the missionaries, the Associates wished to be sure that they were wanted and demanded a letter to that effect. Happily for posterity, this was the trigger that started the Coram/Colman correspondence. Since Coram did not know Colman personally, and having engineered this contact, the first letter was written by way of an introduction. In it Coram gave an account of his life and early achievements, providing one of the most important sources for the main events of his life. He started by apologising for his lack of Latin and learning, and said that, although he believed he should be writing to the President of Harvard, he excused himself on the grounds that he was a poor writer and had no time before the ship sailed.

Coram always felt disadvantaged when writing, knowing that his style lacked polish, but it was direct and vigorous, something Richard Steele would have approved of. In an article in the *Spectator* Steele castigated a world

> grown so full of Dissimulation and Compliment, that Men's words are hardly of any signification of their thoughts; and if any man measures his words by his Heart and speak as he thinks, and do not express more kindness to Everyman, than Men unusually have for any Man, he can hardly escape censure for want of Breeding.

He continued:

---

[16] Coram to Colman, 30 April 1734: 'Letters of Thomas Coram', p. 22.

> The old English Plainess and Sincerity, that generous integrity of Nature,
> Honesty of Disposition, which always argues true Greatness of Mind, and is
> usually accompany'd with Undaunted Courage and Resolution, is in great
> Measure lost amongst us.[17]

Steele might have been talking about Coram who exemplified many of the qualities
he feared lost.

Coram begged Colman to consult with the President of Harvard about the accept-
ability of the books for the missionaries. He wrote that he knew Colman should be
writing to Lord Egmont, who was chairman of the Associates, but taking advantage of
the fact that Egmont was away in the country, he suggested to Colman that it would
be better if the letter was sent to him. He said he would forward it, thus engineering
for himself another important contact in Boston. He noted with pleasure the fact that
Sarah Colman had known Eunice Coram and had asked to be remembered to her. To
further cement the relationship he joined with his wife in sending their utmost
respects to Sarah Colman. To add a personal touch, Coram recalled that when in
Boston he used to meet Sarah's father, Mr Crisp, at the barber, Mr Chickley, where
they both used to be shaved. Coram also took the occasion to mention that he knew
Benjamin Colman's brother, John Colman, a Boston merchant, and asks to be remembered to him.

It took nearly a year before Coram was able to write that an assortment of books
had been looked out, bound and packed in a small chest. Saying that Lord Egmont
had no time to write himself, Coram transmitted his lordship's message to the recipi-
ents of the books in Egmont's own words:

> Be pleased to Intreat your Missionaries to Treat the Indians with Justice and
> Patience and to feed them with milk and not cram them with mistry (those
> are his Lordships words) and have a Care not to put the fire out whilst they
> are endeavouring to Kindle it.[18]

Egmont seemed to take a real interest in the affair, and recommended several of the
fifty-four books that were to be sent, asking only that a catalogue of the books be sent
back to the Rev. Samuel Smith. By this time Coram had quarrelled with the trustees
of Georgia and had ceased to attend the Georgia meetings but did continue to meet
with Dr Bray's Associates. Egmont confided his private thoughts about the books to
his diary:

> Coram never gave up coming albeit irregularly to Dr. Bray's, but it was
> piffling stuff, but gave him occasion for long letters to Colman.[19]

Not content with the gift from the Associates, Coram set about sending tracts and
sermons to each of the missionaries, Stephen Parker, Ebenezer Hindsell and Joseph
Secombe. Secombe had the sense to thank for his gift and sent an account of those
'wild people' which was printed and circulated. To reward him Coram sent him a
bible worth two guineas. Unfortunately Secombe was not so well thought of on the

---

17 *Spectator*, no. 103, 28 June, 1711.
18 Coram to Colman, 13 February 1735: 'Letters of Thomas Coram', p. 24.
19 *Egmont Diaries*, 5 April 1735, vol. III, p. 306.

other side of the Atlantic, but Coram thought he had the harder task 'grapling with the Jesuit and Jesuited Indians' and wished he could have a fellow labourer to carry on 'the Glorious Work'. In his following letter Coram fears that unless it is made absolutely clear that the missionaries are not working for the military garrisons but 'Regaining the perverted Indians out of the Polutions of the F(rench) Jesuits', there will be no more books.

While on a business trip to the northern cities of Liverpool, Warrington and Manchester, Coram tried to get friends there to help with gifts of books. During the course of the correspondence there is much exchanging of tracts and sermons, and the whole tenor of the letters is more serious than the factual and practical letters exchanged between Belcher and Coram. The letters, besides reflecting Coram's fear and hatred of Catholic France's pretensions in North America, also reveal his views, very advanced for his time, on women's education. Commenting on a sermon on the death of a Boston lady who believed in girls' education, Coram thought it would have a good effect on a charity school in Liverpool where there were only eight or ten girls to about sixty boys. He took the opportunity to express his views on the importance of education for girls, which he believed to be underestimated.

> An Evil amongst us here in England is to think Girls having learning given them is not so very Material as for boys to have it. I think and say it is more Material for Girls, when they come to be Mothers, will have the forming of their Childrens lives and if their Mothers be good or Bad the Children Generally take after them, so that Giving Girls a vertuous Education is a vast Advantage to their Posterity as well as to the Publick.[20]

Coram's letters give a picture of a man of boundless energy. In 1737 he was busy with plans for Nova Scotia and for the Foundling Hospital. Nevertheless he found time to get together a parcel of 220–230 books from the SPCK to send to Joseph Secombe. He responded to a request from a Mr Josiah Cotton for books by making enquiries as to his bona fides and then sending him a similar number of books. By his own admission, he was now finding writing troublesome. He was approaching seventy and went everywhere on foot. It is perhaps not surprising that he fell ill later that year.

The letters reveal several examples of Coram's capacity for taking infinite pains to fight for justice for those who could not do so for themselves. Having been through hard times himself he understood better than most what the death of a seaman might mean to his relatives. When told that a New England carpenter had died at sea but the wages due to him had not been paid, although the man was totally unknown to him, Coram set about righting this wrong. He discovered from mess mates that the man's name was Samuel Tucket, he was twenty-four years old, and he was due £16 3s. Nothing would have been known about this story had Coram not had to write to Colman to ask for assistance in finding the man's relatives and arranging for them to get power of attorney to enable them to administer the dead man's affairs. One of the two witnesses had to be from London and Coram suggested Jonathan Belcher might do it for no reward. He calculated that the mess mates who brought the matter to his

---

[20] Coram to Colman, 2 March 1737: 'Letters of Thomas Coram', p. 33.

attention would have to have a guinea each, the receivers who would pay had to have a shilling in every pound, and that Belcher might have administrative expenses. All this involved Coram in a lot of work. Tucket came from Connecticut and Coram calculated that the relatives might get £10, worth £50 to £60 in New England money, with which to buy goods. He ends characteristically in a sentence which encapsulates his philosophy of life:

> I do not desire nor Expect any thanks from whom may be entitled to the Wages for this Information, the favour is Small and I beleive every one ought in duty to do any good they can.[21]

The wrongs inflicted upon Indians were always of particular concern to Coram and in the same long letter he tells how he took up the case of two Mohican Indians. They had come to London with Samuel Mason and his son to apply to the King for redress against oppressive injuries done to the tribe by defrauding them of their land. Bureaucratic delays meant the plaintiffs were unable to make their case before the summer recess. Coram applied to Sir Charles Wager, who spoke to the Duke of Newcastle and the Lord President of the Council on their behalf, resulting in a commission being set up to inquire into the whole affair. Sir Charles went further and got a grant of £300 to cover their expenses. Samuel Mason died before the Indians returned to America, but Coram impressed on the son the necessity of writing to thank Sir Charles. He was incensed to discover that the son had never written. Coram was not only angry, he was embarrassed and ashamed, for Sir Charles was the nearest Coram ever got to having a patron, and the Admiral had enquired to know if Mason and the Indians had got back safely. Coram expressed his disgust at Mason's behaviour in his usual robust way

> Such unthankfull Creatures hurts others who afterwards wants friendship, as bad as he does who puls the plank away after he's got over the Ditch. who can ever show favour to such Creatures of no More thankfullness in them than in the baser sort of horses when they have eaten up their Provender turn their Tailes and Shi-te in the Manger.[22]

Coram saw no need to trim his language even when writing to a minister of the church. He always believed in the basic decency of the Indians and hoped one of the Indians, who could read and write, would thank Sir Charles. He wrote to the Indian and took the trouble to send him an axe which he had specially fashioned out of good elm. Young Mason would appear to have been a thoroughly bad lot and in 1742 was charged by the Indians with making false representations.

Coram was so often in the New England coffee house, where all the merchants and ships' captains involved in the transatlantic trade congregated to exchange news and gossip, that he had to instruct his correspondents to address his letters to the Navy Office because otherwise they would go astray. At the coffee house he heard many stories of real hardship among New England sailors stranded in London. In his typical way he began to think of a scheme to alleviate some of the suffering he saw around

---

[21] Coram to Colman, 21 September 1738: 'Letters of Thomas Coram', p. 40.
[22] Ibid., p. 42.

him. He suggested to Colman that one way of helping would be to set up a bank for the relief of distressed New Englanders. To persuade Colman to help, he sent him a series of accounts of New Englanders in difficulties through no fault of their own.

He quoted the case of John Daffin, who had lost an arm in an engagement and so was made unemployed. He was found starved, in rags and covered in lice. Mrs Coram, learning about the young man, advised him to call on Mrs Alden, Edward Hutchinson's daughter, who was in London with Mrs Noyse, Jeremiah Belcher's sister. Eunice Coram went round in the evening to see what had happened and learnt to her dismay that, not unnaturally, he had been turned away. She then told the ladies John Daffin's story, and they took pity on him and took him in and clothed and fed him. Another John, son of Sir John Hobby, a merchant adventurer who died in 1714 seeking the governorship of Nova Scotia and left his estate insolvent, also came to Coram's attention. Coram discovered that John Hobby, given a berth on a ship trading between Boston, the West Indies and London, had been disgracefully treated by the Captain, 'messing him in the forecastle with a negro' and allowing everyone to beat him. The Captain, seeking to excuse himself, told Coram he had only taken him on at the bequest of his father-in-law, Jeremiah Belcher. Coram arranged for him to continue on the ship under another captain, but unfortunately the lad contracted smallpox. It was again Mrs Coram who came to the rescue, finding him a lodging and a nurse. Coram noted that, although he applied to several merchants who knew his father, none would contribute to pay the nurse and the Corams were left to pay all his fees. Coram wrote uncomplainingly of the young man's subsequent ungrateful behaviour, telling how he left his ship to accompany a young woman who was going out to join her husband in Jamaica. This was hardly a story to stir the compassion of possible subscribers to a bank for Distressed New Englanders. Nevertheless, Coram, ever the optimist, ended his letter by suggesting a list of suitable names to manage the bank, including those of Henry Newman, Richard Partridge (Jeremiah Belcher's brother-in-law), and Jonathan Belcher.

The depth and bitterness of Coram's resentment at his treatment in Taunton surfaces from time to time in the letters, but the extent of the hostility he himself aroused suddenly jumps off the page when a name causes him to remember past injustices. Coram was reminded by Josiah Cotton's request for books of his cousin, John Cotton, a minister in Plymouth Colony. The minister had been charged with being too familiar with one of the church members' wives and had been driven out by the Lieutenant Governor of the colony, William Stoughton. Coram, believing the minister to be innocent, had spoken out, probably in his usual forceful way, thus incurring the displeasure of the Lieutenant Governor when 'at that time it was looked on as a sort of blasphemy to suspect Mr. Stoughton could do any wrong'. Although Coram took no further action, he writes in the same letter that John Cotton's nephew, Cotton Mather, whom Coram had never met,

> spoke many fals and Injuring things of me to Cloath me in a Bares Skin which Hallowed all the Hellhounds in Town and Country on to Wurry me. as I never wanted Resentment, so I gave my self no paines about Mr Cotton Mather's Unkle, and if I had, it would have had no Effect for the Generality of the People were taught to beleive I was a vile fellow an Enemy to Gods People and aboundance of such Kind of Cant and Diabolical practices however I beleive that man Mr Cotton has as much Injustice done him in that

abominable Proceeding against him as those other Innocent men who were
Murdered on account of the Pretended Whitchcraft.[23]

The memory of these events led him on to tell Colman of his endeavours to erect a
lighthouse on the Great Brewster after the ship *Hazard*, bringing news of Queen
Anne's death and George I's accession, had gone down with all hands after hitting the
Conyhasset Rocks. Coram persuaded many owners and masters of merchants' ships
trading with New England to sign a petition to be presented to the King, praying His
Majesty to recommend that a lighthouse be erected on the Great Brewster near
Nantucket. He also prepared a certificate, to be signed by captains of warships who
had been on station, to support his application for a lighthouse. He had a lot of
success, all readily subscribing except two or three New England captains, who were
very cautious, and one captain, who suddenly became very alarmed at what he might
have put his name to, and tore up the petition and ran out of the shop. Not to be
deterred, Coram rapidly got another petition subscribed. In 1716, Nathaniel Byfield,
Coram's old enemy, had been in London trying for the governorship of Massachusetts. Coram believed that he had succeeded in blocking his appointment on that
occasion. He wrote

> I had Stuck in his Skirts to prevent his obtaining to be Governor or so much
> as judge of the Admiralty in New England, for the Intolerable Oppression
> that Proud base Monster had Malliciously brought on me in that Country for
> 3 or 4 years together.[24]

Byfield did later succeed in becoming a judge of the Admiralty. But he now saw an
opportunity to get his own back. According to Coram, to deny him the credit for
taking the initiative over the lighthouse, Byfield arranged for his son-in-law, William
Tailor, then Lieutenant Governor, to get the General Court of Massachusetts to erect
the lighthouse.[25] Coram later complained to Trinity House that no provision had
been made for pilots. The two long letters to Colman, written on consecutive days, on
21 and 22 September 1738, are full of stories of Coram's life. It seems at times almost
as though Coram saw Colman as someone to whom he could unburden himself,
someone who would sympathise and, if necessary, put the record straight.

It was only from 1737 onwards that Coram started to write about his hopes for a
hospital for foundlings. This is perhaps not surprising, as during the early 1730s
Coram was involved with plans for the settlement of Georgia and plans and memorials for consideration by the Board of Trade and Plantations for Nova Scotia. But
from 1737 Coram began to share with Colman the trials and difficulties he encountered in trying to obtain the necessary support for his petition for a foundling
hospital. His account of his struggles to establish what he called his 'darling project'
are better read in conjunction with the history of his final success.

In his last letter to Colman Coram wrote of his wife's death. Eunice Coram had
clearly not enjoyed good health during her last years. Coram seldom referred to her

---

[23] Coram to Colman, 23 September 1735: 'Letters of Thomas Coram', p. 31. The words 'Pretended
Whitchcraft' refer to the infamous Salem witchcraft trials of 1692.
[24] Coram to Colman, 22 September 1738: 'Letters of Thomas Coram', p. 46.
[25] Ibid.

in his letters, but his moving and dignified tribute to his wife makes a fitting end to the letters between the two men. It must have been a sadness to him that, although she was alive to rejoice in 1739 when the charter was granted, she did not live to see the first children admitted to the hospital.

> It having pleased Almighty God to remove my dearly beloved Wife from hence by death in the Middle of July. Worn out by long Sickness, I was Marryed to her a little above 40 years during which time she never once gave me Cause to be angry or vexed at her, she was always a Sincere Christian of an humble meek and Quiet Spirit and Wisely Study's my Peace and Comfort and was to her Life's End a vertuous kind and Prudent Wife without fault. She Chearfully bore an affectionate part in all my Toyls and affections. By her Death I am bereaved of one of the best of Wives but as it is the hand of the God of Mercy, I humbly Submit and beseech His Divine Majesty to Sanctify this Stroke to me.[26]

Before she died Eunice would have known that her husband had achieved his dearest wish, the granting of a royal charter for a foundling hospital. Her death came as plans as to how best to care for destitute and abandoned children were being discussed by the newly constituted General Committee. She would have shared in his joy as well as his frustration at the delay in starting to build. It was perhaps fortunate for her that she did not know how little time was left for him to enjoy the satisfaction of working to ensure a better life for those children. In two years' time there would be an added sadness: not only would he grieve for his wife, but his painful exile from the governing body of the hospital would add to his sense of loss.

---

[26] Coram to Colman, 13 September 1740: 'Letters of Thomas Coram', p. 55.

10

Triumph

Coram's ability to raise money and his willingness to promote a cause in which he believed was known and appreciated by the trustees of Georgia, who had asked him to go to Tunbridge Wells on their behalf to seek supporters willing to give financial backing to the proposed colony. But while talking of the need to support the idea of a new colony, Coram also took the opportunity to talk of his own interest in the creation of a foundling hospital. The fact that he had already obtained the signatures and support of sixteen ladies for his 'darling project' began to encourage some men to add their names to his list. He must have been greatly pleased when in 1732 he received his first large donation of £500 from Josiah Wordsworth, to be paid as soon as a charter for the hospital had been obtained. After his first successes with the ladies, no new names were added to the list until 1733, when the Countess of Harold signed. She was a young widow whose father, the Earl of Thanet, was noted for his charitable giving and great piety. A commissioner of the Greenwich Hospital and an original member of the SPG, he was said to have given away £60,000 in his life and at his death in 1729 he gave £40,000 more to trustees to distribute away to different charities.[1] Coram, must have shrewdly calculated that, coming from such a background, he would be listened to with sympathy by the young Countess and that he might hope for financial support as well. He was not disappointed, for as one of the executors of her father's estate she was later to arrange for the payment of £500 to the hospital out of the funds designated by her father's estate.[2]

Never a man to enjoy working as part of a team, once Coram had cut his links with the Georgia trustees and could follow his own inclinations, he restarted his campaigns to drum up support for a refuge for foundlings, and to promote his newly acquired enthusiasm for a settlement in Nova Scotia. Considering that he had to walk everywhere, carrying quill, ink and paper, the effort required to collect the large number of signatures he required to carry conviction with the relevant authorities was prodigious. It must have taken an enormous amount of time and energy to obtain well over a hundred signatures from the artisans, and they were perhaps the least difficult to convince to sign. But, having almost failed at this time to acquire the signature of any nobleman or courtier on his petition, he was having to use all his powers of

---

[1] *Egmont Diaries*, vol. 1, pp. 57–8.
[2] LMA, General Committee Minutes, vol. 1, pp. 137–8.

persuasion to convince reluctant men of influence of the need to show compassion towards the plight of destitute infants, a subject they were reluctant to address. Coram had set himself a formidable task.

Coram was able to add the names of three more ladies to his list at the end of 1734. Both the Earl and Countess of Albermarle signed on the same day. She was the sister-in-law of the Duchess of Richmond and an habitué of the Holland House set, and was part of the extended Richmond family.[3] Like the duchess, she was also a Lady of the Bedchamber to Queen Caroline. To reinforce the court connection, her husband was Lord of the Bedchamber to the Prince of Wales. After the additional support of two more dukes, Manchester and Kent, another two ladies signed, Baroness Trevor and Baroness Ockham, both widows and neither seeming to belong to the charmed social circle that united the others, although there may have been a particular reason for their inclusion on the select list (both may have been wealthy) since Coram seldom did anything without good reason. The penultimate name and the last lady to appear in Coram's diary list was that of the Duchess of Portland.[4] She had only just married the Duke and was very wealthy in her own right. Her father, the Earl of Oxford, a Vice President of St George's Hospital, signed on the same day, the only recorded instance of a father and daughter signing together. After 19 May 1735 Coram ceased to use his old diary to record signatures because by then he had started to use a more systematic method of recording names.

While gathering the names of the ladies, Coram was obviously able to interest some noblemen in his ideas for a hospital, as is shown by their inclusion on the diary list, although it seems that at this stage none of them was willing to be publicly associated with his project. According to his diary, Coram added the name of the Duke of Richmond on 13 April 1734, and this was soon followed by the name of the Duke of Montagu. There was some degree of overlap between Coram's two projects, for the Duke of Montagu had agreed to be a trustee for Nova Scotia as well as supporting the idea of a foundling hospital, as did Viscount Torrington, whose mother-in-law had been one of Coram's earliest supporters.

Coram, having successfully put his memorial for a charter for Nova Scotia before the King, was anxious to repeat his success with a memorial for the hospital. He had the vitally important petition incorporating the names of twenty-one ladies of quality and distinction, or ladies of charity. He also had a second petition signed by fifty-two gentlemen, among them his old friends from the Navy Office, Thomas Pearse and Robert Norman, as well as William Tillard, a friend of Newman's. But before presenting his petition to the King Coram knew that it needed the signature of at least one nobleman to give it weight. He actually managed to get two signatures, those of Viscount Wallingford and the Earl of Derby. Viscount Wallingford, the style given to the Earl of Banbury, was MP for Banbury. However, his signature did not carry much weight, for the claims of the earls of Banbury had not been recognised by the Parliamentary Committee of Privileges since 1632.[5] He had married Mary

---

3   Tillyard, *Aristocrats*, p. 157.

4   The Duchess of Portland inherited a passion for collecting from her father and her purchases included the Barberini or Portland Vase, now in the British Museum. Cokayne, *Complete Peerage*, vol. 10, p. 593, note a.

5   Cokayne, *Complete Peerage*, vol. 12, p. 325.

Katherine, the daughter of John Law, the financial brains behind the disastrous Mississippi Company, with poor, swamp-ridden Louisiana the bait to entice the citizens of Paris to make their fortunes, which collapsed at the same time as the South Sea Bubble. Coram needed a nobleman of more substance to head up his list of petitioners. While he was in the north talking to the merchants of Liverpool about his plans for Nova Scotia he paid a visit to Knowsley, the seat of the Earl of Derby, and succeeded in obtaining the earl's signature alongside that of Wallingford's at the head of the list of gentlemen. He also took the opportunity to tell Derby of his plans for Nova Scotia and, although the earl did not agree to let his name be used immediately, Coram was satisfied that if the project went ahead Derby would be willing to become a trustee of Nova Scotia. The method Coram used to collect signatures was similar for both petitions. Two sheets of paper were folded into three columns. Gentlemen signed one, artisans the other. As soon as the first column was completed the next one was started. The papers thus signed were then annexed to both Coram's own memorials for presentation to the King.

The 1735 Nova Scotia petition elicited a positive response, but nothing came of the petition for a foundling hospital, presented a few weeks later, despite the distinction of the ladies who had signed it. Their names clearly did not carry enough weight to overcome the paucity of support from influential gentlemen. Coram realised that he needed to persuade the husbands, fathers and relations of the ladies not just to give their tacit support, but to make their support public.

He spent the next two years in a round of visits to these noblemen, at the same time as he was working on his plans for Nova Scotia. But he also realised that he would have to broaden the scope of his support to include professional men of influence. Richard Mead had already shown interest in Coram's ideas; now Coram needed his signature. He was doctor to most of fashionable society, physician to the King and to Robert Walpole, not to mention Henry Newman, who might well have talked of Coram's ideas with him. Mead was a distinguished antiquarian, an interest shared by several of the gentlemen who signed Coram's petition. The Society of Antiquaries had been revived and would receive its charter in 1751. Hans Sloane, also a distinguished physician, would also become an active governor of the hospital. His book on natural history had brought him international fame, and as well as much else he was President of the Royal Society, a society formed to give learned men a venue to discuss philosophical questions and report experiments. Former presidents included Samuel Pepys and Isaac Newton. Sloane had a large circle of friends, and had been interested enough in the Georgia project to send for its prospectus and contribute £20 annually.[6] It may have been through the influence of both these distinguished physicians that six other men concerned with the medical profession signed. Certainly the fact that they gave Coram their support was hugely important to him.

Between 1735 and 1737 Coram added the names of 120 distinguished men to his list. According to his diary he had the support of the dukes of Richmond, Montagu, Kent and Manchester. Coram needed to convert that support into public acceptance. At some point the balance must have tipped and it was seen to be socially acceptable to become associated with this new fashionable venture. It is not possible to pinpoint

6   *Egmont Diaries*, vol. 1, p. 278.

the date when aristocrats and courtiers made the transition from opposition to Coram's ideas to gradual acceptance, because there is no record of the dates when Coram recorded their signatures. As leaders of society they were, in many instances, more interested in being seen to do the right thing than convinced of the rightness of the cause. But even after the hospital was up and running there was still a hard core who thought the whole idea of such an institution a danger to the moral structure of society.

Coram's list of influential supporters and persons of quality and distinction was growing, but he was not satisfied. Talking with friends, he felt it would be important to have the support of members of the judiciary before taking his second memorial to the King. Arguing that the children of destitute parents, if they survived the hazards of childhood, with no education or training could only turn to begging, thieving and a life of crime to survive, Coram thought his project would engage the sympathies of the legal profession. For many years Eunice Coram had been a friend of the wife of Anthony Allan, a Master in Chancery.[7] Allan had signed Coram's first petition and it may have been through his influence that Coram obtained the necessary introductions that enabled him to attach a third petition to his memorial, signed by a significant number of the legal profession. In his will, Anthony Allan wrote that he 'did, at the instance of that indefatigable schemist Thomas Coram, intend some considerable benefaction towards carrying on so good a project, and did encourage the concurrence of other liberal benefactors'.[8]

It was during this period of great activity that the Corams moved to a new address. To begin with, life must have been quite difficult for Eunice, a stranger in a strange land with her husband away for long stretches of time, and she would have needed friends. Because of its docks and wharves along the banks of the Thames, and the number of premises associated with shipping, warehouses for provisions and naval stores, Rotherhithe has always been a magnet for seafaring men. It has always been supposed that this is where the Corams lodged and Brownlow, in his history of the Foundling Hospital, states it as fact, although there is no concrete evidence to back up the assertion. It was not until 1732 that Coram actually gave an address on a letter to the Board of Trade and Plantations. He and his wife were then living at 32 Prescott Street in Goodman's Fields, one of the first streets in which houses were designated by numbers instead of signs.[9] Until then Coram had directed that his letters should be sent to the Navy Office because if they were sent to the New England coffee house they would be lost.[10]

Little is known about Eunice Coram, apart from the fact that she was from Boston, and was a loyal wife, but she clearly must have had a gift for friendship. Coram told Colman that they were invited to share part of their house by the Rev. Samuel Smith, Vicar of All Hallows by London Wall, and his wife, on account of their desire for our company, adding that, 'I believe much more for my wife's than for mine'.[11] The

---

7   Coram to Colman, 12 September 1738: 'Letters of Thomas Coram', p. 44.
8   Brownlow, *History and Objects of the Foundling Hospital*, p. 9, note, quoting the will of Anthony Allan, 1753.
9   Harben, *Dictionary of London*, p. 273.
10 Coram to Colman, 23 September 1735: 'Letters of Thomas Coram', p. 27.
11 Coram to Colman, 24 August 1739: 'Letters of Thomas Coram', p. 51.

Corams were evidently very pleased with this new arrangement and said that the Smiths were 'the best and most agreeable company that can be'. Coram was particularly pleased that they thought none the worse of his wife, who continued to go to Congregationalist meetings; he was proud that Eunice remained firmly attached to her Congregationalist roots, showing herself to be a woman of principle and independent spirit. He was also at pains to make quite clear that, although Smith would have given them house room for free, he rented three or four rooms on the first floor. It was fortunate for the Corams that they were with friends when he was so ill later in 1737 and during the period when his wife became increasing frail. It was from this house that Coram must have walked to Whitehall carrying his precious memorial to present to the King on 21 July 1737.

Coram's final list included the names of twenty-five dukes, thirty-one earls, twenty-six other members of the peerage and thirty-eight knights. His list included the entire Privy Council, headed by the Prince of Wales, as well as the names of Robert Walpole, the Prime Minister, and Arthur Onslow, Speaker of the House of Commons, an old friend. The two archbishops and the Bishop of London were named, presumably because they were members of the Privy Council, but no other members of the clergy appeared on the list. Not all those named had agreed to serve as governors, and Coram may never have met some of the noblemen and gentlemen who appeared on his list, but he had added their names to give weight to his proposal and to indicate that he thought them suitable to promote his charitable design. He guessed, no doubt rightly, that once seeing themselves among such influential and distinguished company none of them would want publicly to disassociate themselves from such a newly fashionable enterprise. Besides the aristocrats, Coram had persuaded bankers, politicians, and country gentlemen to sign, including friends from the Navy Office like Sir Charles Wager, and New Englanders resident in London like Richard Partridge, Jeremiah Belcher's brother-in-law, Lords Commissioners of the Board of Trade and Plantations as well as members of the medical and legal professions. By far the largest category were the merchants, many of whom Coram knew personally. To have collected and transcribed all 375 names, ending modestly with his own name at the foot of the petition, was a prodigious undertaking.[12]

In the memorial[13] Coram, describing himself as 'gentleman' as he always did, made clear that he was writing on behalf of helpless infants exposed to destruction. He then proceeded, step by step, to build up his case, starting first with a description of the usual fate of foundlings. He cited first the petition from many ladies of quality and distinction, invoking their concern at the murder of miserable infant children by cruel parents to hide their shame, and at the inhumane custom of exposing new born children to perish in the streets. He went on to attack the barbarous nurses who took in children but starved them or, if the children lived, turned them out onto the streets to beg and steal, or hired them out to vicious people who sometimes bent, maimed and distorted their limbs to arouse pity and compassion. To redress such a deplorable

---

[12] The full list of names with their addresses is given in Nichols and Wray, *History of the Foundling Hospital*, pp. 345–53. McClure gives a detailed analysis of the way in which Coram selected his proposed governors in *Coram's Children*, pp. 28–31, appendix 11, pp. 259–60.

[13] Copy of The Memorial and Petition to the King's Most Excellent Majesty in Council, 29 July 1739: LMA, A/FH/A01/003/001.

state of affairs, the ladies had, in a written instrument, declared they were willing to encourage and contribute towards the erecting of a hospital, following the example of France, Holland and other Christian countries, for the reception, maintenance and proper eduction of such abandoned helpless children, to prevent horrid murders, cruelties and other mischiefs.

He used the second petition signed by noblemen and gentlemen, who, he is careful to say, had approved of the ladies' charitable inclinations, to ask for a grant of letters patent for a hospital. In the third petition, signed by the Justices of the Peace, Coram now introduced a new argument. The helpless children, rescued from destruction, would be useful to the country in either sea or land service. By making public benefit a further object for the establishment of a hospital he now asked not just for a royal charter but for a royal charter of incorporation to be given to such persons as the King might think fit to receive and apply such charity.

To bolster his case, he stated that he had already received promises of contributions as well as legacies. And to underline the importance of the proposed work he stressed again the public benefit rather than the humanitarian aspect of the work, writing that 'such cast of children will make good servants and when qualified to dispose of them to the sea or land service'. Coram seemed to be writing what he believed would be acceptable. He allowed the ladies to be the ones who were moved by compassion, simply stating the facts himself. He kept to himself his belief that the education of girls was as important as that of boys, and he was certainly wise to do this. One controversial subject was enough: it was sufficiently bold to have forced consideration of the plight of foundlings onto the agenda. The education of the girls was, however, not neglected when the time came.

What Coram proposed was breaking new ground. He had already demonstrated his capacity for innovative thinking by incorporating into his proposals for Nova Scotia a blueprint for a civil government. So also was his proposal that the charter for a purely philanthropic venture be given a structure whereby individuals acting together as a legally chartered voluntary corporate body could receive legacies and undertake together charitable work far in excess of anything that one of them alone could have managed. It was not an entirely new concept, as Thomas Bray had made use of the same method to open over 1,400 charity schools in the 1720s. Coram may well have adapted Bray's idea as a means of financing his own proposal. Since the disaster of the South Sea Bubble there was considerable resistance to any further public subscriptions to joint stock companies, whether profit-making or charitable. Coram needed to overcome public suspicion and to demonstrate that he had solid financial backing. This was where the support of the ladies was so crucial, for not only had they allowed their names to be used but they had all promised financial support as well.

This second memorial had too many great names attached to it to be ignored. On 29 July it was referred to the Attorney and Solicitor General to 'examine into ye same together with Proposals or Heads of a Charter as Mr. Coram shall lay before them',[14] and to report back to the committee of the Privy Council. This clearly indicated that Coram still had a great deal of detailed work to do, but unfortunately this coincided

---

[14]   Copy of Privy Council Minute, 29 July 1737: LMA, A/FH/A01/003/001.

with his falling seriously ill. He announced his recovery three months later by writing to Colman to say that he could still walk ten or twelve miles a day, although he had put on weight.

Coram's next difficulty was to find the money to pay for the expense of getting the charter passed. Coram wrote[15] that by employing one of the top attorneys to draw up the heads of agreement he had lost another three months. In spite of being promised 20 guineas, a donation from Eunice's good friend, Anthony Allan's wife, the rich attorney Coram had commissioned neglected the work and when the attorney went out of town he gave the job to one of his clerks. Coram was very displeased, and rejected the clerk's efforts, and had the charter drawn up to his great satisfaction by a person employed by the Attorney General. However, he now discovered that it would cost in excess of £200 to prepare and pass the charter through all the necessary offices, and wrote in frustration to Colman: 'not withstanding it is on so Compassionate a Case, but I am told and do believe, if it was to prevent the abolishing of Christianity out of the World no Lawyer nor Office man would abate his fees'.[16]

Coram had clearly hoped for the Queen's support, and her untimely death was a setback. He wrote to Colman, 'I was in hopes from her late Majesty's so much talked of extensive Goodness and Charity that the Expence of passing a Royal Charter would have been defrayed but I soon found myself Mistaken.'[17] All the indications are that the Queen was indeed interested in Coram's ideas and might well have given him the financial support he so desperately needed. The problem of how to deal with the rising tide of illegitimacy, infant mortality and abandoned foundlings must surely have been discussed with the four Ladies of the Bedchamber who had already signed Coram's petition. The Queen's interest in the subject of bastardy was also kept alive by Richard Savage, the poet she had saved from the gallows, thanks in part to the intervention of Lady Hertford. Having failed to be appointed Poet Laureate, he had cheekily announced that he had appointed himself Queen Caroline's 'Volunteer-Laureat' and would celebrate her verses annually.[18] His poem for 1735 begins:

> In Youth no Parent nurse'd my infant Songs
> 'Twas mine to be inspire'd alone by Wrongs,
> Wrongs, that with Life their fierce Attack began,
> Drank Infant Tears, and still pursued the Man

It continues, almost substituting the 'maternal' Queen for his supposed cruel mother.

> No loss I mourn,
> Though both from Riches and from Grandeur torn.
> Weep I a *cruel Mother*? No – I've seen,
> From Heaven, a pitying, a *maternal Queen*.
> One gave me life; and would no Comfort grant;
> She more than Life resum'd by giving Want.

---

[15] Coram to Colman, 22 September 1738: 'Letters of Thomas Coram', p. 44.
[16] Ibid.
[17] Ibid., p. 43.
[18] Holmes, *Dr Johnson and Mr Savage*, p. 143.

Would she the being which she gave destroy?
My Queen gives life and bids me hope for joy.[19]

Far from ignoring these annual offerings, the Queen gave Savage £50 a year. Well
might Coram have expected financial support from Caroline.

Sometime before her death, the Queen had asked for information about the Paris
Hôpital pour les Enfants Trouvés. But it was only after her death, when the Foundling
Hospital was a reality, that a pamphlet was published in London entitled *An Account of
the Foundation and Government of the Hospital for Foundlings in Paris Drawn up at the
Command of her late Majesty, Queen Caroline.* The preface stated that

> this Account was drawn up at the Command of her late Majesty Queen Caro-
> line; and would have been published, if there had been sufficient Prospect
> that the Design, which was then much thought of, would have succeeded. In
> Her the Hospital for Foundlings has lost a Protectrix and Benefactrix.[20]

From the evidence, it looks as though there was a deliberate attempt to suppress any
knowledge of the Queen's interest in a Foundling Hospital by those who were
opposed to the whole idea and feared the consequences. Only when the establishment of the hospital had become a reality was it deemed helpful to make the Queen's
potential support public.

Coram, having been deprived of the Queen's support, thought that he might
succeed in transferring her interest to her daughter, Princess Amelia. He had chosen
Innocent's Day as appropriate for the purpose.[21] His sad little note recording the
details of this unsuccessful attempt to engage her sympathy is scribbled at the foot of
a copy of the Privy Council minutes of 29 July 1737:

> On Innocent's day, 28th December I went to St James's Palace to present this
> petition, having first been advised to address the lady of the bedchamber to
> introduce it. But the Lady Isabella Finch, who was the lady in waiting gave me
> very rough words and bid me be gone which I did without opportunity of
> presenting it.

His reception at the hands of Lady Isabella Finch lends credence to the suggestion
that there was a faction at court that was wholly opposed to Coram's proposals. He
then hastily copied out his petition by hand and took it to the Princess of Wales,[22]
with the same result. This is hardly surprising since the relationship between the
Queen and her son was one of unmitigated dislike. According to Lord Hervey, the
Queen called her son 'a nauseous beast', and she hoped daily that the ground would
sink him to 'the lowest hole in hell'.[23] The Princess of Wales had recently given birth
to a baby girl, in rather dramatic circumstances, after having been rushed while in
labour from Hampton Court where the court were in residence to St James's Palace so
that her confinement could take place there, without the Queen being present. The

[19] Miscellaneous poems and translations, 'The Volunteer-Laureat', Most humbly inscribed to Her
    MAJESTY on her BIRTH-DAY, Number iv, For the year 1735, pp. 205, 206.
[20] Quoted by McClure, *Coram's Children*, p. 34.
[21] Petition to Princess Amelia: LMA, A/FH/A1/3/1.
[22] Petition to the Princess of Wales: LMA, A/FH/A1/3/1.
[23] Sedgewick, ed., *Memoirs of John, Lord Hervey*, vol. 3, pp. 671–81.

Prince was immediately ordered from the Palace, and the family moved, first to Kew and then to Norfolk House in St James's Square, where Coram must have attempted to present his petition to the Princess. It is little wonder that he had no success. Later, however, the Prince and Princess of Wales showed their support for the Hospital by attending Handel's first concert in 1749, and the Prince contributed to Coram's pension.

To raise the necessary finance and to explain why the charter lay 'fee bound', Coram started to write letters to his supporters. It was no doubt more expensive because Coram, with his usual attention to detail, had insisted upon several amendments which had been opposed by the Attorney General. He had gone over his head to the Privy Council and got the amendments he wanted, but at a price. His letter to the Countess of Huntingdon shows that the Attorney and Solicitor General were going to make him pay for overruling them:

> The expence for Stamps & Fees are so Excessive high That besides the Attorney & solicitor General's fees Several Times wch they had for Examining the Proposals & Making Reports & preparing a draught of the Charter &c. I also paid Seventy one pounds for the said Bill or Charter for the King to signe, & it will Cost much more for that which the Chancelor must fix the Great Seal unto, The Stamps for each of the skins of vellom will be Six pounds, it has already Cost above 150£ for Fees and rewards, wch are unavoidable, to the Several Officers & offices and it requirs much More.[24]

Coram soon found that writing individual letters was too much of a burden, particularly when he received only five guineas from the Lord Mayor of London, an Alderman and the Duke of Bedford. He had five hundred letters printed to circulate to all supporters. Writing that the expense was too great to be borne by the person who had hitherto solicited the affair, he asks all well-disposed persons to assist by their bounty in defraying the said expense.

> Mr Andrew Drummond, Banker at Charing Cross will receive and account for all such Sums as shall be lodged in his Hands at whose House any Benefactor to this laudable Design, will be welcome to be inform'd of the Progress already made in it.[25]

He sent Colman a copy of his letter of appeal but hastened to add that he did not expect any contributions from New England. But to demonstrate the skill with which he targeted likely prospects, Coram recounts that in sending an appeal to a lady in Northamptonshire he enclosed with it a copy of the King's Order in Council in a letter to Lord Vere Beauclerk whom he knew to be staying there with his wife. Lord Vere, a naval officer whom Coram had known for over twenty years, had just become one of the Lords of the Admiralty, but Coram did not know his new rich wife, said to be worth £45,000.[26] His ploy worked. He received £20 each from Lady Vere Beauclerk

---

[24] Thomas Coram to the Countess of Huntingdon, 22 September 1739: Henry E. Huntingdon Library, Hastings Collection.
[25] Letter from Coram addressed to 'Ladys and Gentlemen', 22 September 1738: 'Letters of Thomas Coram', p. 44.
[26] Cokayne, *Complete Peerage*, vol. 12, p. 256.

and her aunt Lady Betty Germain, and both ladies were to remain closely involved with the affairs of the hospital for many years.[27]

Coram told Colman that it had been even more difficult to convince the ladies than it was the gentlemen that his proposed foundation would not promote wickedness.[28] He told of being at dinner with a nobleman and several learned gentlemen, and having heard that the wife of one of them had been left £3,000 to set up a charity school but the parish officers would not accept the money because the interest was insufficient to pay for their dinners. The gentleman had tried to persuade his wife to give the money to the hospital,[29] but she said 'she would by no means encourage so wicked a thing'. Coram then tried to get one of the learned gentlemen to draw up a paper to refute such ideas but they all refused. Not to be thwarted, Coram persuaded Samuel Chandler[30] to write it and print it. Chandler preached at the Old Jury Meeting House, but he had been obliged to open a bookshop because his wife's fortune had been lost in the South Sea Bubble disaster. Coram wrote exultantly that it was printed and sold by a High Church bookseller 'that nobody might know who or what he is that Writ it, it gives great satisfaction'. He also sent a copy to his wife's niece, Mrs Eunice Greenleaf. Coram's letters to Colman show something of the trouble he took to seek out potential rich benefactors, and the ingenious stratagems he devised to counter opposition to his project. It is no wonder that Coram gave great credit to the ladies: not only had they been the first to lend their support, but they were the ones who finally subscribed the major part of the 217 guineas he needed to pass the charter.

However, when the hospital came into being they had little part to play. All the governors were men, and the ladies, unlike Les Dames de Charité in Paris, had no part in the running of the hospital. In a report to the Court of Governors, the General Committee condescendingly notes that

> your committee will always pay due regard to any advice and information which such persons shall give them, either verbally or by letter. And in this method we hope we may receive the assistance of the fair sex, who altho' excluded by custom from the management of Publick Business, are by their natural tenderness and compassion peculiarly enabled to advise in the care and management of children.[31]

Coram's ladies of distinction took no part in the management of the hospital, although Lady Vere was an exception: her advice was sought on several occasions, as later letters to her from the governors show. Draft letters exist asking her advice as to how to persuade a lady of distinction to act as Chief Nurse,[32] and for her help on

---

[27] Both Lady Betty Germain and Lady Vere refused offers to become Chief Nurse in 1752: LMA, A/FH/A06/001/005/09; A/FH/A06/001/005/10.

[28] Coram to Colman, 3 September 1739: 'Letters of Thomas Coram', p. 55.

[29] Ibid., p. 56.

[30] Ibid., note i.

[31] General Court of Governors, 1 October 1740, quoted in Nichols and Wray, *The History of the Foundling Hospital*, p. 29.

[32] August 1752: LMA, A/FH/A06/001/005/10.

approaching the Bishop of Oxford to give a sermon to mark the opening of the chapel.[33]

The King finally signed and sealed the charter of incorporation on 17 October 1739, not for a foundling hospital, but for the Hospital for the Maintenance and Education of Exposed and Deserted Young Children. During the long years when Coram could make no progress with his ideas for rescuing abandoned children he had plenty of opportunities to discuss with those interested in his designs how the hospital might function once it came into being. As far back as 1732 he had asked Newman to write to Sir Erasmus Phillips, who was travelling in Italy, to find out everything possible about the institution for foundlings in Rome.[34] In his usual methodical way he would have studied how the children were received, how their names and identities were recorded, and how the whole enterprise was managed. As he told Colman, even before the charter was signed he had identified

> 34 acres of Land in the fields before Queen's Square in Ormond Street for a Scite for our Hospital and everything proper belonging thereto it is about an equal Distance from Aldgate and from Whitehall or St. James's Palace.[35]

It was in the expectation that as soon as the charter had received royal assent work on the building would begin. It was on this basis that he had raised many promises of financial support. Coram had already seen that there would be need for a seal and at his own expense had had one designed which he proudly presented to the governors at their first meeting. It was a representation of Pharaoh's daughter and her maids finding Moses in the ark of bulrushes 'which I thought would be very appropo for an hospital for Foundlings Moses being the first Foundling we read of'. He must have sought help with the Latin motto, *Sigillum Hospitii Infantum Expositorum Londinensis*, that was inscribed round the seal, which was cut in steel and, as he noted, by a 'good artist'.

Although there are no recorded meetings among the potential governors before 20 November, the day chosen for the public reading of the charter at Somerset House, a number of decisions must already have been taken. There had to be a President to whom Coram could present his charter, and Vice Presidents had to be chosen in advance. The dukes of Richmond and Montagu had already had a long involvement with the plans for the hospital and it is most likely they who approached the young Duke of Bedford and suggested that he become the first President. He had recently remarried and as yet held no office or public appointment. It was said that 'he possessed very exalted ideas of his rank and no very humble ones of his ability . . . the great object of his life was popularity'. Horace Walpole thought he was a man of inflexible honesty and goodwill to his country, 'if he could have thought less of himself the world would probably have thought better of him'.[36] If he was also Coram's choice, Coram could have done a lot worse, for at least he had had the decency to contribute five guineas towards the payment of the legal fees that had been incurred, and he would take the trouble to preside over half a dozen meetings.

[33] October 1752: LMA, A/FH/A06/001/005/14.
[34] Cowie, *Henry Newman*, p. 102.
[35] Coram to Colman, 24 August 1739: 'Letters of Thomas Coram', pp. 53–4.
[36] Cokayne, *Complete Peerage*, vol. 11, p. 83 note a.

The six Vice Presidents must also have been chosen at informal meetings beforehand, as their names were announced at the first meeting of the governors. Micajah Perry, the ex Lord Mayor, had been a supporter, Lord Vere Beauclerk was an old friend of Coram's, and Sir Joseph Eyles, a rich merchant, had given large sums to the Georgia project. Of the other three, Martin Folkes, Peter Burrell and James Cook, Burrell and Cook were both merchants, but Martin Folkes was to be the one most involved with the management of the hospital, and most influential in guiding its policy in its early days. Folkes, who was a good friend of both Richmond and Montagu, had become President of the Society of Antiquaries but quarrelled with Hans Sloane over the presidency of the Royal Society. He was not a man Coram would find it easy to get along with, particularly when both became members of the General Committee.

Coram was now just on seventy; any hope of starting a new life in Nova Scotia had evaporated; his wife was ill and dying. He had worked at great expense to himself, his thoughts and energies concentrated on what he came to call, in a rare expression of tenderness, 'his darling project' for years with no reward. He had had to face strong opposition, at times both vindictive and personal. Until this moment of triumph his had been the mastermind, he was the one who had directed and driven the project as he thought best. After 20 November, when he handed the charter to the Duke of Bedford, he would no longer be in sole charge. Coram had never found it easy to work alongside others. Did he have any misgivings as to what the future might hold?

Somerset House, one of the most influential buildings of the English Renaissance,[37] was a particularly suitable venue for the first meeting of the governors and the public announcement of the new hospital. Built in 1549 and named after its owner, 'Protector' Somerset, after his execution for treason, Somerset House had become a royal palace. There was a fitness about the choice of venue, not only because the Duchess of Somerset had been the first lady to sign Coram's petition, but also because as a royal palace it had associations with many queens. Elizabeth is said to have stayed there, it was settled for life on Queen Henrietta Maria, and was given to Catherine of Braganza as her residence. Was it Coram's idea to use Somerset House for this great occasion as a compliment to the ladies to whom he owed so much? If not, he would certainly have been pleased at the appropriateness of the choice. On Tuesday 20 November *Read's Weekly Journal* announced:

> On Tuesday last was held at Somerset House the first general meeting of the nobility and gentry approved by His Majesty's royal charter to be governors and guardians of the hospital for the maintenance and education of exposed and deserted young children, to hear their charter read, to appoint their committee and a secretary.

On the previous day London had been bedecked with flags, bells were rung and bonfires lit to celebrate the birthday of the Princess of Wales.[38] The next morning the Strand was full of carriages as coachmen jostled to get to the porticoed entrance to Somerset House and into the gracefully arcaded courtyard to set down their noble

---

[37] John Summerson, *Architecture in Britain, 1530–1830*, 4th edn, 1963, p. 16.
[38] *London Daily Post and Advertiser*, 20 November 1739.

masters. Some might have come by water, as on the south side steps led down directly
to the river.

Once all were assembled inside, Coram took the floor. It was his moment of
triumph. In the company of 170 governors, who included six dukes and eleven earls,
Coram read out the words of the charter and then addressed the new President, the
Duke of Bedford, before handing over the document. His speech had been specially
written for him by Jonathan Belcher.[39]

> My Lord, Duke of Bedford,
>
> It is with inexpressible pleasure I now present your grace, at the head of
> this noble and honourable corporation, with his Majesty's royal charter, for
> establishing an Hospital for exposed children, free of all expense, through the
> assistance of some compassionate great ladies and other good persons.
>
> I can, my lord, sincerely aver, that nothing would have induced me to
> embark in a design so full of difficulties and discouragements, but a zeal for
> the service of his Majesty, in preserving the lives of great numbers of his
> innocent subjects.
>
> The long and melancholy experience of this nation has too demonstrably
> shewn, with what barbarity tender infants have been exposed and destroyed,
> for want of proper means of preventing the disgrace, and succouring the
> necessities of their parents.
>
> The charter will disclose the extensive nature and end of this Charity, in
> much stronger terms than I can possibly pretend to describe them, so that I
> have only to thank your Grace and many other noble personages, for all that
> favourable protection which hath given life and spirit to my endeavours.
>
> My Lord, although my declining years will not permit me to hope seeing
> the full accomplishment of my wishes, yet I can now rest satisfied, and is
> what I esteem an ample reward of more than seventeen years' expensive
> labour and steady application, that I see your Grace at the head of this chari-
> table trust, assisted by so many noble and honourable Governors.
>
> Under such powerful influences and directions, I am confident of the final
> success of my endeavours, and that the public will one day reap the happy
> and lasting fruits of your Grace's and this Corporation's measure, and as long
> as my life and poor abilities endure, I shall not abate of my zealous wishes
> and most active services for the good prosperity of this truly noble and
> honourable Corporation.

It was a dignified and moving speech, and reinforced once again the debt Coram felt
he owed to the ladies. He may not have been able to match the melodramatic tones of
Dr Mead, who spoke next and whose speech was described as setting forth 'in the
most pathetic manner the great necessity for such a hospital and the vast advantages
that must accrue to the nation by this useful establishment'.[40] To have the public
endorsement of so eminent a physician would strengthen the governors' hand when
appealing for funds.

The speech-making was followed by the business of the elections, when the offices
of the President and the six Vice Presidents were confirmed. Lewis Way was

39 Compston, *Thomas Coram*, pp. 98–9.
40 *Read's Weekly Journal*, 20–22 November 1739; *London Evening Post*, 20 November 1739.

appointed Treasurer and Harman Verelst, who had been Secretary of the Georgia project and was Coram's choice, as Secretary. The remainder of the General Committee, who were appointed to serve until the second Wednesday of the following May, included the dukes of Richmond, Montagu, and Portland, the earls of Chesterfield, Cholmondeley, Findlater and Abercorn, Viscount Torrington and Lords Gower, de la Warr, Lovel, Vere Beauclerk and the Speaker of the House of Commons, Arthur Onslow. It was not, however, these men, apart from Vere Beauclerk, who would show any lasting involvement with the affairs of the hospital, but rather the middle class professionals elected to bring the number of governors to fifty. Richard Mead, Hans Sloane, Robert Nesbitt and Edward Wilmot were doctors, and Peter Sainthill a surgeon. Besides merchants, there was a banker, Sir Joseph Hankey, and Theodore Jacobsen, a merchant but also a gentleman architect.[41]

This was the moment of Coram's greatest triumph, but probably his overwhelming feeling would have been one of simple satisfaction. Hogarth, although not among the first fifty governors to be elected, was at the meeting in Somerset House and was one of the gentlemen named in the charter. His admiration for Coram and his support for the objects of the hospital were to be of the greatest importance in the future. Was it at that gathering at Somerset House that Hogarth decided to paint Coram's portrait? Was he inspired by the sight of Coram, small, stout and unpretentious as far as outward appearance went, standing there among that great gathering of the rich and powerful, dressed in his red coat, with no wig (the outward sign of a gentleman), yet dominating his surroundings by force of character? His great portrait is not only a brilliant tribute to an ordinary man; it also captures the look of a man, slightly discomforted at being painted amid the trappings usually associated with the wealthy; it also reflects something of the quiet satisfaction that Coram must have felt on that occasion when he knew that, after such a long struggle, he had at last brought about a public acceptance that there needed to be a change in the way the human casualties of society were treated.

---

[41] The complete list of governors as given in *Read's Weekly Journal*, 20–22 November 1739, apart from the officers already mentioned, included Sir James Lowther, Paul Methuen, Benjamin Avery LDD, James Brudenell, William Fawkener, Richard Hollings, John Hollister, Thomas Hucks, John Milner, Col. J. Mordaunt, Nathaniel Paice, Walter Plummer, Henry Spencer, James Vernon, Anthony Warburg, Edward Walpole, George Arnold, Roger Drake, William Wollaston, Nathaniel Newham and James Marin.

11

'My Darling Project'

A notice had appeared in the *Gentleman's Magazine* on 25 November 1739 duly announcing the passing of the royal charter and great seal,

> to incorporate Charles, Duke of Richmond and several other great officers and ministers of state and their successors into one body politic and corporate, by the name of governors and guardians of the hospital for the maintenance and education of deserted and exposed young children, with powers to purchase lands and mortmain not exceeding yearly value of £4,000.[1]

The governors lost no time in setting about their task. Four days later, on Monday 29 November, thirty-one of the fifty governors elected as members of the General Committee to carry on the business of the hospital met at Mr Manaton's Great Rooms at the Crown and Anchor in the Strand, the Duke of Bedford presiding. Coram proudly presented a pattern of the seal he had had made, and the governors approved the design. The charter had made specific mention of the fact that France, Holland and other Christian countries already had hospitals for foundlings. The Secretary was instructed to write to the ambassadors and ministers in Paris, Florence, Venice, Turin and Holland, asking them to forward any information they could gather as to how the authorities in those cities cared for their foundlings. There was no answer from the Ospedale degli Innocenti, whose graceful building adorned with Della Robbia's blue and white frieze of swaddled babies reminded the citizens of Florence of their obligations to abandoned children, nor from Venice where the children were trained as choristers. But Paris and Amsterdam responded and by February 1740 a Mémoire concernant les Enfants Trouvés de la Ville de Paris was received, followed by one from the city of Amsterdam.[2] The documents were ordered to be translated so that they could be studied, and both the originals and the translations form part of the Foundling Hospital records.

Martin Folkes acquainted the governors with the offer from the Duke of Montagu to lease his house in Great Russell Street for £400 a year. It would have suited the duke to have the house taken off his hands. It may have seemed a generous gesture, but the duke was living comfortably at 6 Privy Gardens and was the owner of

---

1 *Gentleman's Magazine*, vol. 9, 25 January 1739, p. 552.
2 LMA, A/FH/A1/4/1.

Boughton, so the house was more of a burden than a pleasure. His father had spent the better part of his income building it, and it was described in 1736 as

> being ridiculously esteemed as one of the most beautiful buildings about town. I must own it is grand and expensive, will admit of very noble ranges of apartments within, and fully answers all the dignity of a British nobleman of the first rank; but after I have allowed this, I must add that the entrance to the court-yard is mean and Gothic(!), more like the portal of a monastery than the gate of a palace.[3]

The walls and ceilings of the great rooms were richly painted, the subjects generally being of pagan gods and goddesses, not, it might be thought, the most suitable subjects for the decoration of a home for destitute children, but more to the taste of Folkes.

In seeking support for the hospital, Coram had asked for and received many promises of benefactions and legacies. The Treasurer was instructed to apply to 'executors or trustees of persons who have left or shall leave legacies to this charity to receive the same', making use of Coram's subscription books. To ensure no possible source of financial assistance was lost the governors decided to advertise in the *Daily Advertiser* and other newspapers. Money to finance the activities of the hospital would always be of concern, and particularly so at this time. Coram must have been greatly pleased to see the promises he had received begin to materialise, as when the estate of Josiah Wordsworth paid the £500 he had promised ten years earlier. Several of Coram's ladies of charity continued to support the hospital: the duchesses of Richmond, Somerset, and Bedford subscribed ten guineas a year and Lady Betty Germain not only gave a regular subscription, she also subscribed £500 to the building fund in 1741.

Coram, an essentially practical man, knew from the start that the duke's apparently generous offer was a mere distraction; he resented the time the governors took to consider the proposal and knew that it would affect donations to the hospital. He wrote crossly to Colman

> We had an Offer made to lett us Montague House by Lease for an Hospital but that could not be accepted. Yet that offer Hurted the Charity very Much ... Benefactions are at a Stand because we have not began to Build yet which I think we should have done before now.[4]

Since the duke was a friend of most of the governors they had no option but to take the offer seriously, and they engaged a surveyor, Mr Sanderson, to inspect the house and prepare plans. But they too must have had their doubts as to the suitability of the building, for at the same time they asked Coram, possibly at his prompting, to find out from the Earl of Salisbury what price he would ask for his land adjoining Queen's Square. Coram, it will be remembered, had already told Colman that he thought he could have thirty-four acres near Queen's Square on which to build.

Coram together with Mr Fawkener, one of the governors, and Lewis Way, the

[3] Strype, *New Critical Review of the Public Buildings of London*, 1736, quoted in Walford, *London Old and New*, vol. 4, p. 491.
[4] Coram to Colman, 13 September 1740: 'Letters of Thomas Coram', p. 55.

Treasurer, had visited the earl's agent, Mr Lamb, and came to the meeting on 25 January with the information that the earl would only sell the land if a foundling hospital were built on it, and then he would not charge more than the going rate for land outside London. On the same day Sanderson reported that it would cost £2,005 10s 8d to repair Montagu House, making the duke's wish to hand over the house even more understandable. It would cost a further £660 to convert it into a hospital. However, his estimate for a new building of comparable size came out at £10,000 plus the expense of paving, fences and drains, a sum that shocked the governors who promptly resolved, mindful of their limited funds, not to engage in building at present, a decision that dismayed Coram. It was not only that Coram was an old man and not unnaturally impatient, although he made it clear that he did not expect to see the fulfilment of his wishes in his lifetime; what he feared most was that benefactions would fall off if the governors did not start building and there was nothing to excite the public's interest and stimulate their generosity. Two weeks later the Attorney General and the Solicitor General informed the committee that since the Duke of Montagu was only a life tenant he was not empowered legally to permit alterations to the building that would change its use from that of a residence to a hospital. This ruling was reinforced by the fear that a Court of Equity might consider the alterations as waste and prohibit them by injunction. The duke was left with his unwanted house and the governors and Coram could turn their attention to other options.

Five years after the duke's death in 1749 the house was bought from his two daughters by the British government to house the treasures left to the nation by Sir Hans Sloane as well as Lord Oxford's Harleian library of manuscripts and the Cottonian library, which together formed the nucleus of the British Museum.[5] An Act of Parliament was passed in 1754 vesting Montagu House in trustees, enabling them to convey it to the trustees of the British Museum. Sloane's splendid collection of objects of natural history, books, manuscripts and medals was preserved for the nation. While some of members of the public were visiting the splendidly decorated Foundling Hospital and watching the children at play, others went to Great Russell Street to admire the grand staircase at Montagu House and to view, among other curiosities, the stuffed stag in the hall and three stuffed giraffes on the first floor.[6]

The governors in the meantime had other worries to contend with. Despite all Coram's patient and careful thought, the charter was soon discovered to lack some necessary powers, particularly in relation to certain of the Poor Law regulations. To amend the charter an Act of Parliament was required, and it was not until April 1740 that the Act received the King's assent. Coram must have been rather vexed to think that he had not succeeded in finalising arrangements for the organisation, despite his triumphing over the Attorney General. The Act, which Coram asserts he procured to confirm and enlarge the powers in the charter,[7] cleared up various ambiguities, confirmed the hospital's right to purchase lands not exceeding £4,000, and gave the

5   The government raised £100,000 by lottery to purchase Montagu House and the collections. The house was demolished between 1845 and 1849; the present building was started by Sir Robert Smirke, continued by his brother Sydney, and opened to the public on 15 January 1859.
6   Description taken from a print entitled 'Montagu House, Grand Staircase', in Walford, London Old and New, vol. 4, p. 492.
7   Coram to Colman, 13 September 1740: 'Letters of Thomas Coram', p. 55.

governors the right to sue and be sued. Details concerning dates of meetings and the constitution and rights of the various committees were laid down and anyone paying more than £10 to £40 a year was given the right to inspect the hospital. Most importantly, the Act provided that no child or employee of the hospital was entitled to a settlement in the parish where the hospital was located. The governors were given the right to apprentice children and to receive the profits from their work; they could also punish them for idleness, disobedience or misbehaviour. This was not unreasonable, but the children were now entirely under the control of the governors and it was up to the governors to see that their powers over the lives of the children were not abused.

It was while all this was taking place that Hogarth persuaded Coram to sit for him in his house in Leicester Square. Had Hogarth not recognised that a portrait of Coram might give him a priceless opportunity to display his talents as a portrait painter in an entirely novel way, we would not know what Coram looked like, for there are no descriptions of him.[8] Hogarth's first contribution in kind to the hospital was a design for a headpiece for the official fundraising letter, which must have been drawn soon after the meeting in Somerset House. Hogarth's design shows Coram as an old man with long hair, dressed in a loose robe, looking rather like Moses when he came down from the mountain with the tablets of stone, but, instead of the ten commandments, the imposing document under his arm is inscribed in large letters with the words, The Royal Charter. He is looking at a mother, on her knees sobbing, who has just abandoned her infant; the baby, naked and sprawling, lies helpless in the ditch, rather like the baby in his later, famous and much-copied drawing of the baby falling from the lap of its gin-drinking mother. Instead of a mother stupified by gin, in this picture, a dagger lies in front of the woman, a mute witness to her utter despair. The kindly old gentleman is pointing to the house ahead. Behind him a woman is surreptitiously hiding a baby in some bushes while beside him a beadle is carrying a naked infant towards the sanctuary of the house.

Girls and boys are gathered outside, the tools of their future occupations in their hands. A group of boys look towards the sea where two ships are riding at anchor, others destined for the land hold a rake and sickle, while two more hold a trowel and plumb line, tools of the building trade. There is little choice for the girls, one grasping a broom and another a spinning wheel; they will become servants to the wealthy. That the enterprise will be conducted in a spirit of Christian kindness and affection is symbolised by the distant church and a woman hugging one of the children on the

---

8   There is a portrait entitled 'Thomas Coram' in the National Portrait Gallery. It is of a younger man and bears a passing resemblance to Coram but has never been authenticated by the gallery. The gallery's catalogue description states 'own thick iron grey hair, shaded dark sepia, greying eyebrows, dark eyes, no lashes, grey coat, plain white steinkerk with lace, ends brown, grey background; painted oval'. The steinkerk, a cravat twisted and thrust in the sixth buttonhole down, was in memory of the way in which French officers, surprised by the Dutch at Steinkerk, hastily tied their cravats. Cravats thus tied indicated dislike of the French and were nearly always worn by military men – an additional reason for not accepting the portrait as being of Coram. It was in the possession of Miss Dora Brownlow King. She and Johanna Brownlow equated it with the portrait said to be of Coram belonging to Dr Mead. Stated to have been bought in 1841 by Charles Pott, governor of the Foundling Hospital, given to his successor John Brownlow and thereafter by descent. Information from the National Portrait Gallery catalogue, John Kerslake, *Early Georgian Portraits*, 1977, pp. 61–3.

To all to whom these Presents shall come.

Whereas our Sovereign Lord the King hath been graciously pleased to take into His Princely and tender Consideration the deplorable Case of great Numbers of Newborn Children daily exposed to Destruction, by the cruelty or poverty of their Parents, and having by His **Royal Charter** bearing date the 17th day of October 1739, constituted a Body Politick and Corporate, by the Name of The Governors and Guardians of the Hospital for the Maintenance and Education of exposed and deserted young Children; which Corporation is fully impowered to receive & apply the Charities of all compassionate Persons who shall contribute towards erecting & establishing the same. And Whereas His Majesty for the better & more successful carrying on the said good Purposes, Hath by His said **Charter** granted to the said Corporation and their Successors full & ample Power to authorize such Persons as they shall think fit to take Subscriptions, and to ask and receive of all or any of His Majesty's good Subjects, such Monies as shall by any Person or Persons, Bodies Politick and Corporate, Companies and other Societies be contributed and given for the Purposes aforesaid. Now know Ye that We the said Governors & Guardians being well assur'd of the great Charity & Integrity of
and that
greatly desire the Success & Accomplishment of so excellent a Work, Have by Virtue of the said Power granted to Us, authorized & appointed, and by these Presents Do authorize & appoint the said to take Subscriptions and to receive gather & collect such Monies as shall by any Person or Persons, Bodies Politick & Corporate, Companies & other Societies, be contributed & given for the Purposes aforesaid, and to transmit with all convenient speed, the Monies so Collected and Received, into the Bank of England for the use of this Corporation, And the Receipt for the same to our Treasurer for the time being, Together with the Names of the Contributors, except such as shall desire to be concealed, and in that Case to insert the Sums only, in order that We the said Governors & Guardians may be enabled from time to time to Publish perfect Accounts of such Benefactions. Given under our Common Seal the Day of 17

By Order of the said Governors & Guardians.

5. Letter, with the heading designed by Hogarth, authorising the collection of subscriptions in aid of the hospital.

steps of the house. Hogarth had encapsulated in one small drawing Coram's vision of the future.

It was during the bitterly cold winter of 1739/40, while the idea of a hospital for foundlings was newly fashionable and with the Somerset House meeting fresh in his mind, that Hogarth persuaded Coram to sit for him in his house in Leicester Square. Hogarth had been infuriated by the way in which foreign painters like Van Dyke and Van Loo had monopolised the fashionable market for portraits. He wanted to demonstrate that English painters had as great a talent and a right to be considered their equals. With his keen eye for people and his ability to highlight society's absurdities and hypocrisies, he admired Coram's honest and straightforward approach to the problem of caring for destitute children. Both men had had difficult childhoods, and had been brought up in poverty. Hogarth's father had fallen into debt, Coram's father had been unable to maintain a home for his son, so they both had needed to be tough to survive. The relationship between Hogarth and Coram as they talked together during the sittings would have been based on mutual respect and understanding.

Hogarth wanted to make society accept that he was as skilled a painter as any foreign-trained artist from Europe. He had watched Coram holding the floor surrounded by the nobility and gentry in their fine clothes and elaborate wigs. In an act of bravado he chose Coram to be his sitter for this demonstration of his art, and he chose to give him the same grand setting he would have given to anyone of the gentlemen present at Somerset House. The empathy that must have existed between them enabled Hogarth, who was working on the largest canvas he had ever used for a portrait,[9] to produce a picture of stunning originality and dramatic impact. He painted Coram as he always was, a simple man with no pretensions to grandeur surrounded by symbols normally reserved for royalty and the wealthy, the classical column and in the background the draped curtain, with a faint outline of the figure of charity, giving formality to the design. On a table beside him the royal charter tumbles in creases out of its case, Coram gently holding the seal he had designed. On the little finger of his left hand is a gold ring, his only concession to extravagance; otherwise the serviceable great red coat, the black undercoat half unbuttoned, the untidy cravat, the thick gloves, all are workaday clothes unlike the velvets and silks of Hogarth's usual sitters. The normal wig, the sign of a gentleman, is absent. Hogarth painted Coram with his own abundant white hair framing his face. At Coram's feet a globe, turned to show the Western or Atlantic Ocean, its lowly place a reminder of his lost hopes of returning to America. Beside his right foot the large beaver tricorn propped against the table, his gift from the Hatters. The reflection of a window on the globe, near the American seaboard, its bars forming a cross, is emblematic of the church he had hoped to establish in Taunton and of his links with the SPCK. Coram himself sits somewhat awkwardly in a leather backed chair, his feet scarcely reaching the ground, with the air of a man not quite at ease in such surroundings, but at the same time his expression one of quiet satisfaction at all he had achieved. If one of Hogarth's aims was also to fulfil Richardon's aim for a portrait, that men should be 'excited to imitate the Good Actions . . . of those whose Examples are thus set before

---

[9]   Uglow, *Hogarth: A Life and a World*, p. 333.

them',[10] the portrait triumphantly succeeds. As one of Hogarth's admirers commented, 'there is a natural dignity and great benevolence expressed in the face, which in the original is tough and forbidding'.[11]

Seven years later the young Allan Ramsay painted a portrait of Dr Richard Mead, perhaps to challenge Hogarth's portrait of Coram. Mead sits in a similar pose, surrounded by bolder classical symbols; the draped curtain is red with a tassel, the background features, a classical statue of a woman, a reminder of Mead's antiquarian interests. Mead sits, his great wig in place, magisterially clad in a sweeping black gown open to show the rich brown velvet and silk coat beneath, his cravat and ruffled cuffs made of finest linen, the picture of confident affluence. Splendid though the painting is, it is, in a sense, just one of many such portraits, while that of Coram, while it may not have brought Hogarth the renown and the commissions he hoped for, with its exuberant swagger and charitable associations, is not only memorable, it has achieved iconic status. Both now hang in the Foundling Museum.

Hogarth presented his portrait to the governors at their May meeting, but as they had as yet nowhere to hang it, it seems likely that he returned the picture to his studio, because he later presented the frame as a gift in 1741 when the governors had leased a house in Hatton Garden as a temporary measure to allow them to start work. Hogarth later wrote in his autobiography:

> The portrait that I painted with most pleasure and in which I particularly wished to excel was that of Captain Coram for the Foundling Hospital; and if I am so wretched an artist as my enemies assert, it is wonderful strange that this, which was one the first I painted the size of life, should stand the test of twenty years competition and be generally thought the best portrait in the place, notwithstanding the best artists in the Kingdom executed all her talents to vie with it.[12]

He was more right than he knew.

Money was beginning to accumulate and Coram wrote triumphantly in the summer of 1740 to Colman that 'We have between 5 and 6000 pounds in cash paid in, 323 annual Subscriptions and £2300 in legacies not yet received.' The Treasurer had been able to invest £3,000 in New South Sea Annuities in May. That month a special committee of six governors was set up to study the information received from Paris, Amsterdam and Lisbon so that a plan could be prepared. Coram was not included. The committee worked hard and presented a lengthy document divided into twelve chapters to the court meeting in October. They decided that sixty children were all that they could cope with in the first instance, and even that would demand the greatest frugality. They recognised that the health of the children would depend on the quality of care given by the nurses and arranged for a rota of governors to inspect their behaviour.

No child who was over two months or had the French pox, evil,[13] leprosy or disease of like nature would be admitted. Every child would be inspected by the Chief

---

[10] Jonathan Richardon, *The Theory of Painting*, p. 8, quoted in Uglow, *Hogarth: A Life and a World*, p. 334.
[11] Nichols, ed., *Anecdotes of William Hogarth*, p. 379.
[12] Ibid., p. 21.
[13] The king's evil was scrofula and the queen's evil was venereal disease.

Nurse. The Steward was to write down the sex, supposed age, date and hour when the child was brought in together with a description of the child, noting any marks on its body and the child's dress. Particular mention was also to be made of any writing or other thing brought with the child. The Steward was to seal up and number each sheet of paper. He was then to see that the same number was attached by a piece of tape to the child's body, sealing the knot of the tape to prevent it being taken off. The French Foundling Hospital had been using a similar method to keep track of its children, and doubtless the governors made use of their experience.

The governors accepted that it would be better for the children who needed suckling to be reared in the country during their first three years, so they started to enquire as to what parts of England would afford healthy nurses and what their salaries should be. They needed to know how much would be demanded for the maintenance of a healthy child. At the same time that they were engaged in formulating their plans, they were also looking for suitable temporary accommodation in which to start work admitting foundlings. The governors were sent particulars of many unsuitable houses but finally John Milner learned of a house in Hatton Garden that seemed to answer the requirements. The house, formerly occupied by the late Sir Fisher Tench, had four rooms, a second floor reached by two staircases and a yard at the back. Coram had already discovered that the agent, Mr Burnwood, had died, and had arranged for Mr Bincks, his successor, to meet with the governors. By 13 December the committee had completed all the negotiations and the house in Hatton Garden was leased for six years at a rental of £48 a year. Coram was one of the four governors who signed the lease and he signed with a great flourish, with a large strong curling initial C, as if to mark his pleasure at the progress so far made.

In the meantime, the governors had been negotiating in June with Lamb, Salisbury's agent, for the land on which they hoped to build the hospital. Coram, Fawkener and the Treasurer had been empowered to continue negotiations with Lamb for the land. Coram, impatient at not having been able to arrange a meeting with the other two governors, who were away in the country, went ahead and met Lamb and reported back to the general committee that Salisbury would only sell all four fields and not the two the governors wanted to buy. Folkes was in the chair and snubbed Coram by resolving that the matter 'would be referred to Fawkener and the Treasurer so that they could join with Mr. Coram'.[14] When Coram presented the report in July with Fawkener and Way it was no different, and Coram was asked to thank Lord Salisbury and to ask leave to approach him when they were ready to build, Folkes no doubt satisfied at having put Coram in his place. The governors decided they had no option but to buy the entire property and offered £6,500 for all five fields. Salisbury demanded £7,000 but generously agreed to donate the other £500, and the governors authorised the purchase of all fifty-six acres of land on 17 October 1740, the first anniversary of the hospital's first charter. A subscription book was immediately opened to raise funds.

The governors now had to get down to practical details, and decided that a messenger and a housemaid must be employed to live in the house at Hatton Garden. They began to advertise for staff and decided they should be appointed by

14 LMA, General Committee Minutes, 25 June 1740.

ballot. A committee was set up to consider furnishings for the house and it is pleasing
to see that the first two items to be ordered were a screwpress at £4 4s to impress
Coram's corporation seal, and a lock for the table of the screw press at £3 13s.[15] The
committee had to consider what clothing they needed to order for each child and,
doubtless advised by a Mrs Anne Hollings, who attended with samples of linen and
clothing, they ordered her to make samples and if approved to make up sixty
bundles. With no ladies to advise, the governors must have found it a novel experience ordering for each new born child such items as 4 biggens, 4 long stays, 2 caps, 4
neckcloths, 4 shirts, 12 clouts (nappies) as well as grey linsey mantles with grey linsey
sleeves. By February the first appointments were made. Edward Swift and Margaret
Shepperd were appointed Steward and Chief Nurse respectively. The diet for the staff
was generous. They were to have meat every day, roast three times a week with
greens and vegetables, boiled beef and stewed beef with vegetables on the other days,
and the allowance was set at a weight of one pound each day.

There was now so much to be decided that the governors resolved to meet every
Wednesday and Saturday without further notice. This was a lot to ask of governors
and on occasion there were not enough governors present to make a quorum, but
Coram never missed a meeting. It was decided that in addition there should be a rota
of daily visiting governors. An early bylaw had proposed that

> twelve or more Ladies or other Gentlewomen of Good and Benevolent dispo-
> sitions, Circumstances and Characters be Annually requested by the General
> Court to inspect the Behaviour of the Matron, Nurses and other female
> Servants of this Corporation.[16]

Nothing came of this suggestion. In the Paris Hospital the ladies were actively
involved in its administration but in England no lady would have accepted the invitation even had it been offered. The governors, all men, took upon themselves the
responsibility for the welfare of the new born infants. Dr Mead and Dr Nesbitt were
asked to inform the committee as to the medicines that needed to be stocked. A
cowkeeper, servant to Lord Salisbury, was to attend to provide fresh milk, and coals
were ordered. Coram reported to the committee that the Rev. Mr Smith of All
Hallows had offered to attend gratis every Sunday for the first six months to baptise
the children. Perhaps to make amends for the way in which Coram had so often been
excluded from the decision-making process, it was resolved that the first boy to be
baptised was to be called Thomas Coram and the first girl to be named Eunice Coram.
Coram sent a prayer book, one of several given him in 1736 by the Speaker, Arthur
Onslow.[17] Hogarth gave a specially painted shield to hang over the doorway, which
unfortunately has not survived.

Coram was not included among the governors who were to meet at Taylor White's
house to plan how the announcement that children would be received at the hospital
was to be worded. The time and date had been fixed for eight o'clock on 25 March

15   LMA, A/FH/B1/01/1, Furniture Register.
16   LMA, General Committee Minutes, 20 June 1740.
17   Coram is also recorded as having presented other prayer books given by the Speaker to churches in New
     England, including St Thomas's church in Taunton.

1741. On 4 March the advertisement was approved by the General Committee. The governors' notice reads:

> On Wednesday 25th of this instant March at eight at night and from that time until the house is full, their house over against the charity school in Hatton Garden will be open for children under the following regulations; that no child exceed in age two months nor shall have French Pox or disease of like nature; all children to be inspected and the person who brings it to come in at the outer door and not to go away until the child is returned or notice given of its reception. No question asked whatsoever of any person who brings a child, nor shall any servant of the Hospital presume to enquire on pain of being dismissed. . . . The narrow circumstances of the Hospital confining governors to a limited number, that everyone may know when such numbers shall be completed, a notice will be posted that the house is full. If any particular marks are left with the child great care will be taken for their preservation. Each child will be baptised Church of England by a minister of the church unless such child has already been baptised.[18]

The governors seem not to have complied with this last assurance. The mothers of some of the children had left little notes with their child, asking that the child be given a specific name and sometimes stating that it had been baptised.[19] In the early days, as soon as the child was admitted, both notes and a detailed description of the child were immediately sealed up by the Steward. As a result of this system, devised to protect the identity of the mother, the mother's wishes as to the naming of her child were never seen by the governors. The children were all baptised, whether they had already been received into the Church or not, and given names chosen by the governors. The governors had, however, recognised that it would be easier for the women to come under cover of darkness, and on the night the first children were admitted the lights were extinguished outside to preserve the mothers' anonymity.

The vestrymen of the parish of St Andrew were becoming increasingly fearful that the children who had been rejected might be dropped by the mothers and become a charge on the parish. There were several conferences between the vestrymen and the governors, and during the afternoon of 25 March it was decided that the overseer of the poor, two watchmen and two constables would be waiting at eight o'clock and a signal would be given by the Steward when any child was returned. With the appointment of two more dry nurses, all the preparations were complete. By seven o'clock on that important occasion, ten governors waited in the inner room for the admission of the first infants. The Duke of Richmond was there, together with Lewis Way, Theodore Jacobsen, Taylor White, William Hogarth, Samuel Skinner, Peter Godfrey, Robert Nesbitt, Robert Hudson, and Coram. For Coram, this must have been a moment of high emotion. Twenty years had passed since he had first started his campaign. He must have felt pleasure and satisfaction that at last his dream had come true, impatient, perhaps, that more had not been accomplished. But overall he must have had an immense sense of relief, that, after all the setbacks and difficulties that he had had to contend with, his 'darling project' was at last a reality, and that exposed

---

[18]   LMA, General Committee Minutes, 4 March 1742.
[19]   Notes of tokens are among the records of the Foundling Hospital: LMA, A/FH/M01/008/015/24.

and deserted infants had somewhere to be cared for and educated, although their place in society was carefully circumscribed by the governors.

Under the general plan set out by the governors, when the children were returned from the country after three years, they were to be taught reading but not writing, so that they did not get ideas above their station. There was no doubt as to the expectations that the governors had as to their future. The children were to

> learn to undergo with Contentment the most Servile and laborious Offices; for notwithstanding the innocence of the Children, yet as they are exposed and abandoned by their parents, they ought to submit to the lowest stations, and should not be educated in such a manner as may put them upon a level with Children of Parents who have the Humanity and Virtue to preserve them and the Industry to Support them.

It is impossible to imagine that Coram, who knew all too well the problems of a deficient education, and had always been a champion of the poor and oppressed, could have been happy with this edict. Coram had not been included among those chosen to work on the plan. His exclusion may well have been because the governors were aware of his opinions on such matters and did not wish to discuss it with him. This policy may also have been one of the proposals alluded to in his will by Anthony Allan, Coram's friend, who wrote that Coram had had differences of opinion with the governors and that he agreed with Coram's judgements, stating that 'the governors and guardians went counter to our judgements and proposals pressed on them by the said Coram'.[20] The governors, aware that the Foundling Hospital was not without its critics, may have felt that by making plain their intentions they were meeting the objection that the 'undeserving' were benefiting at the expense of the deserving poor, terms not so much in use then as a century later, but whose meaning would have been well understood.

The minutes of the daily committee provide such a vivid description of the actual events that took place, noting the distress and anguish of the mothers as they brought their babies to the door that first evening, that the account is best given as it was written:

> The Committee met at 7 o'clock in the Evening. They found a great number of People crowding about the door, many with Children and others for Curiosity. The Committee were informed that several Persons had offer'd children, but had been refused admittance. The Order of the Gen'l Committee being that the House sho'd not be opened till Eight o'Clock at Night. And this Committee was resolved to give no Preference to any person whatsoever. . . . At Eight o'clock the Lights in the Entry were Extinguished, the outward Door was opened by the Porter, who was forced to attend at that Door all night to keep out the Crowd. Immediately the Bell rung and a Woman brought in a Child. The Messenger let her into the Room on the Right hand, and carried the child into the Steward's Room where the proper Officers together with Dr. Nesbitt and some other Govrs. were constantly attending to inspect the Child according to the Directions of the Plan. The child being inspected was received, Numbered and the Billet of its Discription enter'd by

---

[20] Extract of the will of Anthony Allan, 1753, quoted in Brownlow, *History of the Foundling Hospital*, p. 9.

three different Persons for greater Certainty. The Woman who brought the Child was dismissed without being seen by any of the Govrs. Or asked any questions whatsoever. Immediately another child was brought and so continually till 30 children were admitted 18 of whom were Boys and 12 Girls being the number the House is capable of containing. Two children were refused, one being too old and the other appearing to have the Itch.

About twelve o'Clock, the House being full the Porter was Order'd to give Notice of it to the Crowd who were without, who thereupon being a little troublesom One of the Govrs. Went out, and told them that as many Children were already taken in as Cou'd be made Room for in the House and that Notice shou'd be given by Publick Advertisement as soon as any more Could possibly be admitted. And the Govrs observing seven or eight women with Children at the Door and more amongst the Crowd desired them that they wou'd not Drop any of their Children in the Streets where they most probably must Perish but take care of them till they could have an opportunity of putting them into the Hospital which was hoped would be very soon and that every Body would immediately leave the Hospital without making any Disturbance which was immediately complied with great Decency, so that in two minutes there was not a Person to be seen in the Street except the Watch. On this Occasion the Expressions of Grief of the Women whose Children could not be admitted were Scarcely more observable than those of some of the Women who parted with their Children, so that a more moving Scene can't well be imagined.

All the Children who were received (except three) were dressed very clean from whence and other Circumstances they appeared not to have been under the care of the Parish officers, nevertheless many of them appeared as if Stupified with some Opiate, and some of them almost Starved, or as in the agonies of Death thro' want of Food, too weak to Suck, or to receive Nourishment, and notwithstanding the greatest care appeared to be dying when the Govrs. left the Hospital which was not till they had given proper Orders and seen all necessary Care taken of the children.[21]

The record continued:

the next day many Charitable Persons of Fassion visited the Hospital, and whatever Share Curiosity might have in inducing any of them to come, none went away without shewing the most Sensible Marks of Compassion for the helpless Objects of this Charity and few (if any) without contributing something for their Relief.[22]

The scene the following day must have been fairly chaotic, with the nurses trying to cope with the babies, some of whom were obviously terminally ill, indeed two died the following day, and the fashionable crowd milling around, many of them curious to see for themselves infants whose previously disregarded lives had suddenly been given new hope. The governors, now desperate to keep up charitable donations, hoped that the sight of these helpless infants would induce more than feelings of compassion, and would translate into financial support. By Saturday, two of the

---

[21] LMA, A/FH/A03/004/001, Daily Committee Minutes, 25 March–22 June 1741, pp. 6–7.
[22] Ibid., p. 9.

babies had to be buried at St Andrews, Holborn, and the baptism of a third brought forward, and the Chief Nurse had been dismissed.

The first service of baptism, conducted by the Rev. Mr Smith and held that Sunday, attracted a record number of 'Persons of Quality and Distinction', something that would become a regular feature at the hospital in the early days. The Duke of Bedford, the Duke and Duchess of Richmond, their daughter Lady Caroline Lennox, and the Earl and Countess of Pembroke, Lord and Lady Albermarle and the Hogarths were among those present, and gave their names to some of the foundlings. Both little Sarah and Charles Richmond survived, as did baby William Hogarth, and they were apprenticed in 1754, 1753 and 1755 respectively.[23] Later, some of the persons of quality and distinction were to find that this lending of their names had become embarrassing, a number of the children, when they grew up, claiming to be related to their namesakes. The practice was to be abandoned, and children were named, for a time, after historical figures, poets and writers.

In conformity with the governors' wishes, the first and second children to be baptised were duly christened Thomas and Eunice Coram. Rather touchingly, both these infants received presents from an anonymous donor. Perhaps it was Mrs Anthony Allan, who sent 'some old fine linen, 2 coral necklaces and two corals set in silver for baby Thomas Coram and Eunice Coram'.[24] 'The first child taken in was a baby boy about a fortnight old, cleanly dressed, wrapped in a red cloak which was returned. It was delivered to nurse Webb and numbered 18 in the general register.'[25] Sadly he did not live long. Coram, the man who had no children of his own, must have felt a tender concern for the infant Thomas who bore his name, and sorrow that his wife was not there to see the baby called after her. The little girl christened Eunice Coram lived long enough to be sent to Yorkshire to be cared for by a wet nurse. She died a month later and was buried in Yorkshire. The governors had to pay 13s 9d for her burial, a double expense because there were two sets of fees to be paid. So stretched were the hospital's finances that the governors seriously considered whether in future the little corpses of those who died in the country outside their parish boundary should be sent back for burial to save expense.

A second baby was christened Thomas Coram the following April. This child survived and was one of the first boys to be apprenticed. Fittingly, he was bound apprentice to a shipbuilder, Henry Bird of Rotherhithe, for sea service, as were a majority of the boys. All that is known about him is that he started his apprenticeship on 15 May 1753, but, unlike all the other boys, Thomas was given 40 shillings, to be returned at the end of his apprenticeship. It is more than likely that this lad was one of Coram's many godsons, and possibly the old gentleman was taking a godfatherly interest in his namesake and left instructions that he was to be given an incentive to do well. Morris Lievesley,[26] writing long after the event, is not a reliable source, but it would make for a happy outcome if his story that the apprentice Coram did well in later life, visiting the Hospital, riding in his carriage, were true. Coram is also known

---

[23]   LMA, A/FH/A09/001, Billet Book, Admission Numbers 1741, March–May.
[24]   LMA, General Committee Minutes, 2 April 1741.
[25]   Ibid.
[26]   LMA, A/FH/F14/1/12, Morris Lievesley, Secretary of the Foundling Hospital 1799–1849, MSS Notebook.

to have presented a Beza Testament[27] to a godson, called Thomas Corham, in 1747. It is impossible to know whether this was the foundling Thomas or a relative.

The children's early records make very moving reading. Some have little fragments of material attached, some have short notes, like number 7: 'This child is not baptised and I desire he may be baptised and called Roger Brown.' It was not to be; the little baby whose mother wanted him called Roger Brown may have become Charles Richmond or been given some other distinguished name, but the mother would never have known. Some children had longer notes:

> Gentlemen, this child was born on Tuesday 27th January 1741 and was baptised the same day by a Minister of the Church of England by the name of Charles, his surname is Allen. I hope in a little time to be grateful to so good an understanding, I am gentlemen, your unfortunate well wisher, M.U.

This entry, number 22, suggests that the mother was an educated woman who had been abandoned and left destitute. Overcome by the agony at having to part from her child she was not able to express any feelings of gratitude, such as she felt the governors would expect. In a pathetic last sentence, she nevertheless hoped, when sufficient time had elapsed, she might be grateful. The child was dressed in white rattan sleeves done up with cherry coloured silk and it had another pair of sleeves of white dimity turned up with flowered calico. Some of the names pinned to the papers said it all: one child named Elisabeth Foundling survived, but another named Hopegood Helpless died within a month, as did all too many of the children.

Some children had been sent to the country, but many had died and there were vacancies at the hospital. Out of the first thirty children, twenty-three died within the first months. The governors needed to keep the nurses occupied, so on 17 April a second advertisement went out, and more children were taken in. Despite the governors' best intentions, it was not easy to control what went on outside. The governors learnt that a woman, claiming to be the servant of Lewis Way, was pretending to be able to get children in if suitably rewarded. The Chief Nurse reported that when she took to the inn the children who were going to Yorkshire where suitable arrangements for their care had been put in place, she was surrounded by women wanting details as to how the hospital was conducted. The hospital was established to save exposed and deserted children, but under the arrangements set in train by the governors there was no means of differentiating between those children really in need, and those who might be merely an inconvenience.

By no stretch of the imagination could child number 53, among the next thirty children to be admitted on 17 April, be classified as deserted or exposed. The paper pinned to the child was carefully written by an educated hand. It read

> This is to certify that this infant has been baptised by a minister of the Church of England and named George – whose surname is Hanover, begs if asked for by that name that he may be seen if agreeable to the Rules of the Hospital.

---

[27] Beza was a Protestant reformer.

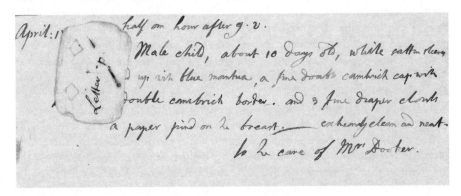

6. a Copy of the letter pinned to the clothes of baby number 53 stating that he was
     baptised 'George – whose surname is Hanover'.

6. b Copy of the entry record for child number 53, with a pin mark where the above
     letter was attached. Both papers were then sealed up.

This was certainly no ordinary foundling. The child is described as male, 'about ten days old and dressed in white satin sleeves bound up with blue mantua, a fine double cambric cap with double cambric border, and three fine diaper clouts. Extremely clean and neat.'[28] Who was this child? The author of the paper, probably the minister who had baptised it, would have known. Did any of the governors read it before it was sealed up? Did they even wonder who this well-dressed infant called George Hanover, with his trousseau of fine diaper nappies, could be? Did some of them know? One of the advantages of getting a child admitted to the hospital was the certainty that its true identity could never be discovered once the admission procedures were complete and its papers were sealed up, safe from all prying eyes. The governors themselves may not have seen the letter. The official entry recording the arrival of baby 53 only gives details of his age and how he was dressed. It merely states that a letter was pinned to his breast and that he was delivered to nurse Booker. There is no way of telling when the seal was broken and the entry and letter became part of the records of the Foundling Hospital. The governors, for the best of reasons, had gone to great lengths to protect the mothers' identities. The child could have been brought in by another woman on behalf of the mother. What is the meaning of the curious wording, 'begs if asked for by that name that he may be seen if agreeable to the Hospital'. Could it be that whoever brought the child to the hospital was aware that if his name was recognised he might not qualify for admission? If so, why call him by a name that could raise questions? Was it in the hope that some day the mother might be able to reclaim him? Was this a royal bastard smuggled into the hospital, and if so who else was party to the deception? The poor little thing was christened John Montagu, after the Duke of Montagu, and died on 2 May 1741, so the riddle of his parentage remains unanswered, as do the many other questions surrounding the admission of the babies. Certainly there were suspicions that the hospital could be used to dispose of unwanted illegitimate children. A satirical song entitled 'Joyful News to Batchelors and Maids . . . in Praise of the Fondling Hospital',[29] is seventeen verses long, and covers all members of society from the farmer's daughter, blithe and gay, to Madam Prim, the Quaker neat, who might benefit from there being a 'fondling' hospital which would take in bastard children with no questions asked. Ladies of the court were seen as legitimate objects for satirical mockery:

> The Court Lady that seemed so shy,
> On John the Skip to cast an Eye,
> But feared a woeful blot;
> Her fierce Desires she may please,
> The burning flames of Venus ease,
> Although a child is got.

The satire is undated and probably was written some time after the hospital first opened.

Coram may have been the only governor not to have been surprised by the numbers applying for admission and the rising demand for help. He had long been aware of the magnitude of the problem, and his dissatisfaction with the governors was partly on account of their slow and cautious approach to the problem. Due in some measure to Coram's continued efforts, and because supporters could see results, the hospital received several large benefactions and was able to acquire the house next door. Thirty children were received on 8 May 1741 and twenty-three more on 5 June. But disorderly scenes outside the hospital were a source of concern, and it was becoming difficult to control the women as they fought to get in at the door. Although the governors visited with great regularity, some of them being present every day, the efficient working of the hospital in reality rested with the Steward and the Chief Nurse. All kinds of difficulties were inherent in an organisation struggling with unforeseen problems. Nurses deemed unsatisfactory had to be discharged and new ones recruited, complaints about thieving investigated, and dissatisfaction because the beer was too weak had to be dealt with. And all the time the babies kept arriving, many so ill they had little hope of surviving their first months. Wet nurses in the country had to be found and supervised by the local vicar or by ladies willing to

---

29 British Library, Shelfmark: 1876, f. i(166) [1 folio]. Anonymous collection of broadsheets, bound, untitled, 1876.

give the time to oversee the welfare of the babies placed out. With the advent of the summer many governors may have left town – certainly meetings were less frequent – but the problems would not have gone away. Coram for the first time missed two meetings, one in July and one in August. At the very end of September a letter accusing the governors of mismanagement was received. It was not considered by the governors at their next meeting on 7 October, when Coram was again absent. It was only discussed at the meeting on 21 October, and by that time the governors must have known that the hospital was confronted with a potential scandal.

12

A Shameful Episode

At the first meeting of the governors in May 1740, a General Committee was formally set up to manage the affairs of the Foundling Hospital. It consisted of fifty members, the President and six Vice Presidents being ex officio members, the other forty-two elected by ballot. All the governors were entitled to attend meetings of the General Court held four times a year. Those governors elected to the General Committee met twice monthly, and sometimes more often. Coram, until 1742, had always been elected to the General Committee with a near maximum number of votes, but in the ballot at the 1742 May Day meeting he received too few votes to qualify, and as a result ceased to have any further say in the management of an organisation which would not have existed but for his efforts. He remained a governor, empowered to attend the four annual General Court meetings of governors, but chose to attend only one further meeting in May 1743.

The reason some of his colleagues took this action was that Coram was said to have spread malicious rumours about the behaviour of two of the governors. His dismissal from the General Committee was the price he paid for having dared to break the code of silence, it being accepted practice that governors could not be seen to have done wrong and their reputations had to be safeguarded. If there was cause for complaint then the matter should be dealt with behind closed doors. But what if Coram had uncovered irregularities in the way the hospital was run? He had already been snubbed and excluded from all the main sub-committees. Would he have been listened to if he made a complaint? Only Dr Nesbitt, who visited almost daily, knew the facts but, although he chose to remain silent, he never denied the truth of Coram's allegations.

A closer look at the events that led to Coram's expulsion from the institution he treasured above all others, and at the personalities involved, reveals an interesting story. There were three main players in the drama: Coram, Martin Folkes, a Vice President, and Sarah Wood, the Chief Nurse. Theodore Jacobsen was the other governor named by Coram, possibly more on account of his friendship with Folkes and thus party to what was going on, than because he played a major role. Martin Folkes[1] was

---

1   Martin Folkes, 1690–1754. Article in the forthcoming *New DNB*, courtesy of Dr David Haycock; see also his ' "The Cabal of a Few Designing Members": The Presidency of Martin Folkes, PRS, and the Society's First Charter', *Antiquaries Journal*, vol. 80, 2000, pp. 273–84.

an ambitious man, very full of his own importance and used to having his own way, by whatever means. He was an antiquary and a natural philosopher, became Vice Chairman of the Society of Antiquaries and had taken part in a heated contest for the presidency of the Royal Society which he lost to Hans Sloane in 1727. On Sloane's retirement, Folkes succeeded him as President. Judging by the unflattering character sketch drawn by Folkes' friend William Stukeley, he would not have been a man with whom Coram would have felt any affinity. Stukeley wrote:

> He chuses the Council and officers out of his junto of Sycophants that meet him every night in Rawthmills coffee house, or that dine with him on Thursdays at the Miter, fleet street. He has a good deal of learning, philosophy: but knows nothing of natural history. In matters of religion an errant infidel & loud scoffer. Professes himself a godfather to all monkeys, believes nothing of a future state, of Scriptures, of revelation. He perverted the Duke of Montagu, Richmond, Ld Pembroke, & very many more of the nobility, who had an opinion of his understanding; and this has done an infinite prejudice to Religion in general, made the nobility throw off the mask & openly deride and discountenance even the appearance of religion w[hic]h has brought us into that deplorable situation we are now in, with thieves & Murderers, perjury, forgery &c. He thinks there is no difference between us & animals; but what is owing to the different structure of our brain, as between man & man. When he lived in Ormond Street in 1720 he set up an infidel Club at his house on Sunday evening, where Will Jones, the mathematician & others of the heathen stamp, assembled. He invited me earnestly to come thither but I always refused. From that time he has been propagating the infidel System with great assiduity, & made it even fashionable in the Royal Society, so that when any mention is made of Moses, the deluge, of religion, Scriptures &c., it is generally received with a loud laugh.[2]

In the absence of the Duke of Bedford, Folkes frequently took the chair at meetings of the General Committee. Even if the sketch was only half true, for Coram, with his strong Anglican convictions, to have to sit under the chairmanship of a man whose views he would have found deeply offensive must have been something of an ordeal, so it is hardly surprising that there was trouble between them. They would have had little in common, and both had forceful personalities.

The story can be said to start with the appointment of the first Chief Nurse, Margaret Shepperd. She was elected from among a number of contenders and won the ballot with fewer negative votes than the other four women.[3] The duties of the Chief Nurse had been spelled out at some length in the plan agreed by the governors. She was to reside in the house, inspect the children and be responsible for their care, and visit frequently. She was responsible for the conduct of the nurses and all the female staff and had oversight of the food. She, alone with the Apothecary, could administer medicines, and with the Steward was the most senior officer. It was on her recommendation that nurses could be dismissed for insubordination, 'sawcisness', or

---

2   This would appear to be a reference to Freemasonry. Martin Folkes had been elected Deputy Grand
    Master of the Freemasons of England in 1721.
3   LMA, General Committee Minutes, 14 February 1740.

other misdemeanours. She was the member of staff with whom governors would have had most contact.

After a month in post Margaret Shepperd was discharged. In her place, with no discussion, it was agreed 'that Sarah Wood, the present laundry maid be appointed chief nurse'.[4] No balloting took place as was usual with the more important appointments. The Duke of Bedford was in the chair at this meeting, but as an infrequent attendee he would have accepted what had obviously been previously agreed. The appointment of a laundry maid, the most lowly and poorly paid member of staff, to the position of Chief Nurse must have caused some raised eyebrows. But Folkes, surrounded by friends and used to having his own way, pushed the appointment through. Nothing was said, and all might have been well had not a letter dated 30 September and signed with the initials GW been received by the governors alleging that many irregularities were occurring at the hospital. Martin Folkes was in the chair and Coram was present when the letter was first mentioned on 21 October, and it was resolved that governors should proceed to examine each of the alleged irregularities.

At the next meeting, on 24 October, the letter was at the top of the agenda and it was decided to set up a group of governors to inquire further into the matter:

> Whereas the Committee is informed that some gentlemen who have attended the Execution of this charity have been grossly aspersed in their characters, resolved that it be referred to Lord Charles Cavendish, Mr. Milner, Mr. Hume Campbell, Mr. Taylor White, Mr. Waple, Mr. Joseph Hankey, Mr. Adair, Mr. Hucks and Mr. Nettleton or any three of them to inquire into the Promoters of such Reports and Report the Facts as they shall appear to them and that they do meet on Saturday next at five in the after noon exactly and have power to adjourn and that Secretary do acquaint them therewith.

The governors were clearly deeply embarrassed by the letter and its contents.

There has been much speculation as to who the mysterious GW, the writer of the letter, could be. It had to be written by someone who was familiar with the way in which the hospital was managed, in effect one of the governors or one of the staff. It is unlikely that visiting members of the public would have had the necessary background knowledge to make the allegations contained in the letter. Since Coram was later to be accused of spreading malicious aspersions upon Martin Folkes and Theodore Jacobsen, it is worth considering if he could have been the author of the letter. He had a habit of writing letters designed to question the integrity of colleagues if he thought them in the wrong, and had done so on several past occasions. Often he was right. He won his court case in Taunton and received compensation (although he could make no immediate use of it); he was right about female inheritance in Georgia, Lord Egmont gracefully noting that he was pleased when the outcome vindicated Coram as he had so much wanted it. If Coram knew, or thought he knew, that a governor or governors had been behaving improperly, what could he have done? He was treated with courtesy, but still seen as an outsider, not one of the small group of powerful and wealthy gentlemen who had taken over the running of the hospital. He

4   LMA, General Committee Minutes, 28 December 1740.

was valued by the governors for his skill in raising funds and as an advocate for the children, but when it came to matters of policy he was never a member of the smaller working parties where such matters were discussed. He had already been snubbed by Folkes for acting on his own, and it is unlikely that if he voiced any dissenting opinion it would have been noted. He might have believed that his only option as a means of bringing matters to a head was to put his accusations on paper, as he had done in the past. There is one further point that could possibly link Coram to the letter. It was signed GW in capital letters, reproduced as such in both minutes. The letters looked as though they had been made by a stamp, possibly to protect the identity of the writer. It so happened that all the bibles and books of religious instruction that Coram sent to New England at this time had his initials TC stamped in red on several of their pages.[5] There is no evidence that the letters GW were made by the same stamp, but it is a possibility. But why the letters GW? They refer to no governor, nor to any member of staff, but if the writer of the letter was Coram he could have chosen them for that very reason, since he was hardly likely to use his own initials.

On 4 November Taylor White reported back that the gentlemen to whom the report had been referred had resolved that they would take the report into consideration on Monday 9 November at eleven in the forenoon precisely. The Secretary was to send a particular summons to every member of the committee 'to attend upon this occasion acquainting them with the business'. It was almost a foregone conclusion that all wrongdoing would be denied, and so it was. Seventeen members were present, including Coram, when the committee met on 9 November. Folkes and Jacobsen withdrew before the report was considered. The minute stated:

> it was resolved, nemine contradicent, that after the strictest Examination and Inquiry it appears to this Committee that the information given by Mary Rayner and others late nurses in this Hospital containing several scandalous Insinuations and Aspersions upon Martin Folkes and Theodore Jacobsen Esquires, two of the Governors of this Hospital are Unjust, False, Groundless and Malicious. Resolved that the promoting and spreading of Accusations or Aspersions upon the Characters of Gentlemen who are diligent in the Execution of this Charity tends to the ruin of it, by preventing their attendance. Resolved that it appears to this Committee that Mr. Thomas Coram, one of the Governors of this Hospital has been principally concerned in promoting and spreading the said Aspersions on the two said Governors. Resolved that it appears to this Committee that Dr. Nesbitt, another of the Governors of this Hospital, was very early acquainted by Mary Rayner and other Nurses with the said Aspersions and did not take Measures proper to discountenance the same contrary to what in Justice is due to the Governors of this Hospital and the Character of the Gentlemen aspersed. Resolved that the diligent and constant Attendance of Martin Folkes and Theodore Jacobsen Esquires, two of the Governors of this Hospital, and their indefatigable Zeal in the Execution of their Trust have been highly beneficial to this Charity and deserve the Thanks of all who wish it well, and that the Thanks of this Committee be returned accordingly, and that this Committee hope they will continue to act in the same Manner, they being satisfied nothing can contribute more to the

---

[5]   A few of the remaining books thus stamped are held by the Old Colony Historical Society, Taunton, and have been seen by the author.

Welfare and Prosperity of the Hospital. Resolved that the Papers this Day read to the Committee from the Gentlemen to whom it was referred to inquire into the Promoters of the before mentioned reports be sealed up by Mr. Milner, Mr. Folkes and Mr. Burrell, Vice Presidents, and be kept by the Secretary.

One can only imagine Coram's feelings while this condemnation of his actions was read out and the governors, whom he believed to be at fault, were so fulsomely praised. There is no record of his having made any reply.

That there was more than meets the eye behind this scandal is reinforced not only by the fact that the papers were sealed up and left in the keeping of one of the accused, Martin Folkes, but also by the fact that they were destroyed at a later date. It is not clear from the report whether Mary Rayner, the nurse who had given the information, was dismissed, but certainly the nurses who supported her are called 'late'. The minutes record that two nurses had been discharged on 26 August, maybe at the request of Sarah Wood. What could Coram do or say? He had the whole body of governors against him, except for Dr Nesbitt, yet he must have known that something was amiss. Sarah Wood, the Chief Nurse, had, in effect, been exonerated from wrongdoing. It must have taken a considerable amount of courage for Mary Rayner and the other nurses to speak up, knowing that in all probability they would be dismissed for their pains. The life of whistleblowers is hard: *plus ça change, plus c'est la même chose.*

Folkes, who must have known about the allegations against him, would have presumed that they would be disregarded. He had not counted on another governor actually listening to what the nurses said and believing their account, still less that a letter would come before the governors making allegations against him and Jacobsen. Dr Nesbitt, the physician in charge, was an almost daily visitor to the house in Hatton Garden and had clearly been told by the nurses of their misgivings but, while not denying their allegations, he had taken the easy way out and said nothing. Someone else who believed that all was not well at the hospital was Anthony Allan, the Master in Chancery and a long-time friend of Coram's. In his will dated 1753 he wrote

> And whereas many years before the obtaining the Royal Charter for the Hospital for exposed and deserted young children, I did, at the instance of the indefatigable schemist Thomas Coram, really intend some considerable benefaction towards carrying on so good a project and did encourage the concurrence of other liberal benefactor, till some of the acting Governors and Guardians of the said Hospital went counter to our judgments and proposals pressed upon them by the said Coram, on several occasions which made me withhold my hand.[6]

Anthony Allan, who was a governor, is recorded as having visited the hospital on several occasions at this period.

The governors had clearly been embarrassed by the allegations, which must have had some truth to them, for while exonerating Folkes and Jacobsen from all blame they had also perforce endorsed the conduct of the Chief Nurse, the former laundry

6   Brownlow, *History of the Foundling Hospital*, pp. 9–10, note.

maid, who was in charge. Just over a month later, on 23 December, the committee came round to considering that the information given by Mary Rayner and other nurses that the 'chief nurse is charged with immodesty, dishonesty and drunkeness' and their insinuations that she had 'miscarried in the hospital' were groundless and malicious. Yet this statement was immediately followed by a second resolution which declared that 'it appears to this committee that the affairs of the hospital have been very improperly managed and that Sarah Wood should be discharged'. She was given two days' wages and directed to deliver over everything in her care to the new Chief Nurse, Bridget Tomkins, who had just been appointed.

In their efforts to distance the two governors from any responsibility for misman-agement or knowledge of Sarah Wood's behaviour, the committee had had to dismiss the allegations made by the nurses, yet it is quite clear from the second minute that Sarah Wood was responsible for this mismanagement. It is more than likely that some of the allegations made by the nurses were true, but too embarrassing to be accepted. The death rate among the first sixty babies admitted was very high. Of the first thirty, only seven survived for more than a year. The second intake of thirty had a higher survival rate, only eighteen dying in the first year.[7] Because Folkes and Jacobsen were frequent visitors, and because responsibility for the way in which the hospital was managed lay with them as governors, and particularly with Folkes, because he was a Vice President, they had to be protected. The records show that Folkes and Jacobsen were in and out of the house in Hatton Garden on an almost daily basis and could hardly not have known what was going on, or have been unaware of Sarah Wood's behaviour. Since the papers were destroyed, the true facts can never be known.

However it is possible to construct a possible explanation for the events proceeding from the strange appointment of a laundry maid, Sarah Wood, the most poorly paid employee, to the post of Chief Nurse, through to her abrupt dismissal in December. Folkes was a man used to having his own way, who clearly enjoyed power. If he wished the laundry maid to be Chief Nurse it is unlikely that he would be opposed. He had been chairing nearly all of the twice-weekly meetings at the Hatton Garden house that had been set up after the children were admitted. A rota of gover-nors had also been set up to visit regularly, but a rough copy of the visiting governors covering the months of May and June shows that Folkes, besides chairing the meet-ings at the Hatton Garden house, was by far the most assiduous, visiting the hospital and the nurseries almost every single day during that period, often accompanied by Jacobsen and sometimes by some other governor.[8] The only other governor with a comparable record was Dr Nesbitt, but the frequency of his visits can be accounted for, as many of the children were ill and needed constant medical attention. It has been noted earlier that the books were not regularly entered, which might account for there being no further records of visits after June; or perhaps it was because during the summer months many of the governors would have been out of town.

---

[7] LMA, A/FH/A09/002/001, General Register: Children's Admission and Discharge.

[8] The notes, among the General Committee Minutes, only cover the months of May and June and are in rough form. They show that Folkes was only absent from the hospital on 9, 12, 13, 24, 25 and 26 May and this pattern of visits continued throughout June.

a. Dr Richard Mead, governor and
eminent physician.
By Allan Ramsay, 1747.

b. Theodore Jacobsen, governor
and architect of the hospital.
By Thomas Hudson, 1746.

c. John Milner, Vice President
1746–50. By Thomas Hudson, 1746.

d. Martin Folkes, Vice President.
Unattributed engraving for the *Universal
Magazine*.

7. Portraits of four governors, all intimately concerned with the early development of
the hospital.

However, it is noteworthy that immediately after Sarah Wood's dismissal, Folkes, who had been so constant in his attendance, is not recorded as having been present at the hospital for the next ten months. Milner, one of the other Vice Presidents, stepped into the breach and from now until October chaired nearly all the meetings until the following October. Jacobsen, on the other hand, continued to attend with great regularity, but there was a good reason for his being present, since by this time he must have been preparing his own plans for a building for the hospital, and no doubt hoped to get the commission. Although unpaid, it would enhance his reputation as a gentleman architect.

By that time Coram had been made to pay the price for his indiscretion in making public his misgivings about the way the hospital was being managed. In retrospect Folkes seems an unlikely man to have interested himself in the welfare of foundlings. A close friend of the dukes of Montagu and Richmond, who had shown their interest in Coram's ideas from early on, did Folkes become involved on their account, so as to be part of what had obviously become a fashionable charity? Folkes' involvement with the Foundling Hospital is not mentioned in any published information about him, including in the *Dictionary of National Biography*.[9] There is only a factual record of his attendance at meetings in *The History of the Foundling Hospital*, yet as one of the first Vice Presidents he played an important role in the development of the hospital in its early days.

The General Committee had been asked to consider a plan to start building a hospital. A sub-committee was set up which included Jacobsen but not Coram. The committee met informally at Meyer's coffee house in King's Street, Bloomsbury. By 30 June 1742, four plans were received, including one from Theodore Jacobsen. Before that point was reached, the building committee had taken upon itself the right to decide the site of the hospital and had proceeded to order bricks.

Relationships between Coram and the other governors must have been somewhat strained after the November meeting of the General Committee, but were perhaps eased by the sacking of Sarah Wood and Folkes' temporary disappearance. Coram was present at several of the subsequent meetings, including the fateful one on 9 March when Milner was in the chair. Sir Charles Wager, Coram's old friend and a fellow sailor, was also present at the meeting. Perhaps Wager, who may have known what was intended, had come to offer Coram his support. When the list of new General Committee members who had been successful in the ballot was read out, Coram's name was not among them and he knew that he must have received too few votes to secure membership. Perhaps the governors could afford to be polite to Coram, who was still reporting legacies he had secured, but it is likely that some of them had already decided on his fate.

Folkes, who had almost certainly orchestrated the move, was absent while this shameful episode was played out. Considering that without Coram's efforts there would have been no hospital, that he was now an old man, and that he had devoted a large proportion of his meagre resources to seeking support for the institution, their punishment was harsh. There was a special cruelty about the governors' decision to

9   I am grateful to Dr David Haycock for this information.

exclude Coram from the executive body. Most of them had many other interests, but for the widowed, childless Coram, the rescue of the foundlings had been central to his life for so long, his 'darling project', the focus of so much time and thought. With no regard to his achievements, the governors had decided not only to humiliate the old man publicly, but to remove his chief joy and pleasure, involvement in the hospital caring for the deserted babies, babies for whom he cared as though they were his own.

Coram behaved with dignity. With the others present he agreed the accounts. But there was one more embarrassment for the chairman before the meeting ended. The General Committee had set up the building committee, but when they were said to have 'agreed the ground on which to build a hospital' there was an objection. The General Committee said 'they did not know the [building] committee had been appointed to fix upon a proper part of the ground and that they had been induced to sign such a memorial from an apprehension that it was only to appoint a committee for that purpose'. Was it Coram who pointed out this irregularity? The question had hurriedly to be put to them again. The governors, having had their protest accepted, gave their assent except for Coram. This must have seemed to him yet one more example of how a small clique of men were pushing through their ideas without due regard to the views of others. Coram may well have had his own views on whether the ground chosen was the healthiest and the most commodious, and the best place for the hospital to be sited. After all, he had given thought to the question long before and had written to Colman on the subject.

Coram believed that the building committee had exceeded their remit. Following his decision to withhold consent to the proposed site for the building, it must have seemed to him only logical to vote against the following motion, which was to authorise a contract for making 400,000 bricks for its building. The contract, agreed by the building committee that Mr Thomas Scott should make a quantity of best stock bricks at 12 shillings a thousand, had not been authorised by the General Committee. The General Committee, possibly at the instigation of Coram, had shown their displeasure by ordering Scott to stop work, and resolved that no sub-committee should have power to make contracts but 'such as are conditional to be approved by the general committee'. When the matter was again put to the General Committee in the following May they agreed the contract, with Coram alone voting against, the only way open to him to show his dissatisfaction at the way the business had been handled. The minute read:

> that the general committee being acquainted that the agreement prepared by the committee for building be made with Mr. Thomas Scott a quantity of best stock bricks for the use of the hospital being well burnt, firm and good to be made at the N-E corner of East Conduit Fields and delivered at the place of the building at 12/- a thousand and it was by the consent of all the governors except Mr. Coram.

Because there had been so much trouble over the contract made by Scott for the bricks, at the formal governors' meeting, which followed that of the General Committee, the matter came up again for ratification at the Court meeting. It must have seemed to Coram only right to vote against the motion. As this was Coram's last action as a governor, his decision to vote against the order for the bricks has often been taken out of context, and seen as a last defiant gesture, a metaphorical thumbing

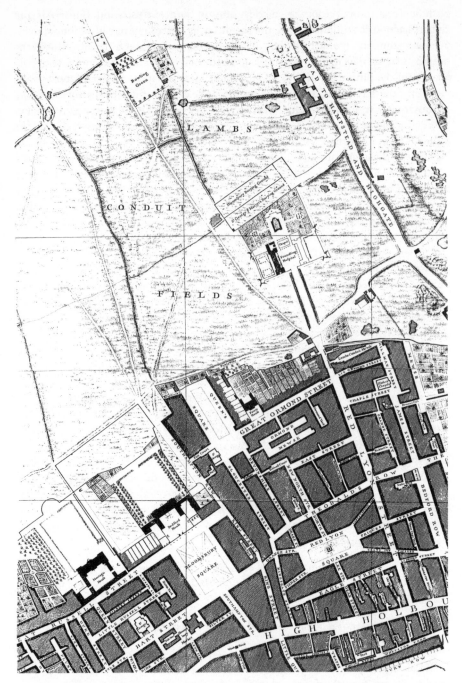

8. Roques' map of London, 1745, showing the half finished Foundling Hospital, the
houses of the dukes of Montagu and Bedford, and Queen's Square where Folkes lived.

of the nose at the governors, a senseless gesture born of frustration. But looking at Coram's action over a number of months, he does seem to have had serious misgivings as to the way in which the hospital was being managed. His negative interventions can be seen as a way of protesting at the small but powerful group who had taken over the running of his beloved hospital, taking decisions without regard to the views of others on the General Committee. It is understandable that men used to having their own way might well have wished to be rid of their awkward colleague, despite the fact that his criticisms might have been valid, and despite all they owed to him.

After his exclusion from the General Committee, Coram made one more appearance at the Court meeting the following May, but thereafter gave up all formal contact with the hospital. Perhaps his reception by the other governors at the May meeting of 1743 was such that he decided to cut all formal links with the organisation he had virtually created single handedly. There is no doubt that the governors did work extremely hard, they had to grapple with problems that they had never had to face before, and they were ultimately successful in creating an organisation that endured for nearly 250 years

That Martin Folkes had behaved in some way that was discreditable to him can hardly be denied. He was responsible for the appointment of Sarah Wood, who had had to be dismissed summarily after months of prevarication. After a long period of denial that anything was amiss, the rumours about her conduct had proved undeniable. All the papers concerned with the matter were sealed up and later destroyed, leading to a suspicion that there had indeed been a cover-up. There is a later account of this affair by Morris Lievesley, Secretary to the hospital from 1799 to 1846, which does not correspond to the known facts, but which nevertheless reveals that memories of this episode persisted, and shows that opinions among the governors had been deeply divided. Lievesley cannot have seen the actual papers referring to the matter as they had been destroyed, so he must have had to rely on hearsay for his account.[10]

Whether the rumours of sexual misconduct were true will never be known, but certainly there was misconduct of some kind. For a man of Folkes' standing, dalliance with a servant would be taken as a matter of no importance. But if that servant happened to be the paid senior officer of a fashionable charity, and another governor was making allegations of misconduct, then the resulting publicity could have been damaging to Folkes as well as to the charity. Folkes' sudden and unexplained ten-month absence from Hatton Garden after the dismissal of Sarah Wood lends further support to the notion that there was something to hide. He lived nearby at

---

[10] LMA, Morris Lievesley, MS Notebook, Private Papers: 'It is scarcely possible to believe that Gentlemen of Education assembled within the walls of the Hospital to carry out works of charity should lose sight of the object, and permit the most hateful passions of hate and jealousy to infuriate their moral character and the best interests of the institution. Coram the great good founder was driven out of his own temple of mercy by a cabal. Sir Thomas Bernhard to whom the hospital owes its building revenue was obliged to resign his office of treasurer by the cabal. A petty quarrel over the supremacy of Mrs Jones, the matron and Mr. McLennon the apothecary agitated a numerous portion of the governors. Those on the side of the matron were arrayed against those on the side of the apothecary. The real interests of the charity were neglected and forgotten. This quarrel occasioned the absence of all the dignified minded governors and threw the whole management of the institution upon the treasurer, whose habits rendered him unfit to bear the burden.' There was no matron or Mrs Jones at that time; Sarah Wood was the Chief Nurse.

6 Queen's Square[11] and had been involved on an almost daily basis with the business of the hospital until Sarah Wood's dismissal. Was Coram's forced departure orchestrated not just to be rid of a difficult character, but rather as part of a deal to ensure that the reputation of a powerful and ambitious man would no longer be challenged? To a lesser degree it also ensured that Jacobsen, who had been implicated with Folkes in Coram's aspersions, would have no further opposition and be able to submit his building plan for the hospital. He gave his services free, and the hospital has since been considered his finest architectural achievement. It must have been a bitter moment and a sad one for Coram, but he would not have regretted doing what he believed to be right.

---

[11] Philips, *Mid-Georgian London*, p. 176.

13

Coram in Exile

The removal of Coram from the General Committee did not go unnoticed. At a stroke the governors had lost their chief fundraiser and their best advocate for the foundlings and the hospital. The dramatic falling off of subscriptions in the two years following Coram's ejection speaks for itself. By May 1742 benefactions to the hospital had reached £9,157, and this together with annual subscriptions of £740 and money from the charity boxes at £170 amounted to over £10,000, collected at a time of financial depression. In the two years following Coram's departure only £1,899 was raised. Anthony Allan cannot have been the only one who stayed his hand, and rumours must have continued to circulate about the management of the hospital as well as about the way in which Coram had been treated.

To safeguard the reputation of the governors, and of Folkes and Jacobsen in particular, the governors needed to undermine Coram's standing. The accusations against him of casting untrue and malicious aspersions on two governors have echoed down the years, as has his reputation for being difficult. Thus the story of his removal from the General Committee has been made to seem regrettable, but inevitable in the face of his unreasonable behaviour. The governors, in their haste to be rid of Coram, failed to count the cost to the hospital. Only he could make the direct approach, his patient determination, his belief in the cause he was promoting, his known integrity and his blunt honest charm winning support from men and women of all ranks in a way no governor could emulate. The men who now spoke for the hospital had their reputations to consider and could not solicit funds in such a manner. They used the anonymity of the charity box, the indirect approach through the charity sermon and fashionable events. Much time was spent in the early years chasing up promises and bequests, taking legal action if necessary when executors sought to avoid paying legacies due to the hospital. Early on, the governors had understood that the infants themselves were an attraction, the emotional thrill of witnessing the anguish of the mothers who surrendered their children and the grief of those refused admittance, brought curious onlookers. The services of baptism became another draw – children rescued from the gutter symbolically admitted to the Christian community, regardless of the fact that some of them had already been christened. It was in the hope that all who came would give generously that such visiting was encouraged. In the following years the picture gallery and the Handel concerts would provide entertainment for fashionable society and help to fill the charity boxes. In the meantime the governors had to struggle with the problem of financing the work they had begun.

9. Thomas Coram with a baby in a basket. Print taken from a painting by R. Nebot, 1741, published in 1751, then in the possession of Dr Nesbitt.

In October 1740 Coram had asked to keep the subscription books for the purpose of promoting benefactions. The General Committee now asked the Secretary to write and ask for their return as 'they have an immediate occasion for them'.[1] Coram also owned the original charter setting up the charity. It is more than understandable that Coram wanted to hold on to both. It was, after all, he who had procured the charter. The subscription books contained the record of his struggles and success in raising money and would allow him to continue. Brocklesby noted that Coram considered each entry with more pleasure than a miser counting his gold.[2]

Now everything was to be taken from him. It is no wonder he refused to surrender these precious records to the men now in charge of his hospital. However, his old friend Dr Mead, who had argued so passionately for a Foundling Hospital at Somerset House, intervened. Coram, perhaps as a measure of his bitterness at being ousted, had sent in an account for the money he had had to pay to the lawyers. Despite all his attempts to raise subscriptions to pay their charges, he had had to pay part of their fees out of his own pocket. The kindly Dr Mead, who no doubt sympathised with Coram, was delegated to settle the account and to ask if Coram would hand over to him the subscription books and papers. Aware of Coram's feelings towards his erstwhile colleagues among the governors, Mead was authorised to say that the books and papers would remain in his hands so they could be read, 'to be returned to Mr Coram afterwards should he desire the same'.[3] It was a generous gesture and Coram eventually returned all the records.

The urge to help those in need was too strong to allow Coram to remain idle. He could see for himself that the Foundling Hospital was only able to deal with a tiny proportion of the children in need. Perhaps he hoped others might follow the model that he had provided. He saw there was still work for him to do. He immediately set about drafting a petition for another foundling hospital, this time addressed to the Princess of Wales. He pointed out that the present Foundling Hospital could not care for half the children brought to it. This petition was in the names of church wardens, overseers of the poor and other principal inhabitants of the parishes and liberties of Westminster. Coram knew the territory well. He had walked these same streets when obtaining the signatures of men willing to go to North America to settle part of Maine. Now, with his quill, ink and paper in his pocket, he walked the parishes of St Margaret's Westminster, St Martin in the Fields, St Paul's, Covent Garden, St Clement Danes, St Ann, St James, St Mary le Strand, St John the Evangelist, St George's Hanover Square and the Precinct of the Savoy.[4] It was a remarkable effort for a man now in his mid-seventies, but perhaps the familiar routine, tramping the streets, arguing his case, obtaining the coveted signatures, helped to fill the gap in his life. How long it took him to collect the 120 names attached to the petition is not known, nor when he presented it to the Princess of Wales. Coram always took a lot of trouble about the appearance of his petitions, and sought assistance with both the drafting

1   LMA, General Committee Minutes, 8 December 1742.
2   Brocklesby, *Private Virtue and Publick Spirit*, p. 120.
3   LMA, General Committee Minutes, November 1739–July 1744.
4   An unsigned copy, almost certainly written in Coram's hand, is at the LMA. McClure, *Coram's Children*, p. 279, note 10, is also of the opinion that the copy is in his handwriting.

and the writing of them. In a letter in 1748 he asked Mr Austin, master of the charity school in St Bartholomew Close, for help.

> Sir, I request That when you send the Draughts of Petitions Tomorrow Morning you will also be pleased to send the 2 Rough Draughts within the brown paper and that you will also be pleased to send me a little of your best Ink in a little vial that I may take it with me for every Subscriber to write his Name with it that it may look all alike (and as tho subscribed at ye same time) and not as tho one name was writen last summer and another Bartholomew tide and one in one county and some in another, I pray you will rule the Lines with ye Black Lead pensils that they may be easily rubd out with bread if needfull.[5]

This letter is worth quoting as it shows the extreme care Coram took over every last detail. The letter talks of two petitions, so it is very likely that at least one of them was the petition Coram wished to present to the Princess of Wales. George Bubb Dodington provided the only other reference to Coram's having gone to see the Princess, reporting in his journal on 9 February 1750 that at Carlton House that evening he saw 'Dr Lee who brought old Coram with propositions for a vagabond hospital', and 'that they were going up to see the Princess'.[6] This time Coram had no great names to head up his petition, and without the support of the nobility and gentry he had no hope of success.

Even though the Foundling Hospital was on a much smaller scale than the Paris and Amsterdam hospitals, it never inspired others to follow its lead. Henry Fielding had published a ringing endorsement:

> At last the long contested Point of establishing a Hospital for Foundlings is carry'd; to the immortal honour of Mr *Coram*, who has pursued it on such noble, and disinterested Motives, and with such indefatigable Zeal and Industry; A Design so truly humane and charitable, that one cannot help wondering, it has been delayed so long; and yet as it results from the voluntary Subscriptions of Individuals, 'tis as much to be wondered that it ever took place at all.[7]

But the antagonism to a hospital for foundlings had not died down. During his life, Coram himself was the subject of personal ridicule and unfounded insinuations, notably in the satirical poem *Scandalizade*. The poem also demonstrates that Coram's efforts to settle Nova Scotia were publicly known. The fact that he figures in the same volume as his contemporaries Hogarth, Handel and Garrick indicates that neither he nor his work had been forgotten in 1750.

> Lo! Old Captain Coram, so round in the face
> And a Pair of good Chops plumpt up in good Case,
> His amiable Locks hanging grey either Side,
> To his double brest Coat o'er his Shoulders so wide

---

5   Compston, *Thomas Coram*, p. 40.
6   *The Political Journal of George Bubb Dodington*, ed. John Carswell and Lewis Arnold, Oxford 1965, p. 48.
7   *The Champion*, vol. 1, November 1739, p. 30. *The Champion* was a periodical produced by Henry Fielding, 1739–41.

Malcontented he cry'd, tis with Sorrow I see
Scheme mad a job of projected by me
This same *Nova Scotia* will hardly succeed,
To provide for a Lobster abroad was the Deed,
Boundry Commissi'ners and Agents and clerks,
Loungers, and Leaches and such king of sharks.

The Architect Biggs so lumbringly full,
Like the Church he erected so expensively dull;
Addres'd the Old Captain; Prithee, why dost thou sob:
Nova Scotia's in very good hands for a Jobb:
For is not the Government civil forsooth
With its free laws in the Governor's mouth.
But this not all the Effects of they Pains
The *Hospital Foundling* came out of thy Brains.
To encourage the Progress of vulgar Amours,
The breeding of Rogues and the increasing of Whores.
While the Children of honest good Husbands and Wives
Stand exposid to Oppression and Want all their Lives.
Was it conscious of revelling erst in the Sport,
That hath prompted thee thus to deprecate for't?
For, methinks, I can still in they Countenance see,
Thou hast many a Lass grappl'd under the Lee,
But thou'rt in thy Projects so wonderously nice
Thou quit'st them as soon as they're set to a Price,
So testily honest thou art in thy choice.[8]

The *Gentleman's Magazine* ran a facetious article on the hospital for foundlings, pretending to see advantage in that the boys could be bred to military discipline and form a great army, and that the females might follow as wives, sutlers and laundresses for this body of men. But the real attack on it came from the lips of a 'gay young fellow' who said

> he saw no Objection to the Proposal, since most of these Foundlings, being by-blows, begot out of the dull Course of Matrimony . . . He added that he should certainly contribute to the undertaking, since provision was made here for helpless Issue, and thereby the only Objection against the Freedom of Love was removed.[9]

There were other attacks on the hospital in print. Christopher Smart, the poet, under cover of his pseudonym Mrs Midnight, wrote to the governors of the Foundling Hospital pretending to give her reasons for not applying to be of their society.

> In the first place you are guilty of the most scandalous Misnommer (as the *French* Phrase is) for you call your Hospital an Hospital for exposed and deserted Children, when exposed and deserted Children are absolutely

---

8   *Scandalizade: a Panegyric-Satiri-Serio-Comic-Dramatic Poem.* First printed in 1750 it included skits of Coram, Hogarth, Handel and Garrick. In 1760 it was included in *The Remarkable Satires of Porcupinus Pelagius*, attributed to Macnamara Morgan, pp. 116–17.

9   *Gentleman's Magazine*, vol. 10, January 1740, p. 24.

excluded by the Laws of your House, and the whole business is entirely left to
Fortune, so the Bastard of a L—d, has an equal Chance with an helpless
Wretch, who, perhaps, *was* (as *Shakespear* had it), *Ditch-delivered by a Drab!*[10]

While infants with a pedigree like that of George Hanover were being admitted, Mrs
Midnight might have been nearer the mark than she knew.

Coram's last effort, unsurprisingly, came to nothing and, although the establishment of a foundling hospital in the teeth of the kind of opposition so pointedly
expressed in the poem was a remarkable achievement, sadly the workhouses, with
their appalling child mortality rates, were to remain the main refuge for destitute
infants who, at this time, could only be admitted with their mothers. Indeed, Jonas
Hanway, who became a governor in 1756, wrote that if the Poor Laws were properly
executed as they ought to be, he believed England would not need a foundling
hospital as such.[11] He thought the role of the Foundling Hospital ought to be as an
intermediary between the parish officers of London and rural nurses.[12] Despite being
the most fashionable charity in London, it did not inspire others to follow its
example. For nearly 150 years it remained the only charitable organisation to care for
illegitimate children. Not until the 1870s, when Protestant evangelical organisations
like Barnardo's came into being with the proud boast 'no destitute child ever refused
admission', did the hospital have any competition. Although Barnardo's was a
Protestant Christian organisation, it was not directly linked to any church, but nearly
all the child rescue organisations, like the Church of England's Waifs and Strays
Society and the Methodists' National Childrens' Homes, were church based. The
Foundling Hospital remained the only one without any specific church affiliation,
and, although the children were brought up according to the teachings of the
Anglican Church, there was no attempt to proselytise.

In the years that followed Coram's death there was a surge in the number of charitable institutions: the Marine Society, the Magdalen Hospital, and the Female
Orphan Asylum among others were founded between 1756 and 1758. These three
had one thing in common: they were incorporated charities, a form pioneered by
Coram for the Foundling Hospital. Even the Society of Antiquaries, which until 1751
had been a voluntary body, followed suit. Since it was Folkes who led the petition to
the King for the incorporation of the Society of Antiquaries by a royal charter, which
gave it, like the Foundling Hospital, the right to hold property in perpetuity and to
receive benefactions, it appears that he too had learned from Coram's example.

While Coram was endeavouring to set up a second foundling hospital events were
moving fast in Hatton Garden. In June 1742 four plans were under consideration by
the building committee.[13] Two were judged unsatisfactory: that of George Sampson
was thought too small and the other, by George Dance, too expensive. The remaining
two plans, one by John James, surveyor of the fabric of Westminster Abbey, and the
other by Jacobsen, met with the specifications laid down by the governors. The
hospital was to be built in stages, the first stage to be capable of holding two hundred

---

10 Smart (1722–71), 'A Letter from *Mrs Midnight*', pp. 60–1. Mrs Midnight was a pseudonym for
     Christopher Smart himself.
11 Taylor, *Jonas Hanway*, p. 104.
12 Ibid., p. 112.
13 LMA, General Committee Minutes, 30 June 1742.

children. The building was to be composed of two storeys and an attic storey, the wards were to be 24 feet wide, and there was to be an arcade to each wing the whole length of the building. It is unsurprising that when the detailed comparisons came to be made Jacobsen's plan was deemed the most suitable. He was, after all, a governor and knew what the governors required. He was also a friend and shared the anti-quarian interests of Folkes and other governors, and also became a founder member of the Society of Antiquaries when it received its royal charter. He was a member of the Royal Society, like Sloane and Mead, had designed the new East India House and had been involved with the rebuilding of the Bank of England.[14] Jacobsen proved to be an excellent choice and remained involved with building of the chapel and the east wing, earning the thanks of the General Court 'for his great attention and care in carrying on the Buildings of this Hospital on the approved plan made out by him'.[15]

The foundation stone was inscribed: 'The Foundation of this Hospital was laid on 16th September 1742.' There is no record that Coram was present, or even knew that a start had been made to bring his vision to reality. By February 1744 the fitting up of the interior was underway and by May it was decided that the still unfinished hospital should be insured for £4,000 against fire. The final details took longer than expected and in September 1745 the governors held their last meeting in Hatton Garden. The hospital had no direct access to the nearest paved carriage way, Red Lion Street leading to London, and the trustees had had to negotiate with the owner of the intervening land, the trustees of Rugby School, for a right of way, which became Lambs Conduit Street and the hospital's main access route. Did Coram walk across the fields where cows quietly grazed to view the west wing rising up in splendid isola-tion? When funds allowed, an east wing would be built; the east and west wings were to be linked by a chapel and all built round a courtyard. In identifying this remote spot so early on Coram had recognised, as did the governors, the benefits of clean air for the children and the importance of keeping them away from the temptations of the great city.

The building into which the children moved on 1 October 1745 was a simple, well-proportioned structure of no great pretension. Its plain exterior must have pleased the practical Coram and was in marked contrast to the opulent court room the gover-nors had designed for themselves. It would have seemed that the magnificence of the room was designed to emphasise the gulf between the rich and the poor, but it was also designed to attract the rich and the wealthy and to persuade them to support the work of the organisation. It is not clear who designed the court room, but it had many characteristics in common with that designed by Jacobsen for the East India Company, where six oil paintings representing Calcutta, Madras, Bombay, Tellichery, Cape Town and St Helena are set in architectural frames.[16] If the suggestion and design came from Jacobsen, he found a more than willing collaborator in Hogarth, who had already given his magnificent portrait of Coram to the hospital. Hogarth admired Coram and had given the enterprise his wholehearted support. There was little opportunity at the time to practise history painting, and no public galleries in

---

[14] I am indebted to Dr Alan Borg for this information: Borg, *Theodore Jacobsen and the Building of the Found-ling Hospital*, forthcoming.

[15] LMA, General Committee Minutes, 13 June 1752.

[16] Borg, *Jacobsen and the Building of the Foundling Hospital*, p. 16.

10. The court room as it was when still in the original eighteenth-century building.

which to display it. Hogarth had already completed the decoration of the staircase at St Bartholomew's Hospital, free of charge.[17] He seems to have had little difficulty persuading his fellow artists to become associated with the newly popular and fashionable Foundling Hospital, particularly when it was known that Rysbrack, the reputed sculptor, had designed the marble bas relief depicting charity, over the grand chimney-piece.

The governors, struggling to raise money for their building, could not be seen to be spending money on works of art, so in return for the gift of their paintings the artists were all made governors, many of them in 1746. There is no way of knowing whether Coram was aware of the way in which his straightforward concern for abandoned children had fired the imagination of the artistic world, stimulating artists to provide the themed decoration of the court room. As he went about the streets of Westminster, collecting the signatures of the ordinary men who dealt with the needy poor, one cannot but admire his steady hope, and the way that the humanitarian impulse that drove him was strong enough to appeal without the need to entertain and delight the wealthy and powerful. Living now in poverty, sustained by the charity of a few friends like Anthony Allan and the Smiths, with whom he still lived, Coram might well have viewed this ostentatious display of wealth, this marking out of the

17 Allan, 'Art and Charity in Hogarth's England', p. 8.

social distinction between the degradation of the needy poor and the superiority of the powerful, with some dismay. If he was unhappy at all the magnificence on display, he would not have been alone. The poet Christopher Smart continued his attack, writing:

> Extravagant Feasts, Musick, Revelling and Dancing are of the Species of Charity, which Pride and Gluttony are ever ready to bestow on themselves and their Associates – But to Fast for a Friend in order to serve him; – to Pray for him in order to promote him; – to undergo Pain to give him pleasure, is Christian Charity. – All the rest is Ostentation, Nonsense, Noise , and something yet worse than all of them, which I forbear to mention because I wou'd give Offence to Persons of Distinction.[18]

The sentiments may have been a little extreme but there was truth in them. There is no doubt, however, that these attractions brought the *beau monde* flocking to the hospital, eager to see and be seen, were financially beneficial to the hospital and kept it in the public eye.

Coram cannot have had much in the way of personal belongings. He is spoken of as still wearing the red coat that he was painted in, but it was getting shabby. It had seen good service, an eminently practical garment, with its single cape that could button up as a collar, made of a heavy, napped woollen cloth, sometimes known as a Watchcoat it was large and loose with a vent at the back to allow for riding a horse. Used by continental armies, it became popular with civilians in the eighteenth century, an ideal garment for a man who rode and walked everywhere in all weathers.[19] One of his prized possessions would have been the book by Samuel Pepys, *The Memoires relating to the State of the Royal Navy*. It was inscribed , 'Presented by one C. Jackson to Thomas Coram'. The book is now very rare. Some copies have no imprint and were probably run off for friends in 1689, and many copies have manuscript corrections.[20] Coram's copy is dated 1690, so the likelihood is that he was given it when he was commissioned by the Navy Office go to Liverpool to detect frauds in the ships taken on to transport soldiers to Ireland at that time. Coram in his turn inscribed the book 'To Mr. Mills, worthy sir, I happened to find among my few books Mr Pepps, his memoires, which I thought might be acceptable to you and therefore pray you accept it. I am with much respect, sir, your most humble servant Thos. Coram June 10th 1746.'[21] It is thought that Mr Mills might have been Peter Mills, a shipwright.

It is certain that Coram was not invited to the splendid entertainment to view the newly completed court room where governors and artists alike hoped to reap the rewards of their effort and labour in the shape of donations and commissions. Hogarth had contributed a fine painting of Moses brought before Pharaoh's daughter, and Francis Hayman a painting of the finding of Moses in the bulrushes, both continuing the Moses theme of Coram's seal; James Wills provided the illustration to

---

[18] Smart, 'A Letter from *Mrs Midnight*', pp. 60–1.
[19] Ralph and Mary Briggs, *Watchcoats* (www.nwta.com/couriers/11–96/watchcoats.html). I am grateful to David Coke for drawing my attention to the provenance of Coram's coat.
[20] I owe this information to Dr Richard Luckett, Pepys Librarian.
[21] Dobson, *Eighteenth Century Vignettes*, p. 45.

Christ's admonition, 'suffer little children to come unto me and forbid them not'; the least satisfactory of the four paintings was Highmore's depiction of the angel surprising Hagar with Ishmael, the child she had borne for Abraham, asleep in the desert, an outcast. Between the large biblical paintings, eight enchanting roundels proclaim the charitable virtues of the laity, the earliest examples being Christ's Hospital, Bethlem and the Charter House (painted by the young Gainsborough), followed by the Chelsea, Greenwich, St Thomas's and St George's Hospitals, and finally the Foundling Hospital itself painted by Richard Wilson. All the paintings were elaborately framed, possibly the work of William Linnell.[22] The ornate plaster-work ceiling and the relief work and decoration on the walls, the work of William Wilton, all added to the sumptuous feel of the room.

Samuel Smith, who had baptised many infants and had been made a governor, could have been present at the gathering. If so he would have been able to give an account of the occasion to Coram, who was still living with him. George Vertue, that indefatiguable chronicler of the London art world, noted that

> Wednesday the first of April 1747, at the Foundling Hospital was an enter-
> tainment of publick dinner of the Governors and other gentlemen that had
> inclination – about 170 persons great benefactions given then to the hospital
> – at the same time was seen the four paintings newly put up, done Gratis by
> four eminent painters – by Hayman Hogarth Hymore & Wills – & by most
> people generally approved & commended. As works in history painting in a
> higher degree of merit than has heretofore been done by English Painters –
> some other portraits are done & doing by Ramsay, Hudson & landskis &c.[23]

While all this flowering of artistic activity was taking place, Coram, sitting alone in his room, received an unwelcome letter from Boston. The King's Chapel in Boston needed rebuilding, and the minister and committee appointed to oversee the work had written to Coram seeking his help.

---

[22] Borg, *Jacobsen and the Building of the Foundling Hospital*, p. 16, note 16.
[23] *Vertue Note Books*, vol. III, Walpole Society, 22, 1933–4, p. 135.

14

A Gift Misused

Coram was unmoved by the letter he received from the minister and committee appointed to oversee the rebuilding of the King's Chapel in Boston. In that letter they reminded him of his attachment to the Church of England and of the many occasions on which he had exerted his interest and influence in favour of the infant churches in New England. They wrote that the rebuilding placed a great burden upon the infant people, and was made the more so by the 'violent oppression of dissenters and the unreasonable charges they have imposed on us for the purchase of a small piece of ground needed and for its rebuilding'.[1] It is a measure of Coram's renown in Boston that his name appears alongside that of Archbishop Herring in a list of those to whom the committee were appealing for help. However, Coram did not answer the letter, though six months later he was to receive a visitor.

Coram was a man who rarely held grudges, but the treatment he had received from the men of Taunton had ruined the life he might have had in New England, and he never completely forgave those who had wrecked his early career. Now, however, his resentment was directed against the vestrymen of the King's Chapel. They were the people he had entrusted with the responsibility of seeing that his gift of fifty-nine acres was put to good use. He accused them of doing nothing to ensure that his gift of land was properly used.

Coram had been following events in Taunton, and was aware that there had been changes following a militant crusade started by William Cutler. When, in 1722, Cutler returned to Boston to become minister of Christchurch, he started to agitate for religious liberty for Anglicans in New England. Something of this fervour had reached Taunton. In 1728 a plot of land had been deeded for the erection of a church building near Three Miles River, on what is now Tremont Street, but the congregation lacked the money to build. Although Coram was busy with his work for the royal charter, he had heard that at least thirty families in Taunton had got together to request a missionary to come to preach. 'On 17th January, 1739 the Rev. Ebeneezer

---

1   Foote, *Annals of the King's Chapel*, vol. 11, p. 70. The Church of England in America felt threatened by a revival known as 'the great awakening' which swept through the country at this time. George Whitfield had come from Savannah, Georgia, with crusading zeal, preaching 175 sermons in seventy days while covering 800 miles. The Church of England was alarmed at the inroads Dissenters were making, and fearful that its precarious hold in America would be further undermined.

Miller was engaged to preach next Sunday by a request of the committee of those of the Church of England in Taunton.'[2] The wish to have a church was growing. Three years later twenty-six subscribers had raised £528 to build their first church on the Glebe, and called it St Thomas. This was exactly the kind of development that Coram wished to support, and he wanted his gift to be used for the benefit of this fledgling church. He wrote to the SPG in 1740 saying that the Bishop of London and his secretary had written several times to Mr Miles, the minister in charge of the King's Chapel, to ask for news concerning his gift and that there had been no reply.[3]

Coram believed that he knew the reason for the neglect of his gift. At the time the deed for the fifty-nine acres was given over to the vestrymen there were two ministers at the King's Chapel, a Mr Bridge and a Mr Miles, who were at odds with each other over the relative social status of their respective wives. The story has a Trollopian flavour, but there is evidence to show that Coram's account of the dispute between the two ministers and the effect it had on his gift had a great deal of truth in it. Coram's account of the story appears in the annals of the King's Chapel.[4]

> The said Mr Bridge was a sober man, well esteemed and married to a sober, virtuous and well bred young lady out of one of the best families in that country at which the church was highly pleased and made her a handsome present of plate. At which, Mrs Miles, the other minister's wife, who was not so well respected, was filled with resentment and she incensed her husband, who was a very fiery man against Mr. Bridge, who soon after left for England for a short time. Then Mr. Miles, by his influence with Mr. Hall, the secretary to Bishop Compton, prevailed upon his lordship to order Mr. Bridge to remove from Boston, first to one place, then to another in some remote country where he and his wife died.

The correspondence that passed between the Bishop of London and Mr Miles bears this story out.[5] The chapel record merely states that

> Captain Coram attributes vestry neglect to the fact that he lodged the deed with Mr Bridge, for which reason Mr. Miles disrespected the said deed of gift and prevented the vestry from taking any notice of it.

Coram then wrote in 1740 to the Secretary of the SPG asking the organisation to make inquiries through their American agents into the neglect of his gift, 'due to wilful prejudice and mismanagement', and that 'if the vestry should neglect it, let them make the deed over to the corporation [SPG], who may perhaps think fit to place a missionary there'. He added characteristically, 'I am persuaded that the present inhabitants will not adventure to play their tricks with the corporation as the last generation of vipers did.'[6]

Coram may well have upset the vestrymen when he very first went to Boston, by complaining to the Archbishop of Canterbury about the behaviour of their minister,

2   Emery, *History of Taunton*, pp. 241–2.
3   Coram to Secretary of SPG, 18 September 1740: Perry, *Historical Collections*, vol. 3, pp. 342–5.
4   Foote, *Annals of the King's Chapel*, vol. 1, p. 356.
5   Mr Miles to Dr Beveridge, 4 January 1704: Perry, *Historical Collections*, vol. 2, p. 75; Mr Bridge to the Secretary, 7 October 1706: Perry, vol. 2, p. 80; Perry, vol. 2, p. 246.
6   Coram to Secretary of SPG, 18 September 1740; Perry, *Historical Collections*, vol. 3, p. 245.

and it may be for this reason that they were somewhat suspicious of him. After living in Boston for only two years he had written to the Archbishop of Canterbury disparaging a certain Mr Hatton who had taken over the pulpit at the King's Chapel in 1696. The young Coram was writing to complain about his behaviour:

> The said Minister, Mr. Hatton, was a very worthless man. He resided in Boston and was utterly unfit to gain and reconcile to the church such dissenters so strong and inveterate against it; but he was far from attempting to do so for he frequently sat up on Saturday nights to play cards at all or the greatest part of the night in company with an Irish butcher and an Irish barber and another or more of such his acquaintance. Whereby he was usually so much disordered and prevented from officiating the next day at Church which gave numerous enemies great opportunities to ridicule against him.

This was part of a letter pleading for more missionaries to be sent to the 'inhabited parts of the British empire', and an early example of Coram's habit of writing to complain of behaviour that he thought was injurious to any cause to which he was committed. The vestry were not impressed: '. . . of Mr. Hatton we have an account by a not unprejudiced witness in Mr. Thomas Coram'.[7] By 1745 the vestrymen may have forgotten or forgiven Coram's criticism of their minister, for it did not then stop them appealing to his generosity; but in the 1730s it may have made them less receptive to his complaints about their neglect of his gift.

It is clear that Coram was taking a great interest in the little church of St Thomas's in Taunton. In 1742 he sent them a very fine book of common prayer, a companion to the one he had given to the Foundling Hospital, both given to him by Arthur Onslow. The inscription reads: 'The Rt. Hon Arthur Onslow, Esq., Speaker of the House of Commons and Treasurer to His Majesty's Navy to Thomas Coram of London, gent., for the use of the church lately built at Taunton in 1742.' It is now one of the most valued treasures belonging to the present St Thomas's Episcopalian church. The church also received a valuable gift of books for their library, stamped throughout with initials TC in red. Sadly, many of the books have been lost, but seventeen have survived. An old mutilated record book, dated March 1742–43, belonging to the church provides evidence to show how Coram's gift of books was valued. It was noted that 'Abraham Waldron returned his 2 borrowed books on 2 April, 1743 to James Briggs, in good order, having retained them for one month. Pledge of 15/- [15 shillings] was returned.'[8] Some of the other pledges have a more homely feel to them: 'the hed of a riden hood – one pare of balens – one hankicher' and 'one sheet coten and Linen and one Pilowe'.[9] Money was obviously scarce but if the citizens of Taunton were prepared to pledge their bed linen, it shows how much the books were valued.

All that remains of that first church are a few crumbling tombstones in the Episcopalian burying ground, two miles west of the Green. They provide startling evidence of the changes in religious allegiance that had taken place among the people of

[7] Foote, *Annals of the King's Chapel*, vol. 1, p. 365.
[8] Emery, *History of Taunton*, p. 255.
[9] *St Thomas's Church*, p. 2.

Taunton. Nathanial Burt, one of the first rectors of the church, who died in 1765, his wife and Mr Thomas Burt as well as Peter Walker are buried there. It was the earlier dissenting members of the Burt and Walker families who had hounded Thomas Coram, not least because they suspected him of wanting to establish the Anglican form of worship in Taunton.

By January 1743 the parish was able to buy a glebe for the use of the rector.[10] Unable to help the church in Taunton through his gift, as he had hoped, Coram decided to sever his last link with Massachusetts. He sold the house he had had built in 1700 for himself and his newly married wife, as well as the land with apple orchard, to Nathaniel Blagrove, a merchant of Bristol, on 23 February 1743.[11] There is no proof that he gave the money from the sale of his house to the church to build a dwelling for a permanent minister. However, it seems more than likely, since the house was to have been called Coram Hall. The glebe land is described in the deed 'as a certain parcel of land with a dwelling house thereon, which house when enlarged, shall be called Coram Hall'.[12] The church was blown down in a gale in 1815 and a new church was built in 1828 when the glebe was sold. The congregation outgrew that church and the present church, the third St Thomas's, was built in 1857 in 'English gothic cathedral style'. A stained glass representation of Coram in his red coat in one of the windows commemorates his association with the church. It is a memorial to the man who had tried so hard to encourage the establishment of an Episcopalian church in Taunton and worked to support it. His work for the Foundling Hospital is also honoured there.

The King's Chapel vestrymen were not put off by the lack of response from Coram to their letter of 1745. Six months later Coram received another letter, saying that Mr Trecothick, a lawyer, had been sent to London to appeal personally to those he hoped might help raise money for the chapel. Trecothick asked permission to call on Coram and said he would give him a 'particular account, together with an estimate of expense'.[13] Coram agreed to see him, and in a letter to Boston Trecothick gives a very vivid account of his interview.

> I had almost forgot to give you an account of my embassy to Capt. Coram. I waited on him and was very graciously received; but when I opened the occasion of my visit he broke out into the most passionate reproaches against the vestry of the King's Chapel for slighting the present he made of a piece of land. I found it would not do to insist they were to a man another set of people and not chargeable with the misconduct, with whatever else I could think of to cool the old gentleman, but all in vain. After several attempts to soothe him, he flatly told me 'he knew it in his power to serve God, but if the twelve apostles were to apply to him on behalf of it he would persist in refusing to do it'. This I thought a definitive answer.

10 Article in the *Church Militant*, May 1975, p. 9, *Collections of Old Colony Historical Society*.
11 *Taunton Daily Gazette*, 20 August 1904, *Collections of Old Colony Historical Society*.
12 *St Thomas's Church*, p. 3.
13 Foote, *Annals of the King's Chapel*, vol. 11, p. 88.

It looks very much from Coram's furious reply, that Mr Trecothick was trying to persuade him to give the land in Taunton to the King's Chapel. Mr Trecothick was nothing if not persistent. He paid Coram another visit and was again courteously received, 'But on mention of the church he has directly relapsed into his passion, so that you can lay aside all help from that quarter.'[14]

In his deed of 1703, Coram had stated that forty rateable men from Taunton had to make application to the vestry in Boston; however, when they did apply there were only twenty-six Taunton men qualified to do so. The King's Chapel has always maintained that this was the reason why his gift had not been used. This cut no ice with Coram, and it must have been clear to Mr Trecothick and the other vestrymen that Coram would have altered the deed he had made, in different circumstances, in 1703, to suit the situation in Taunton as it was in the 1740s. His letters to them, which had remained unanswered, must have made it clear that he wanted his land to be used for the benefit of the church in Taunton. It was no wonder that Coram was angry. As for the excuse that they were no longer the same men who had signed the deed, that too was brushed aside. Coram had specifically mentioned in his deed that not only the present vestrymen were responsible for his land, but also their successors in office.

The subsequent actions of the vestrymen did them little credit. It seems that after Coram's death in 1751, the vestrymen were nervous that a suit might be brought against them, showing how unsure they were as to their legal right to claim the lands in Taunton, which they now proposed to do. In 1753 a guinea each was given to Jeremiah Gridley and James Olis as a retaining fee for the church's right to the land in Taunton. Eliakim Hutchinson, one of those who had sat in judgement on Coram in 1700, was asked to take charge of the affair on behalf and for the benefit of the church.[15] In direct opposition to Coram's known wishes, they did what they had not dared do in his lifetime: they transferred the gift, meant for the church in Taunton, to the benefit of King's Chapel.

At a vestry meeting in May 1754, Hutchinson reported that he had settled the affair of the land in Taunton. The son of the original owner, Stephen Burt, was happy to pay the gentlemen of the vestry £100 lawful money, with the proviso that there would be no recovery against them in the next inferior court in Taunton.[16] Eliakim Hutchinson was empowered to proceed, and the £100 lawful money, when recovered, was to be applied to the building of the new chapel.[17] A more dishonourable outcome is hard to imagine. Stephen Burt was the son of the man who had shot at Coram and threatened him with violence if he tried to take possession of the fifty-nine acres that were legally his. It must be remembered that those acres were given as compensation for the damage Coram had suffered to his shipyard at the hands of Burt, which amounted to far more than £100. Coram had never been able to use the land, but the vestrymen knew very well how he wished it to be used. Yet only four years after his death, the men he had trusted to defend his interests had betrayed his wishes. The deed putting the transaction into effect was signed and witnessed on 22 July 1755. To the church in Taunton, justice was not seen to be done. The powerful vestrymen in

14 Ibid., p. 92.
15 Ibid., p. 117.
16 Ibid.
17 Ibid.

Boston justified their behaviour by asserting that a claim had never been made by forty rateable men from Taunton. Refusal to answer his requests for information as to what was being done with his gift, and holding on to the original document, then claiming, in contradiction to Coram's known wishes, to be applying a stipulation made fifty years before in different circumstances, may be legally defensible, but even that defence could be challenged. Coram had no family with an interest in continuing the fight. He was a relatively poor man and there was no one to see that his wishes were carried out. That Coram's name is still remembered with gratitude by the church in Taunton is a fitting memorial.

15

The Pensioner

After an absence of nearly four years Coram began once again to visit the Foundling Hospital and started to attend the baptismal services of the children. This became a regular habit, and he stood godfather to more than twenty of these tiny infants, enabled in this way to feel part again of his hospital.[1] In a little note he wrote to Hans Sloane, preserved with Sloane's papers, Coram humbly asks him to visit a pretty girl and another child with eye problems, showing the interest he took in all aspects of the children's welfare.[2] There were undoubtedly other unrecorded instances of his kindness to the children he loved. It showed how far removed Coram was from the everyday affairs of the hospital that when he wanted to gain admittance for friends to see the children, he did not even know to whom to write, but addressed the letter requesting permission for a visit to 'sir or madam'. His emphatic signature, with its huge capital letters made its own statement.[3]

Plans were now being drawn up for the building of the chapel but money had yet to be raised for the building. When the foundation stone was laid in May 1747, the governors, building on the hospital's social success, turned the occasion into a celebration with a public breakfast in the hospital attended by a 'great concourse of Nobility and Ladies of distinction'. Realising that the small children themselves were very effective in helping with the fundraising, the governors had the children present baskets of flowers to the guests, swiftly followed by them making the rounds with collection boxes. There are no records of those who attended, but among them must have been a number of the ladies who signed Coram's original petition. Lady de Vere[4] and Lady Betty Germain[5] both remained involved with the hospital, and no doubt persuaded their friends to attend. The occasion was a great success and, although the expenses slightly exceeded receipts, donations and the sale of the tickets at 2s 6d each

---

[1] LMA, A/AF/A14/004/00/002, Register of Baptisms 1741–1838.
[2] Original letters to Hans Sloane, vol. xxii, 1740–4: BL, Hans Sloane MS 4057 40 80.
[3] State Papers, 1567–1760, BL Stowe 155 28, f. 114.
[4] A draft letter to Lady de Vere discusses the problems of appointing a lady of distinction to the post of Chief Nurse and suggesting she herself might be interested, August 1752: LMA, A/FH/A06/001/005/10.
[5] In 1752 Lady Germain refused the offer of the post of Chief Nurse on the grounds of age and infirmity: LMA, A/FH/A06/001/005/09.

brought in £596 for the building.[6] The building fund had got off to a flying start and the governors, quick to build on this success, turned it into an annual event.

The chapel, although not finished, was also seen as an attraction, and large numbers of the public attended every Sunday to see the children baptised. The governors, realising that this presented yet another opportunity for fundraising, formalised the occasion. Four governors with white wands passed up and down the middle of the chapel after prayers while foundling children went along the rows of seats with collection plates. These fundraising activities were crowned by the most spectacular event of them all, when George Frederick Handel joined the list of artists giving their services for the benefit of the hospital. His offer of a performance of vocal and instrumental music was accepted with gratitude by the governors. The proceeds were to be used to finish the chapel, and tickets for the first concert were much sought after when it was known that the Prince and Princess of Wales were to attend. Hogarth designed the tickets for the performance, using the coat of arms he had also designed as a heading, and included the request that gentlemen were desired to come without their swords and ladies asked not to wear hoops on their dresses, such were the numbers expected.[7] Tickets were advertised in the *London Gazeteer* and sold at White's chocolate house and Balston's coffee house in Cornhill. Originally scheduled for 24 May 1749, the concert was delayed with good reason until 27 May at the Prince's request. The *Gentleman's Magazine* recorded that on Saturday 27th:

> The P. and Prss. of Wales, with a great number of persons of quality and distinction were at the chapel of the Foundling hospital; to hear several pieces of vocal and instrumental musick, compos'd by Georg Frederick Handel, Esq., for the benefit of the foundation. 1. The musick for the late fireworks, and the anthem of peace. 2. Select pieces from the oratorio of *Solomon*, relating to the dedication of the temple; and 3. Several pieces composed for the occasion, the words taken from scripture, and applicable to the charity, and its benefactors. There was no collection, but the tickets were at half a guinea, and the audience above a thousand.[8]

One of the pieces composed for the occasion was the Foundling Hospital anthem, with its rousing alleluia chorus borrowed from the *Messiah*. This concert marked the beginning of Handel's long association with the hospital. Handel, following in Hogarth's footsteps, may have used the Foundling Hospital concerts to promote his work, particularly performances of the *Messiah*. The success of the concerts, which became an annual event, raised large sums of money for the hospital over the years. Handel, like Hogarth, had an instinctive sympathy and belief in the necessity of its work. He had been influenced, while working at the University of Halle, by the passionate devotion of Professor Francke to the needs of orphans. It is strange that the governors never consulted Francke's account of his orphan house in Halle, which was founded in 1695.[9] Francke's account of its history was translated as *Pietas Hallensis* and

6   *Gentleman's Magazine*, vol. 17, 1 May 1747, p. 245.
7   O'Connell, *London*, 1753, p. 160.
8   *Gentleman's Magazine*, vol. 19, 29 May 1749, p. 235.
9   *Segensvolle Fusstpafen*, 1790, was translated as *Pietas Hallensis*.

11. Invitation to a performance of Handel's *Messiah*, 1750, with the hospital's coat of arms, which had been designed by Hogarth.

was well known at the time, inspiring George Whitfield to open his orphan house in Bethesda in Georgia in 1740.

Coram, Hogarth and Handel were all childless, and all three felt a special sympathy for children, particularly orphans and foundlings. The words of Sir Oliver Knox in Thomas Middleton's play *The Chaste Maid in Cheapside*, 'for having none, I mean to make good deeds my children', seem particularly applicable to them, who by their actions were indeed giving effect to his words.[10] By the time he died in 1759, Handel had raised £6,725 in total for the hospital. Having first declined the honour of becoming a governor because 'he would serve the charity with more pleasure in his way than being a member of the corporation',[11] he allowed the governors to elect him the following year, giving an organ for use in the chapel.[12] Gifts to the hospital continued to be received. Andrea Casali's painting, *The Offering of the Wise Men*, was

---

[10] Middleton, *Five Plays*, p. 181.
[11] LMA, General Committee Minutes, 9 May 1749.
[12] LMA, General Committee Minutes, 9 May 1750.

installed over the altar in the chapel.[13] It is not known when Coram expressed a wish to be buried in the chapel, but he must have decided that this was the place where he wished his bones to rest, despite the fact that his wife was buried at All Hallows, London Wall. The chapel was in fact only dedicated the week before Coram died in 1751[14] and not opened for regular Sunday services until 16 April 1753.

In 1750 Hogarth made a well-publicised gift of his painting *The March to Finchley* to the hospital, a gift which combined a mixture of commercialism and altruism. Hogarth had meant to dedicate it to King George, as it showed his guards about to depart to put down the 1745 uprising when the Young Pretender got as far as Derby before being stopped. The painting shows a typically chaotic Hogarthian domestic street scene in the foreground, with the soldiers drunk and disorderly, while in the background the men are shown marching off in good order to Finchley. The King was most displeased by Hogarth's painting and is reported to have said 'what a painter burlesque a soldier; he deserves to be picketed for his insolence'.[15]

Hogarth, unable to sell his picture, had prints made and advertised at 7s 6d, and for an extra 3 shillings each subscriber was entitled to a lottery ticket for the original painting. Of the 2,000 tickets printed, 167 were unsold and given to the hospital. The *General Advertiser* reported that 'at two o'clock the Box was open'd and the Fortunate choice was Number 1941, which belongs to the said Hospital; and the same Night Mr. Hogarth delivered the Picture to the Governors'.[16] The *Gentleman's Magazine* reported that it was in fact a lady who had drawn the winning number, but that it was feared that it might be seen as scandalous if she gave the ticket to the hospital so Hogarth was asked to present it as coming from him.[17] Whether true or not, it was one more indication of the public's ambivalent attitude to the work of the hospital, despite the fact that it was becoming an ever more popular venue for social functions.

Hogarth remained devoted to the hospital. He had designed a coat of arms – a naked baby under a half moon and two stars on the shield, with a many breasted Diana of Ephesus symbolising charity as a supporter on one side while Britannia holds the cap of liberty as the supporter on the other side; the crest is a lamb and the motto the single word, help. He also designed the children's uniforms, coats of brown drugget trimmed with scarlet and dresses made of brown serge for the girls. All the children, boys and girls, wore white hats tied with red binding.[18] Both Hogarth and Jane, his wife, had babies named after them. Jane supervised the boarded-out children in Chiswick, writing that she thought the children should spend several weeks longer in the country during the summer months. She continued to supervise the children until at least 1762, when she made out a bill showing she had paid two nurses £13 13s, while another nurse got £10 10s for nursing a child through smallpox.[19]

13 Nicolson, *Treasures of the Foundling Hospital*.
14 *Read's Weekly*, 6 April 1751, n. 1388: 'Last week the new Chapel belonging to the Foundling Hospital was consecrated with due solemnity.'
15 Binney, *A Guide*, p. 13.
16 *General Advertiser*, 1 May 1750.
17 *Gentleman's Magazine*, May 1750.
18 LMA, Sketch and Description of the Children at the Breakfasting, General Committee Minutes, 1 May 1747.
19 LMA, Misc. A/FH/M01/1–17, Mrs Hogarth's account of the Foundling children under her care, October 1765.

It was not until Coram was in his eightieth year that his friend Samson Gideon became aware of how impoverished Coram had become. Gideon[20] was the son of a Jewish Portuguese emigrant who had made his own fortune; an amiable and generous man, he had become a governor in 1747, paying £50 for the privilege, as did many who wished to become governors. It is typical of the way in which Coram had been treated by the governors that it was an outsider, in many ways an outsider like Coram himself, who took steps to see that the old man did not sink further into poverty and got up a subscription for him, writing that 'his little fortune being gone and being far advanced in age and utterly incapable of providing for himself by any business . . . [the signatories] do of their own accord and free will resolve to grant to the said Thomas Coram one guinea yearly, to be paid May 1st'.[21] But first, Dr Brocklesbury, the friend who knew Coram best, was deputed to discover if he would be offended by this action. Coram is said to have replied

> I have not wasted the little wealth of which I was formerly possessed in self-indulgence and vain expenses, and am not ashamed to confess, that, in this my old age, I am poor.[22]

The subscription brought in a total of 161 guineas, the Prince of Wales subscribing 20 guineas. Although some of the names on the roll have faded, they do not appear to include any of the great men who became so keen to associate themselves with the hospital just ten years before. It was Coram's merchant friends who subscribed most of the money. They had not forgotten what he had done to increase trade in his early life, writing that he had been the procurer of great good to the people of Great Britain and citing his work to procure the Tar Act, his action in arranging for the importation of deal from the Netherlands and Germany as well as his work to obtain the charter for the Foundling Hospital as evidence as to why he deserved help.

The old man could now live the last two years of his life in relative comfort. He no longer had to rely on the charity of friends, and he moved out of the Smiths' house to lodgings of his own in Spur Street, now Panton Street, off Leicester Fields, where it would not have been so far for him to walk to the hospital. He was said often to be seen sitting in the arcade of the hospital, dressed in his well-worn red coat, 'distributing with tears in his Eyes Gingerbread to the Children, himself being at the time supported by Subscription'.[23] Simply having the money to buy the children little treats must have given the old man so much pleasure. He must also have been gratified to receive from the mayor and corporation of Lyme the compliment of the freedom of the borough in 1749. His letter acknowledging the honour is now on display in the museum in Lyme Regis. The kindly Dr Mead arranged at the same time to present Coram with prints of the hospital. Two perspective views of the hospital with emblematic figures of the hospital had recently been engraved by Charles

---

[20] Samson Gideon of Eardley Grange, 1699–1762, left substantial sums to charity. His son, Sir Samson Gideon, also became a governor of the Foundling Hospital and became Baron Eardley. Cokayne, *Complete Peerage*, vol. 5, p. 1.

[21] LMA, A/FH/Ao1/7/2: subscription list 1749.

[22] Brocklesby, *Private Virtue and Publick Spirit*, p. 97.

[23] LMA, Morris Lievesley, Notebook. According to Lievesley's notes he had heard the story from Thomas Collingwood, Secretary of the Hospital 1758–90, who said he remembered seeing Coram with the children.

a. Children dance round an emblematic figure of Venus while benevolent, unpretentious English visitors stroll past overdressed French gentlemen shown sneering at the hospital.

b. Fortune stands beside her wheel outside the hospital, while Charity, holding a child in her arms, is within. A sad line of mothers wait there to surrender their babies.

12. Perspective views of the Foundling Hospital, 14 April 1749, published to raise money for the hospital

Grignion and Pierre Canot and published to encourage donations.[24] They were dedicated to the Duke of Bedford, and perhaps it was these that were given to Coram, a gracious and thoughtful gesture on the part of Mead.

America was never far from Coram's thoughts. He had always wanted the teachings of the Church of England to be more widely known in New England, and had used every occasion open to him to advance the interests of the Church of England in America. He had watched the growing importance of Harvard as a centre of learning and had proposed to the Archbishop of Canterbury a scheme for founding an Anglican College in Cambridge to counter the influence of the Dissenters. He wrote in 1748 suggesting that land be bought in Cambridge, New England, 'and thereupon be built and properly Furnished a good College to be named the King's College'.[25] He may have chosen the name as a challenge to the vestrymen of the King's Chapel. He particularly wanted the college to be able to instruct the children of the native Indians, saying they were grateful and kind if well used. He thought, with his usual optimism, that 'His Majesty's good subjects would doubtless most chearfully contribute towards carrying forward so good a work.' Two years later, in 1750, he followed up this petition with a letter to George Onslow, the brother of the Speaker, Arthur Onslow. He now said that he knew of twenty acres of ground in a convenient spot in Cambridge, which he proposed to purchase. He said there were two colleges for Dissenters in New England and not one for the Church of England. He intended to make a present of the land for the erecting thereon of a 'College for a University of Learning according to the Church of England'.[26] In his memoir of Coram, Brocklesby also writes of him wanting to set up an establishment for the education of Indian girls.[27] There is no record of such a petition, apart from the ideas in Coram's letter to the archbishop, but it would have been very much in character. Coram had always believed that women had an important role to play in society: as mothers they were models for the next generation of girls, and he thought they needed to be educated to be able to fulfil that role. He had always had a concern for the native Indians in America, and all his experience had taught him that if they were treated with kindness and generosity they would become useful allies, as the French had demonstrated. He had been angered by the way in which they had been cheated out of their lands by the British and New Englanders, so he would have seen his proposals as a way of making amends. It remains a mystery as to how Coram proposed to find the money needed for the land. He may have been intending to exchange his fifty-nine acres in Taunton for the twenty he wanted in Cambridge. What makes these accounts of his last ideas so poignant is the fact that he was always very conscious of his own limited education. It was as if his own lack of scholastic attainment had given him a greater respect for and understanding of the value of education, and his own beliefs reinforced his wish to see the spread of Anglican-based education in America. Coram was now a very old man, and none of these later initiatives would ever be more than

[24] O'Connell, London, 1753, pp. 158, 159; BL, Crace XXXI.67 1880–11–13–4786; Crace XXXI.68 1880–11–13–4787.

[25] Thomas Coram, Memorial and Petition to the Archbishop of Canterbury, 1748: Perry, Historical Collections, vol. 3, pp. 64–7.

[26] Coram to George Onslow, 12 May 1750: 'Letters of Thomas Coram'. New England Genealogical & Antiquarian Register, vol. 41, reprinted in Notes and Queries, 7th series, vol. 4, October 1887, p. 142.

[27] Brownlow, History and Objects of the Foundling Hospital, p. 123.

ideas. What is interesting is that in his final years Coram never changed. He had always wanted to see the American colonies more closely linked to Britain and to see the spread of Anglicanism in America. He no longer had a part to play in the rescue of destitute children in London, although his love and concern for them remained as strong as ever. Perhaps the idea of helping Indian children provided him with another outlet for his desire to assist the underprivileged.

There is no one to tell how Coram passed his last few months. Did some kind friend care for him during his last illness or did death come suddenly? All that is known is that the governors were notified on 29 March 1751 that Thomas Coram had died. They knew that Coram wished to be buried in the vault under the altar of the chapel and they immediately set about making arrangements for the funeral.

The following day the death of the Prince of Wales was announced, and London was plunged into mourning. The Prince's funeral, which was to be private, was scheduled for the day following that of Coram. It was to take place in the painted chamber of Westminster Palace. It is a strange coincidence that the day before Coram had handed over the charter to the Duke of Bedford, London had been joyfully celebrating the birthday of the Princess of Wales. Now, the day after Coram's death, the city was mourning the death of the Prince.

If the governors had sidelined Coram in his lifetime, they did him proud in death. The chapel had already become a renowned venue for concerts as well as services and baptisms. It was well adapted to serve as the theatre for the last act of Coram's life. Some of the gentlemen of the choirs of St Paul's Cathedral and Westminster Abbey had spontaneously offered to perform the choir service. Charity sermons were preached at St Paul's and the gentlemen of Westminster would have been aware of Coram's efforts to help their poorer parishioners, so their offer to sing was a genuine tribute. Dr Boyce, the organist at St Paul's, composed a special anthem for the occasion. The governors asked the High Constable of Holborn to attend with six constables and their staves, and they ordered twelve workmen of the hospital to attend to secure the doors. No one was to be admitted into the chapel except in mourning, and six of the governors were to support the pall, the rest to follow the coffin into the church. They also realised that a book would be needed to register the names of all persons buried in the vault under the chapel of the hospital.[28]

The funeral was reported very fully by the newspapers and journals in the following days.[29] Read's Weekly Journal reported that the galleries were filled with gentlemen and ladies, all dressed in mourning and with great decency, and the order with which the whole was conducted made it 'a very awful sight'. The London Evening Post gave a vivid account of the occasion:

---

[28] When the chapel was pulled down in 1927, 142 more coffins were discovered, some in a very deplorable state. A new coffin was made for Coram and he was reburied, first in unconsecrated ground at Kensal Green cemetery, where he remained until he could be re-interred in the chapel at Berkhamsted, to where the institution moved in 1935. When those buildings were sold and the Foundling Hospital returned to London he was brought to his final resting place in St Andrew's church, Holborn, where his tomb can be seen in a chapel in the church. LMA, Letters re reburial, FH Vaults, 1927.

[29] London Advertiser, 4 April 1751; Read's Weekly Journal, 6 April 1751; London Evening Post, 2–4 April 1751; London Penny Post, or The Morning Advertiser, 3 April 1751; Whitehall Evening Post, 2 April 1751; Remembrancer, 1741–51; Gentleman's Magazine, vol. 21 (1751), pp. 141, 183.

13. The Foundling Hospital from the top of Red Lyon Street in 1751, as it was at the time of Coram's death.

> Last night the Remains of the excellent Capt. Coram were interred pursuant to his Desire in the Vault under the Chapel of the Foundling Hospital. The body was brought in a Hearse from his Lodgings near Leicester Square, attended by one Mourning coach in which were his Relations.

We know from his father's will that Coram had a half-brother, John, who had predeceased his father. John Coram and his wife Ann (Anna) had had two children, Richard and Anna. Letters of administration were later granted to Ann Coram, spinster and next of kin (the duty would surely have been Richard's had he been alive), so it must have been Coram's niece who rode in the mourning coach, perhaps with her friend Joyce Baker. Little else is known about Coram's relations. A godson called Thomas Corham had been given a Beza Testament, and Coram had also given a Baskett Bible to a Miss Spes Corham.[30] Apart from the fact that Thomas Coram's mother was also called Spes, a very unusual Christian name, nothing is known of the lady or if she attended the funeral. Ann Coram died three years later on 18 June 1754, thus bringing to an end that branch of the family.[31]

The account continues:

> The Corpse was met at the gate of the Foundling Hospital by the Governors and the children of both sexes (a most affecting sight) who walked two and two before the coffin which was immediately preceded by a Person carrying the Charter on a Crimson Velvet cushion. The Pall was supported by Sir Joseph Hankey, Kt., Peter Burrell, Joseph Fawthorp, John Milner, Paul

[30] John Baskett, King's Printer, claimed a monopoly to print bibles. After his death in 1742, his sons printed bibles in 1743.
[31] PROB 11/809, Q. 191. She left one shilling to her cousin, Ann Canner, and the residue to her friend, Joyce Baker, who had looked after her during her illness.

Joddrel, Samuel Clarke, Stephen Beckingham and Samson Gideon Esqs and followed by a great number of gentlemen, walking two and two. Taylor White, the Treasurer attending as Chief Mourner. As soon as the Corpse entered the Chapel (the galleries of which were fill'd with gentlemen and ladies) some of them from the choir of St Paul's who attended, began to sing the Burial Service, which was composed by Dr. Boyce who played the same on a small organ set on one side of the Chapel.[32] When the Minister had read all the Service but the last collect, the following anthem, composed by Dr. Boyce, was sung by Mr. Bear, Mr Meace and Mr. Savage and the Chorus Parts by the other Gentlemen of Westminster and St Pauls.

The words of the anthem were reported in *Penny Post*:

If we believe that Jesus died, and rose again; Even so them also which sleep in Jesus, will God bring with him.
For this we say unto you by the Word of the Lord, That we which are alive and remain unto the Coming of the Lord, shall not prevent them which are asleep.
For the Lord Himself shall descend from Heaven with a Shout, with the Voice of the Archangel, and the Trump of God: And the Dead in Christ shall rise first.
Then we which are alive and remain, shall be caught up together with them in the Clouds to meet the Lord in the Air; and so shall we ever be with the Lord.
Wherefore comfort ye one another with these words.[33]

The *London Evening Post* continued:

The clergyman then read the last collect after which the corpse was carried down into the Vault and laid under the Communion Table. The inscription on the coffin was Capt. Thomas Coram, died March 1751, aged 85 years. The spectators seemed greatly moved at this last Duty paid a Man who had spent the great Part of a long Life in Service to the Publick, with uncommon zeal and Spirit and with a total Disregard to his Private interest – rare Example of a Patriot Persevering in which few could equal nor can ever excel.

Such a spontaneous contemporary tribute to a man who had been so little regarded during his final years was perhaps a surprise to some of the governors. The newspaper account ended with a very bad poem, which is nevertheless worth quoting for its sentiment:

From Coram learn that wealth seldom is consig'd
To Those whose Passion is to serve Mankind:
But to the grasping wretch too often given,
Such is the Will of Man – not that of Heaven.

[32] The organ had recently been given to the Hospital by Handel, and still belongs to the organisation.
[33] This same anthem was played at Dr Boyce's own funeral in St Paul's, where he was buried in the vault under the dome of the cathedral.

The Governors, in having the word 'Capt.' inscribed on his coffin, were giving him a title he had never claimed for himself. He had always described himself simply as 'gentleman' or 'gent.' and that is how he wished to be known.[34] They have also caused some confusion over his age, as, if he was born in 1668, he could at most have been 83 when he died. The governors had proposed putting up an inscription in the chapel but in the end arranged for a monument to be erected at no expense to the charity. It seems likely that it was his friend Dr Brockleby who composed the words for his monument. They had to be written by someone who knew him well, and the admonition to the reader at the foot of the inscription could be seen as an implied rebuke to those who had virtually ignored his achievements during his life. The inscription gives a fitting summary of his life.

Captain THOMAS CORAM
Whose Name will never want a Monument
So long as this Hospital shall subsist,
Was born in the year 1668.
A Man eminent in that most eminent Virtue, the Love of Mankind.
Little attentive to his Private Fortune,
and refusing many Opportunities of increasing it,
his Time and Thought were continually employed
In Endeavours to promote the Public Happiness,
both in this Kingdom and elsewhere,
particularly in the Colonies of North America.
and his Endeavours were many Times crowned
with the desired success.
His unwearied Solicitation, for above Seventeen Years together
which would have baffled the Patience and Industry
of any man less zealous in doing Good.
and his Application to Persons of Distinction, of both Sexes,
obtained at length the Charter of Incorporation
bearing the Date 17th October 1739.,
FOR THE MAINTENANCE AND EDUCATION
OF EXPOSED AND DESERTED YOUNG CHILDREN,
by which many Thousands of Lives
may be preserved to the Public and employed in a frugal
and honest Course of Industry.
He died the 29th of March, 1751, in the 84th Year of his Age,
poor in Worldly Estate, rich in Good Works,
and was buried at his own Desire in the Vault underneath this Chapel
(the first there deposited) at the East End thereof, many of the Governors
and other Gentlemen attending the Funeral
to do Honour to his Memory.
READER
Thy Actions will show whether thou art sincere
in the Praises thou may'st bestow on him,
and if thou hast Virtue enough to commend his Virtues,
forget not to add also the Imitation of them.

---

[34] Letters of Administration, April 1752, accord Thomas Coram the status of Esq. PROB 6/127, f. 216v.

Epilogue
A Short History of the Foundling Hospital and Successor Bodies

Because of financial constraints, in the fifteen years between the opening of the hospital in 1741 and 1756 the governors had been able to receive only 1,384 children into their care. Because of limited capacity and the clamour caused by women trying to force their way into the hospital, they had been obliged to institute a selection process. John Milner, a Vice President as well as a member of the Society of Antiquaries, would have been familiar with the Society's system of blackballing the names of undesirable potential members. He now suggested an adaptation of this method for the selection of mothers. Women who drew a white ball out of a bag were admitted immediately, those who had the misfortune to draw out a black ball were turned away. Those who picked a red ball were allowed to wait to see if any of the infants belonging to women who had been admitted with a white ball were not deemed suitable. They then had a chance of gaining admittance for their infant. The enactment of this miserable lottery attracted the attention of outsiders, who were allowed in to watch the anguish of the mothers and it became a public spectacle, testimony to the inability of the hospital to meet the demand for places.

The governors decided that the only way they could expand their activities was by appealing to Parliament for a grant. In 1756 the House of Commons granted the sum of £10,000 to the hospital on condition that *all* children should be admitted. This was a disastrous decision. The flood of children pouring in was more than the governors could properly cope with. Children were now arriving at the rate of more than a hundred a week, the governors precluded from refusing admittance to any child. Stuffed into panniers tied onto donkeys, they came from all over the country. Many died on their way, tossed aside by carriers only interested in the money they could make by offering to transport the babies. Many children were so ill that they hardly had time to be admitted before they were buried. Of the 15,082 children admitted between 1756 and 1760, more than 9,000 died. The hospital came in for renewed criticism, not only on account of the scandals and abuses the governors were powerless to control, but also because the high mortality rate made Members of Parliament feel they were not getting an economic return for their money.

In February 1760 the House of Commons passed a resolution terminating support of the policy of general reception. So ended the most turbulent period in the history of the hospital. It was no wonder that Parliament thought the whole venture an unmitigated disaster. No consideration had been given to the potential size of the demand, nor of the financial implications of meeting the needs of unwanted children

14. Mothers, watched by society ladies and gentlemen, picking black, white and red balls from a bag in the hope of gaining the admission of their infants to the hospital. Print by Bripham Dickinson, 1749.

countrywide, nor of the number of wet nurses and nurses needed to manage such a huge increase in numbers. The hospital received more adverse criticism during those few years than at any other time, and the old idea that children conceived in sin should not be better rewarded than those of the industrious poor made itself heard again.

Parliament, recognising that it had a responsibility for the children admitted under its aegis, tapered the grant accordingly. It also recommended the sale of the six branch hospitals that the governors had acquired at Ackworth, Aylesbury, Barnet, Chester, Shrewsbury and Westerham. The governors had no option but to close their country hospitals, and Ackworth, which had cared for 2,664 children, finally closed in 1773. It was bought by the Quakers in 1786. The governors had also to change their working practices and dispose of the children more rapidly. Apprenticeships had to start earlier, at eight or nine years old instead of fifteen or sixteen. It was no longer so easy to send the boys to sea service, and the governors were grateful to anybody who offered to take the children. Mass apprenticeships were agreed. Careful investigation of masters and follow-up visits were impossible to maintain, and a system that had held so much to recommend it became open to abuse and to opportunities for neglect because the administrative machinery was overloaded. Parliament had given a total of £548,798 to the hospital. The first experiment by central government in using the services of a charitable organisation to care for the nation's unwanted children was seen as a complete disaster.

By the following century, there was a change in policy. In 1801 a resolution was passed stating that, instead of restricting entry to foundlings, the principal object of the Hospital was the maintenance and support of illegitimate children, whose mothers it now sought to rehabilitate. The governors now required a mother to prove that her good faith had been betrayed, that she had been promised marriage or had been raped or seduced and deserted, before accepting her child. Françoise Barret-Ducrocq, in her fascinating book *Love in the Times of Victoria*, used the Found-ling archives to argue that the governors were projecting their own class values onto the women, who themselves had a much more pragmatic attitude to sexual morality. Pregnancy among the London poor did not mean social disgrace or family rejection, but it did mean economic disaster. Hospital policy in the early days reflected the public perception that the very act of giving birth to an illegitimate child – in whatever circumstances – was shameful if the mother was working class and poor; now the governors adopted a more tolerant attitude.

Financial necessity forced a further change on the governors. They decided that they had no option but to develop the land on which the hospital stood. Although some objected that the benefits to the children of the hospital's relative isolation would be lost if the estate were developed, the majority of governors were in favour of granting leases for the development of the hospital's lands. Guilford, Bernard and Coram Streets, and Tavistock Square were constructed in 1794 to give better access to the property. By 1799 rows of plain four-storey houses constructed of cream coloured brick and with slate roofs had been built on each side of the streets. Brunswick and Mecklenburgh Squares became central features, with commercial activities being relegated to the street north of Guilford Street and west of Grenville Street. Despite many legal problems and the need to see that the buildings reached an acceptable standard, there was the issue of safety and the attempt to ensure that law and order prevailed in this relatively uninhabited area where the risk of being robbed was always present. Although this was a common hazard in London, this area was still relatively isolated.

Future governors had cause to be thankful for the decision taken at the end of the eighteenth century to develop the land. The rentals continued to increase in value by leaps and bounds, going from £13,628 in 1893 to £25,000 in 1908. Throughout this time the hospital continued its work with children, with only small changes to the daily routine, continuity being a marked feature of the organisation. The children were still dressed in the uniforms designed by Hogarth in 1745 or 1746. Charles Nalden,[1] in *Half and Half: The Memoirs of a Charity Brat*, has left a vivid account of what life was like for a small boy in his time there, 1908–22. He writes that an unsuccessful attempt was made to change the uniforms in 1922 and visitors still came to watch the children eat their Sunday lunch, an experience no less humiliating to him than it must have been for those earlier generations of children. The young children still returned from the country, wrenched from the care of foster parents they had grown to love, and felt the same painful sense of bereavement experienced by older generations of children. The infant school, where they first went to be initiated into the routine of life in a large organisation, was housed in 40 Brunswick Square, known as Forty House. Where before girls and boys had played together in the foster homes, now the sexes were strictly segregated, a system that made for difficult relationships in later life.

The hospital, surrounded by buildings, was no longer isolated, as it had been originally. By 1926 it was considered that the children would benefit from country air. Negotiations for the site to be used for the new Covent Garden market came to nothing but the hospital was eventually sold for £1,650,000. The buildings were demolished, but the court room and parts of the building were dismantled and preserved. The children went to St Anne's School, Redhill during the time a new school was being built for them in Berkhamsted, complete with chapel. Coram's remains were brought from the unconsecrated ground in Kensal Green cemetery in 1935 and reinterred under the altar.[2] The children moved to their new home in 1935 but, although the accommodation was better, the children were living in a time warp, discipline was lax, the children were unhappy and admissions were falling. Child care policy was changing and institutional care as practised by the Foundling Hospital was out of favour. By 1954 a decision was made to sell the buildings and to board out the remaining children. After two hundred and thirteen years as a residential child care establishment the Foundling Hospital closed its doors. But continuity was not lost; on the site of the old hospital, the Thomas Coram Foundation for Children started to work with local children and their families.

Loathe to see the disappearance of such a precious open space, Lord Rothermere had got up an appeal in 1929 to buy nine acres of the old site, to be kept for the use of children;[3] the land is still known as Coram's Fields. For their part, the governors

---

1 Charles Nalden was in the care of the Foundling Hospital from 1908 to 1922. He emigrated to New Zealand and on his retirement was elected Emeritus Professor of Music at the University of South Auckland in 1974; he was awarded the CBE in 1976 for services to music.
2 See note 28 of chapter 15.
3 No adult is allowed to enter Coram's Fields unless accompanied by a child.

decided to purchase two and a half acres of land originally belonging to the hospital and to start welfare work with children in London. They began by supporting the St Leonard's nursery school, already on the site. They decided to rebuild 40 Brunswick Square and make it their administrative headquarters as well as a place to house their art collection. They were able to reconstruct the court room in all its glory. The picture gallery and committee room had been preserved together with the original staircase from the boys' wing of the hospital and all could be incorporated in the new building, which has now become the Foundling Museum.

The Thomas Coram Foundation for Children faced the difficulty of running modern child care services, including an adoption centre, after-care facilities, a children's day care centre as well as other children's services from a building that was essentially a museum. It was an intimidating building for the families to use and it also sent out all the wrong messages. With so many treasures, what need was there to raise funds for the work? Yet the governors could not sell their artistic inheritance, which had become part of the nation's cultural and social history.

There was room on the site adjoining 40 Brunswick Square to build another children's centre. This building now became the administrative centre for the expansion of the services for children and became known as Coram Family. In a radically different way, Coram Family is continuing the work started by Thomas Coram of promoting resilience in vulnerable children and young people, enabling them to take responsibility for their own lives and to achieve their full potential. Services provided by Coram Family include an adoption and fostering service, a leaving-care service, a child contact service, a parents' centre and family support service as well as preventative work and a voice influencing policy and practice nationwide. The Foundling Museum and Coram Family, now separate charities but closely linked both by their history and a happy interdependence, are free to develop in their different ways.

But what of Coram, the man whose initial vision made all this possible? He suffered the fate of many founders, replaced by others and his name all but forgotten by the outside world. He might have had one of the two squares named after him, but the governors thought it more appropriate to flatter their patron, the Hanoverian King George III, by naming the squares Brunswick and Mecklenburg. Coram had only a street named after him. However, Coram had one big advantage: Hogarth's great portrait ensured that he would always be remembered as he was in the year of his great triumph. The public might have forgotten him, but the children did not. His portrait hung in the dining hall of the Foundling Hospital and many of the children thought of him as their father. The Hogarth portrait was lent to the Manchester Art Treasures Exhibition in 1857 and most probably was seen by the artist Edward Matthew Ward. In a typical Victorian sentimental recreation of fact and fantasy, Ward created a picture entitled, 'Hogarth's studio 1739 – a Holiday Visit of the Foundlings to View the Portrait of Captain Coram'.[4] Behind the easel, where his portrait is on display, Coram and Hogarth are shown listening to the comments of the children. The portrait by Hogarth was lent to the Tate Gallery for their Swagger Exhibition, held over the winter of 1992–93, where, among the dashing portraits of the wealthy and powerful, it made its own statement. Here was the picture of a simple man whose

---

[4]   The painting hangs in the York City Art Gallery and is inscribed E.M. Ward, R.A., 1863.

goodness and honesty had been recognised by the greatest painter of his time. Its inclusion in the exhibition underlined how brilliantly successful Hogarth had been in giving Coram his rightful place in society.

With the demise of the Foundling Hospital, an evocative name that had all but eclipsed that of the founder, the Thomas Coram Foundation for Children and its successor, Coram Family, have once again brought centre stage his name and the values that Coram embodied. He is commemorated in the stained glass window in Taunton, Massachusetts, and in his birthplace, Lyme Regis, by Coram Tower. A fine statue of him by W. Calder Marshall was erected a hundred years after his death and stands outside 40 Brunswick Square, the home of the Foundling Museum. Encapsulating, as it does, so much of the history of child care through two centuries, the museum will be a fitting memorial to all those who, over the years, did so much to better the lives of children who might otherwise have died.

Appendix
The Ladies of Quality and Distinction

Names of the ladies of quality and distinction and the dates when they signed Coram's Petition.

Charlotte Finch, Duchess of Somerset	9 March 1729
Ann Vaughan, Duchess of Bolton	22 April 1729
Henrietta Needham, Dowager Duchess of Bolton	25 April 1729
Sarah Cadogan, Duchess of Richmond	22 December 1729
Isabella Montagu, Duchess of Manchester	6 January 1730
Anne Egerton, Duchess of Bedford	7 January 1730
Elizabeth Knight, Baroness Onslow	6 April 1730
Anne Pierrepoint, Dowager Baroness Torrington	14 April 1730
Frances Berkeley, Baroness Byron	14 April 1730
Selina Shirley, Countess of Huntingdon	21 April 1730
Juliana Hele, Duchess of Leeds	24 April 1730
Frances Fielding, Countess of Winchelsea and Nottingham	25 April 1730
Frances Hales, Countess of Lichfield	27 April 1730
Dorothy Savile, Countess of Burlington	19 May 1730
Elizabeth Bruce, Countess of Cardigan	19 May 1730
Frances Thynne, Countess of Hertford	26 May 1730
Mary Tufton, Countess of Harold	6 November 1733
Anne Lennox, Countess of Albermarle	6 November 1734
Anne Weldon Bernard, Baroness Trevor	2 December 1734
Anne Seys, Dowager Baroness Ockham	21 January 1735
Margaret Cavendish Harley, Duchess of Portland	7 May 1735

Bibliography

ABBREVIATIONS

BL	British Library
CO	Colonial Office MSS
CSP, CS: A and WI	*Calendar of State Papers, Colonial Series, America and West Indies*
DAB	*Dictionary of American Biography*
DNB	*Dictionary of National Biography*
DRO	Dorset Record Office
HMC	Historic Manuscripts Commission
LMA	London Metropolitan Archive
MHS	Massachusetts Historical Society (Boston)
MS(S)	Manuscript(s)
NEHGR	New England Historical and Genealogical Register
PRO	Public Record Office
Proceedings MHS	*Proceedings of the Massachusetts Historical Society*
SPCK	Society for Promoting Christian Knowledge
SPG	Society for Propagating the Gospel in Foreign Parts

PRIMARY SOURCES

Manuscript sources

British Library:

Additional MS 32692, f. 536: Letter from Thomas Coram to the Duke of Newcastle
Hans Sloane, MS 3986, ff. 38–39v
Hans Sloane, MS 4051, f. 311
Hans Sloane, MS 4057 40 80: original letters to Hans Sloane, vol. xxii, 1740–4
Shelfmark 1876, f. i (166)0 (1 folio): 'Joyful News to Batchelors and Maids, Being a Song in Praise of the Fondling Hospital, and the London Hospital, Aldersgate Street'
State Papers, 1567–1760, Stowe, 155 28, f. 114: Letter from Coram, 'To admit a visitor', 4 May 1747

College of Arms – Visitations of the County of Devon:

MS Harl., f. 2626, ICI 262b: Visitations of the County of Devon, 1620

Dorset Record Office:

Combe Raleigh Register of Burials, 1721–1731–1741
Lyme Regis Baptismal Register, 1653–1958
Lyme Regis Register of Burials, 1653–1958
Lyme Regis Register of Marriages, 1653–1972

London Metropolitan Archive: Foundling Hospital Records

The majority of the extensive Foundling Hospital records were first stored with the Greater London Record Office. They were uncatalogued. With the abolition of the Greater London Council the records came to the London Metropolitan Archive. They have been catalogued and indexed in three volumes. I have made extensive use of the General Court Minutes and the General Committee Minutes. There are also minutes of the Foundling Hospital's sub-committees and a large number of registers relating to the admission and discharge of children and the disposal of apprentices. John Brownlow, Secretary to the hospital 1844–72, collected items of interest and had them bound in books without arranging them chronologically or classifying them. The volumes all have numbers which I have quoted. In one such volume the written entries with respect to the first babies to come into the hospital are in their original state, complete with scraps of identifying material pinned to their papers with their original seals, now broken open.

General Court Minutes, 1739–99, 4 vols available on microfiche
General Committee Minutes, 1739–99, 23 vols (A/FH/M01/002/234–241) available on microfiche

A/FH/A01/003/001: Copy of Memorial and Petition to the Kings Most Excellent Majesty in Council, 29 July 1739
A/FH/A01/7/2: Subscription List, 1749
A/FH/A03/002/001: General Committee Minutes, Nov. 1739–July 1744
A/FH/A03/004/001: Daily Committee Minutes, 25 March–22 June 1941
A/FH/A06/001/005/09: Letter from Lady Germain refusing post of chief nurse
A/FH/A06/001/005/10: Letter to Lady Vere
A/FH/A06/001/005/11: Letter from Lady Vere declining post of chief nurse
A/FH/A06/001/005/14: Letter to Lady Vere
A/FH/A09/001,2,3: Billet Book, 1741–46
A/FH/A09/002/001: General Register, 1741–57: Children's Admission and Discharge
A/FH/A1/3/1: Petition to Princess Amelia
A/FH/A1/3/1: Petition to the Princess of Wales
A/FH/A1/4/1: Mémoire concernant les Enfants Trouvés de la Ville de Paris, pp. 1–33; Besigt Wegens Het aal Moeseniens Waeslangs den Stadt Amsterdam, pp. 63–116
A/FH/A1/7/1: Coram's Pocket Notebook
A/FH/A12/003/001: Apprentice Books
A/FH/A12/003/008: Disposal of Apprentices
A/FH/A14/004/00/002: Register of Baptisms, 1741–1757
A/FH/B1/01/1: Furniture Register
A/FH/F13/001/00: Miscellaneous Private Papers
A/FH/F14/1/12: Morris Lievesley, Manuscript Notebook
A/FH/M01/005/176–202: Copy of Affidavit relating to the Spoyling and Plundering of the Ship *Seaflower* on the River Elbe, 2 June 1719
A/FH/M01/008/015/24: Notes of Tokens, 1741
A/FH/M01/1–17: Miscellaneous – including Mrs Hogarth's account of children under her care
A/FH9/9/1/1: Papers relating to Register of Children Admitted, 1741
Morris Lievesley, Notebook, vol. 24
Morris Lievesley, Secretary to the Foundling Hospital 1799–1849, Manuscript Memoir

Public Record Office:

C9/466/84: Hunt v Thomas Coram, 1704
C11/1320/46: Jacob Coram v Davy, 1740
C1/484/15: John Coram v Richard Dollyng
C11/107/9: Answer of John and William Coram to Samuel Lyme, 1734
PRO C11/1711/31
C16/192/26: William Coram v George Berry, 1678
C9/458/120: John Coram v Katherine and Robert Tom, 1704
CO 217 Colonial Office and Predecessors: Nova Scotia and Cape Breton, Original Correspondence 1710–1867, vol. 7
CO, vol. 1717–1720
PC 90 2: Petition of Thomas Coram for employment in the Royal Navy, 8 February 1727
PROB 6/127, f. 216v: Letters of Administration, Thomas Coram, April 1752
PROB 11/579, sig. 66: Will of John Coram, 25 March 1721
PROB 11/809, Q. 191: Will of Ann Coram, 18 June 1754

St Mary's Church, Ottery St Mary:

Transcripts of Registers of Births, Baptisms and Burials, 1600–1652

Massachusetts Archive:

Vols 1, 3, 28, 40

Newberry Library, Chicago

Edward E. Ayer Manuscript Collection:
Letter from T. Coram to the Honourable Society for Propagating the Gospel among the Indians of New England, 17 June 1745

Taunton, Mass., Bristol County Court House:

Bristol County Registers Offices
Deed Books, 3, 4, 31, 41
Records of the Court of General Sessions for the Peace for Bristol County, 1697–1701
Records of the Inferior Court of Common Pleas for Bristol County, 1696–1702; 1702–1720

Printed sources

Historic Manuscripts Commission Reports:

Egmont Diaries, 3 vols, 1730–33; 1734–1738; 1739–1747
Portland MSS, vol. V, 1899
Reginald Rawden Hastings MSS, vol. 3
Townshend MSS, Eleventh Report, App. IV

Public Record Office:

Calendar of State Papers, Colonial: America and West Indies, vols for 1701, 1712–14, 1714–15, 1716–17, 1717–18, 1728–29, 1731, 1734–35, 1735–36, and 1737

Boston, Massachusetts Historical Society:

Collection of Charles Greenough
Colman Papers, vols 1 and 2
Col. Edward Hutchinson Papers, 1679–1753
Miscellaneous Bound Items, 1698–1702
Nova Scotia Papers (Gay Transcripts). *Proposed Colony of Georgia in New England, 1713–1733*, pp. 256–71, Colonial Society of Massachusetts

Boston, Massachusetts State Archives:

Vols 3, 28 and 40 653; 40 649 56
Minutes of the Council of the Province of Massachusetts, CO 5 788, pp. 221–4, 229, 232, 231–41, 241–4

Maine Historical Society:

Documentary History of the State of Maine, Collections of Maine Historical Society, 2nd series, vols 9 and 10

Old Colony Historical Society, Taunton, Massachusetts:

Collections of the Old Colony Historical Society, vol. 2, 1880, Appendix A, pp. 28–30
Collections of the Old Colony Historical Society, V D569H, C.W. Chase, 'Houses of Dighton', *Taunton Daily Gazette*, 20 August 1904
Collections of the Old Colony Historical Society, V W151E

Public Archives of Nova Scotia:

Halifax, NS 1900, Governor's Letter Book, Annapolis, 1713–17
F100/B71: 'Thomas Coram and the First Proposals for Foreign Protestants as Settlers', in *The 'Foreign Protestants' and the Settlement of Nova Scotia*, 1990, pp. 32–58

University of Georgia Library:

'Letter of John Martin Bolzius to Thomas Coram, 28 July, 1737', Egmont Papers, vol. 14203, part 1, p. 73

SECONDARY SOURCES

Acts of the Privy Council, Colonial Series VI: Unbound Papers, London 1912, Chancery Records

Acts of the Privy Council of England, Colonial Series: 1713–1783, ed. W. L. Grant and J. Munro, 6 vols, London, 1908–1912

Allan, Brian, 'Art and Charity in Hogarth's England', in *Enlightened Self-Interest: The Foundling Hospital and Hogarth*, ed. Rhian Harris and Robin Simon, London 1997, pp. 8–11

Andrew, Donna T., '*Noblesse Oblige*: Female Charity in an Age of Sentiment', in *Early Modern Conceptions of Property*, ed. John Brewer and and Susan Staves, London 1985, pp. 275–300

Anderson, Robert Charles, *The Great Migration Begins*, vol. III, 'Immigrants to New England, 1620–1633', NEHGR, Boston 1897

Bailyn, Bernard, *The New England Merchants in the Seventeenth Century*, Cambridge, Mass. 1979

———, *The Ordeal of Thomas Hutchinson*, Cambridge, Mass. 1974

Balen, Malcolm, *A Very English Deceit: The Secret History of the South Sea Bubble and the First Great Financial Scandal*, London 2002

Banbury, Philip, *Shipbuilders of the Thames and Medway*, Newton Abbot 1971

Barret-Ducrocq, Françoise, *Love in the Time of Victoria*, London, 1991

Barry, Jonathan, ed., *Medicine and Charity before the Welfare State*, London 1991

Battis, Emery, *Saints and Sectaries: Anne Hutchinson and the Antinomian Controversy in the Massachusetts Bay Colony*, North Carolina 1962

Belcher Papers, *Proceedings of the Massachusetts Historical Society*, sixth series, vol. VI, parts 1 and 2

Bell, Winthrop, 'Thomas Coram and the First Proposals for Foreign Protestants as Settlers', in *The 'Foreign Protestants' and the Settlement of Nova Scotia*, ed. Fredericton and Sackville, New Brunswick 1990 (reprint of 1961 edition)

Bellamy, R.R., ed., *Ramblin' Jack: The Journal of Captain John Cremer, 1770–1774*, London 1936

Bernard, Thomas, *An Account of the Foundling Hospital in London, for the Maintenance and Education of Exposed and Deserted Young Children*, 2nd edn, London 1799

Binney, Margaret, *A Guide: Thomas Coram Foundation for Children*, London, undated

Black, Jeremy, *Walpole in Power*, London 2001

Borg, Alan, 'Theodore Jacobsen: A Gentleman Well Versed in the Science of Architecture', paper read to the Society of Antiquaries, London 2003

———, 'Theodore Jacobsen and the Building of the Foundling Hospital', *Georgian Group Journal*, London 2003

Boorstein, Daniel J., *The Americans: The Colonial Experience*, London 2000

[Bray, Thomas] *A Memorial Concerning the Erecting in the City of London or the suburbs thereof, of an Orphanthropy for the Reception of Poor Cast Off Children or Foundlings*, n.p. n. d., Houghton Library, Harvard

Bremer, Francis, *The Puritan Experiment: New England Society from Bradford to Edwards*, Boston 1976

Briggs, Ralph and Mary, *Watchcoats* www.nwta.com/couriers/11-96/watchcoats.html

[Brocklesby, Richard], *Private Virtue and Publick Spirit display'd in a Succinct Essay on the Character of Capt. Thomas Coram*, London 1751

Brownlow, John, *The History and Objects of the Foundling Hospital, with a Memoir of the Founder*, London 1865

Carswell, John, *The South Sea Bubble*, rev. edn, Stroud 1993

——— and Lewis Arnold, eds, *The Political Journal of George Bubb Dodington*, Oxford 1965

Catholic Record Society, *Blue Nuns of Paris*, Paris 1910

Clark, Andrew Hill, *Acadia: The Geography of Early Nova Scotia to 1760*, Madison 1968

Climenson, Emily, *Elizabeth Montague, the Queen of the Blue Stockings: Her Correspondence from 1720–1761*, London 1906

Cokayne, George Edward, *The Complete Peerage of England, Scotland, Ireland, Great Britain and the United Kingdom*, ed. Vicary Gibbs, 13 vols, London, 1910–59

Colley, Linda, *Britons, Forging the Nation 1707–1837*, New Haven 1992

Compston, Herbert Fuller Bright, *Thomas Coram, Churchman, Empire Builder and Philanthropist*, London 1918

Cowie, Leonard Henry, *Henry Newman: An American in London, 1708–43*, London 1956

Coxe, William, *Memoirs of the Life and Administration of Sir Robert Walpole, Earl of Oxford*, 3 vols, London 1800

Crane, Verner W., 'The Philanthropists and the Genesis of Georgia', *The American Historical Review*, vol. 27, 1921

——, *The Southern Frontier*, Durham NC 1928

Davis, R., *The Rise of the English Shipping Industry in the Seventeenth and Eighteenth Centuries*, Newton Abbot 1972

Dillon, Patrick, *The Much Lamented Death of Madam Geneva*, London 2002

Dobson, Austin, *A Paladin of Philanthropy*, London 1899

——, *Eighteenth Century Vignettes*, vol. 1, London 1891

Documentary History of the State of Maine, Collections of Maine Historical Society, 2nd series, vols 9 and 10

Emery, Samuel Hopkins, *History of Taunton, from its Original Settlement to the Present Time*, Syracuse, NY, 1893

Enlightened Self-Interest: The Foundling Hospital and Hogarth, catalogue, ed. Rhian Harris and Robin Simon, London 1997

Ettinger, Amos Aschbach, *James Edward Oglethorpe, Imperial Idealist*, Oxford 1936

Fairclough, K.R., 'Thomas Coram: His Brief Period as a Gunpowder Producer', *Surrey Archaeological Collections*, vol. 86, 1999, pp. 53–72

Fant, H.B. 'Picturesque Thomas Coram, Projector of Two Georgias and Father of the London Foundling Hospital', *Georgia Historical Quarterly*, vol. 32, 1948, pp. 77–104

Fielding, Henry, *The History of Tom Jones*, Harmondsworth 1985

Foote, Henry Wilder, *Annals of the Kings Chapel from the Puritan Age of New England to the Present Day*, 3 vols, Boston 1882–1940

Forbes, A. and Ralph M. Eastman, *Town and City Seals of Massachusetts*, Boston 1950

Fowles, John, *A Brief History of Lyme*, Friends of the Philpot Museum, Lyme Regis 2000

Glendinning, Victoria, *Jonathan Swift*, London 1998

Griffiths, Naomi, *The Golden Age: Acadian Life 1713–1748*, Toronto 1984

Grundy, Isobel, *Lady Mary Wortley Montagu, Comet of the Enlightenment*, London 1999

Hanway, Jonas, *A Candid Historical Account of the Hospital For the Reception of Exposed and Deserted Young Children; representing the present Plan of it as productive of many Evils, and not adapted to Genius and Happiness of this Nation*, London 1759

——, *Serious Consideration of the Salutory Design of the Act of Parliament for a regular uniform register of the parish poor in all the parishes within the Bills of Mortality*, 1762

Harben, Henry, *A Dictionary of London*, London 1918

Haycock, David, ' "The Cabal of a few Designing Members": The Presidency of Martin Folkes, PRS, and the Society's First Charter', *The Antiquaries' Journal*, vol. 80, 2000

—— and G. S. Rousseau, 'Voices Calling for Reform: The Royal Society in the mid eighteenth century – Martin Folkes, John Hill and William Stukeley', *History of Science*, vol. 37, part 4, no. 118, December 1999

Henderson, Tony, *Disorderly Women in Eighteenth Century London, 1730–1830*, London 1999

Hill, Hamilton Andrews, 'Thomas Coram in Boston and Taunton', *American Antiquarian Society, Proceedings*, Worcester, Mass. 1892, pp. 133–48

Hinde, R.S.E., *The British Penal System*, London, 1951

[Holliday, John] *An Appeal to the Governors of the Foundling Hospital; on the Probable Consequences of Covering the Hospital Lands with Buildings*, London 1787

Holmes, Geoffrey, *The Making of a Great Power, Late Stuart and Early Georgian Britain, 1660–1722*, London 1993

—— and Daniel Szechi, *The Age of Oligarchy: Pre-Industrial Britain, 1722–1783*, London 1993

Holmes, Richard, *Dr Johnson and Mr Savage*, London 1993

Hughes, Helen Sard, ed., *The Gentle Hertford: Her Life and Letters*, New York 1940

Hutchinson, Thomas, *The History of the Colony and Province of Massachusetts Bay*, ed. L.S. Mayo, Cambridge, Mass. 1936

James, Lawrence, *The Rise and Fall of the British Empire*, London 1994

Jones, George Fenwick, *Henry Newman's Salzburger Letterbooks*, Athens, Georgia 1966

Jones, M. Gwladys, *The Charity School Movement: A Study of Eighteenth Century Puritanism in Action*, Cambridge 1938

Jones, Stephen Kay, *Dr. Williams and his Library*, Cambridge 1948

Kamenisky, Jane, *Governing the Tongue: The Politics of Speech in Early New England*, Oxford 1997

Kennedy, Paul, *The Rise and Fall of British Naval Mastery*, Harmondsworth 1976

Kerslake, John, *Early Georgian Portraits*, London, 1977

Knight, C., ed., *London*, London 1841

Kurlansky, Mark, *Cod: A Biography of the Fish that Changed the World*, London 1998

Lane, Helen, *A History of the Town of Dighton*, Dighton, Mass. 1962

Laqueur, T.W., *Religion and Respectability, Sunday School and Working Class Culture*, New Haven 1976

Lemprière, William, ed., *John Howes' MSS 1582*, London 1904

'Letter of Thomas Coram to H. Newman, 20 November 1732', *Notes and Queries*, 8th series, vol. 4, 1893, p. 266

'Letters of Thomas Coram', *Proceedings of the Massachusetts Historical Society*, vol. 56, 1922, pp. 15–56

Lewis, W.S., ed., *The Yale Edition of Horace Walpole's Correspondence*, 48 vols, New Haven 1937–83

Macaulay, T. B., *History of England*, 4 vols, London 1863

Mahaffie, Charles, *A Land of Discord Always: Acadia from its Beginnings to the Expulsion of its People, 1604–1755*, Maine 1995

Mayer, Andre, *King's Chapel: The First Century, 1668–1787*, Boston 1976

McClure, Ruth, *Coram's Children: The London Foundling Hospital in the Eighteenth Century*, New Haven 1981

Melville, Lewis, *Lady Suffolk and her Circle*, London 1924

Middleton, Thomas, *Five Plays*, ed. Brian Loughry and Neil Taylor, London 1988

Moorhead, Warren, 'Ancient Remains of Pemaquid, Maine', in *Old Time New England*, vol. xiv, Maine 1924

Morgan, Macnamara, attrib., *Scandalizade, A Panegyric-Satiri-Serio-Comi-Dramatic Poem*, London 1750, reprinted in *The Remarkable Satires of Porcupinus Pelagius*, London 1760

Mowl, Timothy, *Horace Walpole: The Great Outsider*, London 1996

Nalden, Charles, *Half and Half: The Memoirs of a Charity Brat, 1908–1989*, New Zealand 1990

Nelson, Robert, *An Address to Persons of Quality and Estate, to which is added a Representation of the Several Ways of Doing Good*, London 1715

New England Historical and Genealogical Register, vols 3, 24, 25 and 31, Boston 1849–77

Nichols, J. B., ed., *Anecdotes of William Hogarth, annotated by himself, with Essays on his Life and Genius*, London 1833

Nichols, R. H. and F. A. Wray, *History of the Foundling Hospital*, Oxford 1935

Nicolson, Benedict, *Treasures of the Foundling Hospital*, Oxford 1972

North, Roger, *The Life of Francis North, Baron of Guildford*, London 1642

O'Connell, Sheila, *London, 1753*, catalogue published to accompany the exhibition at the British Museum, London 2003

Ollivier, B., *Eighteenth Century Shipbuilding: Remarks on the Navies of the English and Dutch (1737)*, trans. and ed. David H. Roberts, Robertsbridge 1992

Owen, David, *English Philanthropy, 1660–1690*, Cambridge, Mass. 1964

Pennington, Edgar Legare, *Anglican Beginnings in Massachusetts*, Boston 1941

Perry, William S., ed., *Historical Collections Relating to the American Colonial Church*, 5 vols, Hartford, Conn. 1870–78

Philips, Hugh, *Mid-Georgian London*, London 1964

Phillimore, W.P.W. and G. E. Cokayne, eds, *London Parish Registers, 1168–1683*, London 1900

Pinchbeck, Ivy and Margaret Hewitt, *Children in English Society*, London 1696

Porcupinus Pelagius (pseud.), *see under* Morgan, Macnamara

Porter, Roy, *English Society in the Eighteenth Century*, London 1982

Reed, Charles A., *The Province of Massachusetts in the Seventeenth Century: Enrolment of the Precincts*, Boston 1880

Report of the Record Commissioners Containing Boston Births, Baptisms, Marriages and Deaths, 1630–1699, Boston 1883

Report of the Record Commissioners of the City of Boston Containing Boston Marriages from 1700 to 1751, Boston 1898

Ridge, C. Harold, *Records of the Worshipful Company of Shipwrights*, vol. 1, Chichester 1939

Roberts, David H., ed., *Eighteenth Century Shipbuilding*, London 1992

Robins, Joseph, *The Lost Children: A Study of Charity Children in Ireland, 1700–1900*, Dublin 1980

Robinson, C.N., *The British Fleet*, London 1894

Rodger, N.A.M., *The Wooden World: An Anatomy of the Georgian Navy*, London 1986

St Thomas's Church through Two Centuries, 1728–1928, Taunton, Mass. 1928 (pamphlet)

Savage, Richard, *Miscellaneous Poems and Translations*, published by Richard Savage, 'son of the late Lord Rivers', London 1726

Schwoerer, Lois G., *Lady Rachel Russell, 'One of the best of women'*, London and Baltimore 1988

Sedgewick, Robert, ed., *Memoirs of John, Lord Hervey*, 3 vols, London 1931

Smart, Christopher, 'A Letter from Mrs Midnight to the Governors of the Foundling Hospital', *The Midwife, or the Old Woman's Magazine*, 3 vols, 1751–3 (Mrs Midnight was the pseudonym for Christopher Smart)

Smollett, Tobias, *A letter to the Rt. Hon the Lady V . . . SS V . . . occasioned by the publication of her memoirs in 'The Adventures of Peregrine Pickle'*, London 1751

Some Considerations on the Necessity and Usefulness of the Royal Charter Establishing an Hospital for the Maintenance and Education of Exposed and Deserted Young Children, London 1740

Statutes of the Realm, vol. viii, chapter ix, p. 354: an Act for encouraging the Importation of Naval Stores from HM Plantations in America

Stephens, William, *The Castle Builders: A Political Novel*, London 1759

Stewart Brown, R., *Liverpool Ships in the 18th Century*, London 1932

Tague, Ingrid H., *Women of Quality: Accepting and Contesting Ideals of Femininity in England, 1690–1760*, Woodbridge 2002

Tattersfield, Nigel, *The Forgotten Trade, Comprising the Log of the Daniel and Henry of 1700, and Accounts of the Slave Trade from the Minor Ports of England, 1698–1725*, London 1991

Taylor, James Stephen, *Jonas Hanway, Founder of the Marine Society*, London 1985

Thomas, M. Halsey, ed., *Diary of Samuel Sewall, 1674–1708*, Boston 1973

Thompson, H.P., *Thomas Bray*, London 1954

Thomson, Mrs, ed., *Memoirs of Viscountess Sundon, Mistress of the Robes to Queen Caroline, Consort of George II*, 2 vols, London 1847

Tillyard, Stella, *Aristocrats: Caroline, Emily and Sarah Lennox, 1740–1832*, London 1994

Town & City Seals of Massachusetts, Boston 1951

Turrell, E., *Life and Character of Dr. Benjamin Colman*, Boston 1749; reprinted Oxford 1972

Uglow, Jenny, *Hogarth: A Life and a World*, London 1997

Wagner, Anthony and Antony Dale, *The Wagners of Brighton*, Chichester 1983

Wagner, Gillian, 'Spreading the Word: The Church and SPG in North America: Thomas Coram and Anglicanism in New England', *Journal of the Canadian Historical Society*, vol. XLV, 2003, pp. 65–76

Walford, Edward, *London Old and New*, vol. 4, 1856

Index